THE GOLFING MACHINE

IT'S CONSTRUCTION
OPERATION
AND ADJUSTMENT

THE

GOLFING MACHINE

By
Homer Kelley

The Star System
of
G.O.L.F.™

(Geometrically Oriented Linear Force)

COPYRIGHT © 1969 HOMER KELLEY
COPYRIGHT © 1971 HOMER KELLEY
COPYRIGHT © 1975 HOMER KELLEY
COPYRIGHT © 1979 HOMER KELLEY
COPYRIGHT © 1980 HOMER KELLEY
COPYRIGHT © 1982 HOMER KELLEY
COPYRIGHT © 2006 THE GOLFING MACHINE, LLC 7th Edition
COPYRIGHT © 2006 THE GOLFING MACHINE, LLC Edition 7.1, 12.15.15
COPYRIGHT © 2006 THE GOLFING MACHINE, LLC Edition 7.2, 3.3.17

All Rights Reserved. No portion of this book may be reproduced — mechanically, electonically, or by any other means, including photo-copying — without the express written consent of the publisher. All inquires should be addressed to The Golfing Machine, LLC.

For information address:
The Golfing Machine
6107 SW Murray Blvd. #405
Beaverton, Oregon 97008
(877) 647-G.O.L.F.

Visit our website at: www.thegolfingmachine.com

For inquires and questions, contact us via
E-mail: moreinfo@thegolfingmachine.com

Library of Congress Catalog Card Number: 78-65234

ISBN: 978-0-932890-06-1
Printed in the U.S.A.

The Golfing Machine, LLC dedicates the 7th Edition to Homer and Sally Kelley.

With Homer's quest for truth in golf, he gave us a solid base for G.O.L.F. instruction; and without Sally's assistance in bookkeeping during his life and her desire to keep his life's work available in the years following his death, the world of golf and golf instructors would not have "the Duffer's Bible, the Golf Nut's Catalog, the Circuit Players handbook or the Instructor's Textbook," as Homer described The Golfing Machine.

We owe a debt of gratitude and thanks to Homer and Sally for continuing the legacy of The Golfing Machine.

The Golfing Machine modifies the 7th Edition and names it The Golfing Machine Edition 7.1

This modified edition of The Golfing Machine comes eight years after the 7th edition revisions, which stemmed from the copious notes taken by Mr. Kelley prior to his untimely death in February 1983. Mr. Kelley spent an enormous amount of time placing, aligning and adjusting his model for the effect he intended "The pictures depict exactly what they are intended to depict and as near to "Zero Tolerance" as is humanly possible and then only because they were carefully and expertly posed." (2-R). Over the past eight years digitization technology has vastly improved Mr. Kelley's beautiful and accurate photographs making it easier for the reader to discern the alignment. The black and white medium enhances the story.

Edition 7.1 has a larger and more complete Index which allows the reader to reference a topic more thoroughly and completely. The advantage of a more complete Index is the ability to study topics from the different Chapters and subchapters in the text and follow them throughout the book.

Lastly, Edition 7.1 has two further additions which many students have asked for – a lie-flat book which will make reading and studying easier, and Note Pages. These long sought-after note pages will give the student a place to put their thoughts and questions inside the text where they will be readily accessible.

We hope you enjoy this modified edition of The Golfing Machine.

Joe Daniels, PGA, MS, GSED
President
The Golfing Machine, LLC.

Homer Kelley 1907-1983

Many people might be surprised that Homer Kelley's first love in sports was tennis, rather than golf. Growing up in Minnesota, he took up the sport at an early age and over the years became very proficient at the game.

He left Minnesota in 1929 with a friend, with a plan to drive to Seattle and get a job on a ship heading to New Zealand. They arrived on October 29, 1929 — the day the Stock Market crashed.

With his trip cancelled, Homer worked as a cook, in a Tacoma, Washington billiards hall during The Great Depression. The owner was an avid golfer and gave Homer a series of golf lessons. This was his first exposure to the game and he approached it with a great deal of curiosity. He was always asking questions which the local golf professionals couldn't answer and these unanswered questions set the stage for the development of The Golfing Machine.

During World War II, Homer landed a job at Boeing, the country's foremost manufacturer of aircraft. There, working in the engineering department, Homer found a home for his mechanical curiosity. Somewhat of an inventor, there he created solutions to problems that seemed to elude others. He also became an instructor; teaching Boeing engineers how to apply the problem solving skills that came so naturally to him.

Beginning in 1940, Homer began making notes on the concepts which would evolve into The Golfing Machine. This was the "incubation period," for his thoughts and he would later use this same term in the book. Taking an idea that you don't understand and turning it over and over in your mind will eventually yield the answer. His ideas about golf were "percolating" in his mind. They had begun years ago with those first golf lessons and continued with his persistent and relentless questioning of the golf stroke and its hidden concepts.

During that time, he would often work through the concepts in his mind at the local driving range. There, he would take the time to observe others on the range hitting balls. He once made a comment about a golfer he had seen at the range many times: "10 years from now, that guy won't be any better; all he needs is a little information." Homer was always analyzing, refining and working on his own swing as well. The golf professionals at the range would point him out to people and say to their students "See him? That's how you should do it!"

Homer felt strongly that there should be no reason for the lack of knowledge about the golf swing. As a result in 1960 he quit his job to work on the book full-time. He set up a studio in the garage at his home where during the day he continued his research, capturing his findings — "hunting and pecking" — on the typewriter every night.

When The Golfing Machine was first published in 1969 — 40 years after his first series of golf lessons — there were both skeptics and followers to Homer's work. To the skeptics, Homer would always patiently approach criticisms with "That's an interesting thought, but what if you thought about it this way?" He made sure that people understood that he did not create the information in the book; that, in fact, The Golfing Machine is based on scientific principles covering physics and geometry. Homer — using the same problem solving techniques that he used with any job — explained that he simply applied these proven principles to the golf swing. And with that, The Golfing Machine was born.

Soon after the book was published, Homer realized that he needed to pass on the information to professional golf instructors. So, he set forth to develop an authorization program that would allow the instructors to easily explain these scientific concepts to their students.

While Homer's death in 1983 was untimely — The Golfing Machine's authorization program was just hitting its stride —
The Golfing Machine, LLC and its current Authorization program continues to reflect Homer's vision, appreciation for knowledge, and his application of scientific principles to G.O.L.F.

— as told by Sally Kelley

A Note From The Golfing Machine, LLC

The Golfing Machine, LLC is proud to take Mr. Kelley's notes, thoughts, and final changes and put them into this 7th edition. Although these changes were made by Mr. Kelley before his death in 1983, it has taken 22 years to take more than 90 pages of hand-written notes and directions and compile them into this text. The burden of putting them into the correct chapter and place, reformatting, renumbering and proof-reading the text was time consuming but also an incredible education. With these changes Mr. Kelley continues to show us how precise he was in delivering his information by illuminating some of the more difficult concepts in the book and making them easier to understand.

All the changes were made exactly as Mr. Kelley directed. We only changed and improved the Index; increasing the number of items in the Index in order for the students of The Golfing Machine to find key topics more easily. The changes to the Index were compiled over 28 years of reading and studying The Golfing Machine, taking notes and writing down concepts which were difficult to find.

We hope you enjoy studying this 7th edition of Mr. Kelley's timeless work. As he tells us, G.O.L.F. is "the guided struggle versus the blind struggle." If you choose self-directed education to best use the book, read Roman numeral page XIV and follow Mr. Kelley's directions carefully, or per his directions find an Authorized Instructor of The Golfing Machine to assist you in your journey through G.O.L.F., the most precise way to learn your golfing procedure.

For more in-depth instruction, there are Authorized Instructors of The Golfing Machine throughout the world. They are Professional Golf Instructors who have been trained to interpret and teach G.O.L.F. to the golfing public. You can find them and more Information on The Golfing Machine at www.thegolfingmachine.com.

FOREWORD

It was in 1969 that I first met Homer Kelley. After 28 years of work, he had just completed The Golfing Machine and had come to the Pro Shop to interest me in teaching the system of G.O.L.F. We talked for 6 hours. He showed me how he had traced the golf stroke pattern CHAPTER 12, to 24 basic components CHAPTER 7, and that each component had from 3 to 15 variations CHAPTER 10, summary CHAPTER 11, and that some variations were not interchangeable, CHAPTER 13. I knew right then that The Golfing Machine was the book my students and I were waiting for. Homer went on to explain the 12 sections of every stroke CHAPTER 8, and I could see at once how duffers and hackers were out of sequence, trying to release the power package before it had been assembled, loaded and delivered. I have come to appreciate CHAPTER 9, as all my lessons start basically from one of these 3 zones depending on the ability of the student; Body Control, Club Control, then Ball Control. As Homer explained CHAPTER 6, the difference between Power Source and Power Application, the words "accumulator," "plane," "lever assembly," "pressure points," "clubhead drag," and "clubhead lag" have become good friends over the years. Chapters 4 and 5 — Educated Hands — were fun to learn, and it is now my conviction that anyone with "clubhead throwaway" will never improve until he gets these chapters into his coconut. I remember telling Homer I could "hit it" with almost any kind of grip — "that's right, you always had lag," he said. Chapters one, two and three in all of the revised editions have been polished and refined since the first edition. The 21 facts in the third edition, 1-L, have been so useful for precision golf and I will still treasure Homer's original meanings of the generation of angular momentum in 2-K. CHAPTER 2 (Golf as a Science) takes some study but is worth the effort as empirical knowledge is worse than useless. Homer explains how he used CHAPTER 3 to translate mechanics into feel, and these first 3 chapters give both the instructor and student the background of good golfing.

After our six-hour visit, I arranged for Homer to put on a series of evening classes at his studio for a few fellow professionals so that I could get their thoughts. I asked Homer to help me with my classes at the Club to get student feedback and to audit my teaching. In 1973 we were invited to present the book to the National PGA Education Committee. I'll never forget Homer's talk on what the book would do for golfdom. I

FOREWORD

spoke on the practical application of teaching the Star System of G.O.L.F. However, even though I knew from my students' progress that The Golfing Machine was the truth in teaching, it seemed that my assignment was to continue teaching, and Homer polishing, knowing it would be a Bobby Clampett who would put it into his computer, CHAPTER 14, and demonstrate The Golfing Machine to the "Golf World."

One of the Nation's most highly regarded teachers told me in 1973 that I was "ten years ahead of us." I replied I had only been studying and teaching The Golfing Machine for 5 years; it's been 37 years now, and my intention has always been to share it. As the book says, mandatory positions mean nothing without principle, and it is obedience to principle that gives one power and accuracy.

Thanks, Homer for explaining G.O.L.F. and, in doing so, making the job possible to inform the student who must absorb and apply. So — take one component at a time using the sequence in CHAPTER 9 plus the index, and in 24 hours, days, weeks, months, or years you will be able to "sustain the line of compression" . . . the lag . . . impact.

Ben Doyle, GSED, PGA Teaching Professional
The First Authorized Instructor of The Golfing Machine
b. 1932   d. 2014

PREFACE
INTRODUCTION TO THE BOOK

It may be that an octopus, or a thing from outer space, would need a different procedure, but for people-shaped golfers, there is actually only "one swing," as depicted in Chapter 8 and discussed in Chapter 7. This Basic Stroke is not a basic *procedure*, but it is basic *geometry*. Almost anyone can do a basic imitation that could appear to the untrained eye to be as good looking as those of many experts. All that would need to be added would be more precision in the Component relationships, and *that* this book can supply. In fact, that is all it is intended to supply. Without that "Basic Motion," it couldn't even do that. See 3-0.

The relationships in the Golf Stroke can be explained scientifically only by geometry; because geometry is the science of relationships. So, learn Feel from Mechanics *rather* than Mechanics from Feel. "Alignment Golf" — Feel from Mechanics — dispenses with all dependence on "mandatory" Positions, which can be perfectly executed and still miss the ball. They facilitate things but guarantee nothing — unless you know the relations they are supposed to facilitate. "ALIGNMENT UTILIZATION" provides these "MANDATORY ABSOLUTES" and "UTILIZATION PROCEDURES" provide "OPTIONAL FLEXIBILITY". See 14-0. Alignment Golf simply smothers Position Golf; so, translate your "Position Procedures" into "Alignment Procedures" as fast as you are able to do so. Feel no concern for THE Perfect Stroke. There are trillions of precision Patterns — with totally correct Alignments and Relationships which are *perfect* for some application or preference.

The number one alignment is the Flat Left Wrist (Law of the Flail 2-K). The Flat Left Wrist is a Golfing Imperative (2-0). Without it, more information means only more confusion. There is much information herein that you won't need but there is none that someone won't need. This system ultimates in its own simplification — The Triad, mentioned below. But, without the supporting detail herein, that simplification could not have been conceived or supported. This textbook can support individual "MY Way" procedures but no "THE Way" theory.

The Golf Stroke involves, mainly, two basic elements — the Geometry of the Circle and the Physics of Rotation. There are only two Basic Strokes — Hitting and Swinging. The geometry (for "uncompensated" Strokes) is the same for both. And for all Clubs and Patterns. But, basically, the

PREFACE

Physics of Hitting is Muscular Thrust, and of Swinging, Centripetal Force. Herein, "Motion" is Geometry — "Action" is Physics. Hitting and Swinging seem equally efficient. The difference is in the players. If Strong – Hit; If Quick – Swing; If Both – Do either, as they are Mutually Exclusive (10-19-0).

The definition of the Geometry of the Circle has two aspects: the facts and the illusions, visual and sensory. When the facts are understood, the illusions not only cease to mislead, but also can be utilized (2-N).

The definition of the Physics of Rotation does not specify "Golf Laws" — only the simple, universal Laws of Force and Motion that you use every day because you cannot move yourself or anything else except in compliance with them. Physics merely takes the "seems as if" out of things. Including Golf (2-K).

The Incubator and Computer (14-0) deal with the Mental Aspects of Golf and its programming, reducing the complexity to a repeatable but adaptable sequence of alignment-sustaining motions and "feels" as the player has selected them for the situation at hand.

It's not instant perfection but continuous progress toward a practical goal — mastery of the STAR SYSTEM TRIAD: The Three Imperatives (2-0) applying the Three Functions (1-L-A/B/C) through the Three Stations (12-3) — which should be sought.

As you apply this System you may suddenly realize you are now *actually* doing what you had always merely *thought* you were doing.

First use of this system might be to understand your present game before you abandon, replace or scramble it. It may not be all that bad. At least it's familiar. Besides, habits can be harder to break than to reshuffle a little. This book may point up why you don't play better but also why you play as well as you do. (See 1-H and 14-0.) Does it all seem as if it would just "take too long"? What if you had worked out one step each week — or each month — for the last two years? Or the last five years? How about the next two? Or five? At the very worst, it's the guided struggle versus the blind struggle. With this book you can do a lot of learning in your armchair.

The "Uncompensated" Stroke is recommended simply because — for example, per 7-13 — if you cannot take the Shoulder Down the Clubshaft Plane, you must take it along some other path and add compensations — now, instead of one motion to remember you wind up with <u>at least</u> two.

PREFACE

The principles set forth in this book will greatly benefit many other activities where manual dexterity is required. It will be realized that *conscious* hand manipulation is indispensable in the learning process. Those involved with swinging components will grasp the geometry of their Force and Motion. And it will be seen that great diversity of procedure can be differentiated and patterned in total detail. Every part is carefully related to every other part to be one complete harmonious whole — as a whole or piece by piece. It is arranged in the order best suited to point up its continuity and completeness and the flexibility inherent in its use of the reference numbered headings for research and lesson assignments and for the location of Stroke Pattern selections. Chapter 12 and the Index contain detailed instruction on this invaluable feature of Cross-referencing.

Please remember that this handbook is intended to serve as a manual and tries to adhere to a textbook style of writing which customarily eschews selling, debating, reminiscing, opinions and hilarity. The presentation is basically "technical writing" but, for its emphasis, with a definitely conversational style throughout the book. The capitalization, as discussed in 1-H, may seem unfamiliar and confusing but only at first glance. The "un-golf-like" terminology has no hidden or "cute" applications — they're just plain dictionary English. Uncovering previously unknown elements of Golf simply mandated that terminology be adopted to express them. Don't turn away because the truth looks too complex. Stay with it a while and you'll soon find it all very helpful and comfortable. After all, complexity is far more acceptable and workable than mystery is.

PREFACE

Approach the book as a four step process using the lists below:
1. Follow List #1 as sequenced (ignoring cross-reference numbers) until you grasp the essentials (more or less) of each group;
2. Move to List #2. Study each Chapter as sequenced, ignoring all cross-reference numbers;
3. Start the preliminary assembly of your selected Pattern from Chapter 12, checking all cross-reference numbers;
4. Use the book as an encyclopedia (or tips) on subjects of interest.

List #1

1. Preface, Table of Contents
2. Chapters 1, 12-0, 14-0
3. Chapters 8, 9, 7-0
4. Chapters 10-0, 11-0
5. Chapters 12-1-0, 12-2-0
6. Chapter 13, Index (General)
7. Chapters 2-0, 6-0
8. Chapters 3-0, 3-A

List #2

Chapters 2, 6, 7, 3, 12-1, 12-2, 9-1, 4, 5, 9-2, 9-3, 12-3.

This book is dedicated to Joe Duffer and Joe Pro for keeping golf alive and is intended to serve as the Duffer's Bible, the Golf Nut's Catalog, the Circuit Player's Handbook and the Instructor's Textbook.

Homer Kelley

Homer Kelley

CONTENTS

TITLE	CHAPTER	PAGES
Homer Kelley		VI-VII
A Note From The Golfing Machine, LLC		VIII
Forward		IX-X
Preface		XI-XIV
Golf as an unmapped frontier		
Table of Contents		XV
Golf as areas of interest		
Introduction	1	1-11
Golf as a game		
Statements of Principle	2	12-45
Golf as a science		
Component Translation	3	46-55
Golf as a personal program		
Wrist Positions — Individual	4	56-62
Golf as a handful		
Wrist Positions — Combinations	5	63-65
Golf as a double handful		
Power Package	6	66-92
Golf as a mechanical device		
Twenty-Four Basic Components	7	93-115
Golf as a basic assembly		
Twelve Sections	8	116-120
Golf as a standard sequence of motions		
Three Zones	9	121-133
Golf as a three lane freeway		
Catalog of Basic Component Variations	10	134-210
Golf as a parts catalog		
Summary of Chapter 10	11	211-220
Golf as a shopping list		
Stroke Patterns	12	221-230
Golf as instant simplification		
Non-Interchangeable Components	13	231
Golf as square pegs and round pegs		
The Computer	14	232-234
Golf as a programmed computer		
Glossary	15	235-240
Golf as a point of view		
Index	16	241-245
Golf as a warehouse inventory		

CHAPTER ONE

INTRODUCTION
INTRODUCTION TO THE GAME
FUNDAMENTALS

1-0. GENERAL Is Golf an easy game or a difficult game? It is both. It is many things to all participants.

It is an easy game, in that no amount of ignorance about the technique can, alone, prevent players from completing the trip from Tee to Cup. If an urge to reduce this ignorance seizes one, this can be done in easy steps — over the centuries. Or at as fast a pace as the individuals can assimilate and apply massive doses of scientific explanations in their drive toward the "Ideal" in understanding the technique of Faultless Golf, or just something in-between these extremes. Are there any shortcuts? Indeed, and typical of short-cuts, they can easily turn out to be the longest route. Chapter 12-0 has an example of a safe one.

It is a difficult game in that total perfection is virtually unattainable because the Golf Stroke is fantastically complex demanding of mechanical precision — whether consciously or subconsciously applied — and ruthlessly deviates with every slightest stretching of tolerances during application.

1-A. LAW All the laws operating in the Golf Stroke — Force and Motion, Geometry and Trigonometry, Materials and Structure etc., have been known since at least the days of Isaac Newton. No instructor or player put these laws into anything. Nor can they or anyone else be exempted from compliance with them. Laws are the Modus Operandi of their Principle and it is their unalterable Identity. Only clear Identities can produce precise applications.

1-B. SIMPLICITY Treating a complex subject or action as though it were simple, multiplies its complexity because of the difficulty in systematizing missing and unknown factors or elements. Demanding that golf instruction be kept simple does not make it simple — only incomplete and ineffective. Unless this is recognized, golf remains a vague, frustrating, infuriating form of exertion. "Simplicity" buffs may find Chapter 5-0 or 12-5 sufficient.

INTRODUCTION

FUNDAMENTALS

1-C. GEOMETRY It's not the *theorems* but merely the *shapes* and *lines* of Plane Geometry — familiar to all — that are used herein. Most useful are lines and relationships that are flat, parallel, horizontal, vertical, straight, On Plane or centered because their precision can be checked visually — there is no question of degree in such alignments.

1-D. STRUCTURE Then, there is the matter of structure. The house that is built plumb, square and level is geometrically correct. But there is also the matter of proper materials. The vertical wall will support a load that would crumple a leaning wall. But a vertical picket fence will never support the load easily handled by a vertical brick wall.

So, besides being geometrically correct, a structure must not be loaded beyond the strength of its materials. The small frame may be capable of greater speed but incapable of supporting a sharp acceleration force. While the heavy-weights can develop tremendous acceleration, they may be able to move fast enough to keep up with it only briefly. So the length of the Stroke should vary with a player's speed and strength and the Thrust demands of the selected Stroke Pattern.

1-E. PATTERN DEVELOPMENT To adjust, compensate, interchange, and correct every component, and to detect imprecisions, is the instructor's function. The students need to know only the factors and components, etc., of their particular Stroke Patterns as recommended and assembled by the instructor. Or themselves. The student who can play and practice only occasionally should not be induced to proceed on the lines of detail and precision that a prospective champion would need.

The process does have a degree of latitude but this latitude in instruction is invariably reflected in a latitude of scoring potential. The instruction should fit and fill the student's capacities and opportunities. The student must not expect to play a game with more precision than is built into it. But every student should achieve a commensurate degree of consistency and play with a satisfying assurance of competence to perform within these built-in limitations and that, at any time, the limitations can be reduced by merely increasing the precision of all or any part of the present game.

The student must approach instruction as a step-by-step process. The only real short cuts are more and more know-how. A careless beginning can be disastrous. Every board and every panel must be cut to fit its place and cut to fit in with the overall design. It's as premature to expect the *complete* results of instruction before the last factor is fitted in, understood and mastered.

INTRODUCTION

FIRST STEPS

1-F. RIGHT ARM OR LEFT The "mystery" of the Mechanics of Golf fades away when Right Arm participation is understood (7-3). Whether its participation is active or passive is difficult to detect visually because in either case the Left Arm is ALWAYS SWINGING and the Right Forearm is ALWAYS DRIVING. It is always a Left Arm Stroke unless the Right Elbow replaces the Left Shoulder as the center of the Clubhead Arc. (10-3-K)

This, alone, does not properly separate "Hitters" and "Swingers" because it is possible to "Swing" the Club with either Arm but only the Right Arm can actually "Hit." (See 10-19.) However, you will save yourself much anguish by using the Right Hand just for sensing and controlling acceleration and the Left Hand just for sensing and controlling alignments. Right Hand — Clubhead. Left Hand — Clubface. Essentially, the Left Hand should be consciously Monitored (5-0) from Start up (8-4) to Finish (8-12) so there will be no unintentional or panicky wobble. (See 6-M-0.) And variations in Elbow Bend and/or location during Release will disturb Clubface control by the Right Arm, making it an inferior procedure (7-2). Only the Right Arm and Shoulder are in a position to "Push." Everything else in the Stroke "Pulls." (Study Component 19.) Therefore, with or without Shoulder Turn, the Right Arm can contribute Hand Acceleration to the Downstroke and support all elements of "Resistance To Deceleration." (See 7-3.)

1-G. APPROACHING THE GAME Actually, this entire first Chapter concerns the change of *approach* required by the advent of G.O.L.F. (2-0). Scientific Golf means you can never consider the game an enigma. Whether you approach the beginning, per 9-0 (Putting), or the end, per The Preface (The Triad), or somewhere in between, without the Key of Educated Hands per Chapters 4 and 5, more information only means more confusion. G.O.L.F. is a game for thinkers, and as detailed as this book is, it is still greatly dependent on thinking players. Therefore, it is very important that the player have an understanding of the laws of geometry, structure, force, motion, etc., to properly apply these Mechanics as the player's increased skill requires a tightening of tolerances of permissible deviations in execution. Hitting the Ball is the easiest part of the game — hitting it effectively is the most difficult. Why trust instinct when there is a science. The instructor can only inform and explain — the student must absorb and apply. When better judgment is the margin of victory, it is misleading to give unscientific procedures the credit.

INTRODUCTION

GENERAL INFORMATION

1-H. MISCELLANEOUS NOTES Terminology is a matter of selection. Selections herein are based on the power to describe, differentiate and categorize — and also on brevity and euphony. The appropriate term promotes communication. The extreme brevity herein is dictated by the advantages of holding such voluminous information to a one volume Handbook. Because of questions of all kinds, reams of additional detail must be made available — but separately, and probably endlessly.

Every separate item in the Stroke is properly understood only when learned and mastered separately and its separate identity maintained. The Golf Stroke is one piece like an ocean liner — not like an Indian dugout canoe. Proper design and assembly are required. Then interchangeability, correction or refinements are simple adjustments. Consider the Crash and Relative Translation Procedure alternatives in 3-C and 3-D.

There is little excuse for forcing the average week-end golfer — *who has some strong tendency or other* — to adopt any procedure or Stroke Pattern that calls for the elimination of that tendency. It is far easier to develop a Stroke Pattern that properly compensates for it. Change the factors that are easily controlled to fit those that are difficult to change.

There is no effort to classify any Stroke Pattern as best or worst, except on the basis of Mechanical Advantage. But there is undoubtedly a best "central" Stroke Pattern for each individual. An Authorized Instructor's assistance should be employed to work out the most suitable basic Pattern. Component Variations (Chapters 10 and 11) are listed progressively — that is, where possible, from the simplest to the most sophisticated or else from the least restrictive to Zero. Especially regarding Pivot or Body Position Categories because these have, for that reason alone, been considered as required — or "standard" — for centuries. The same applies to Wrist Action (10-18-A). Now, herein, they are just a basic Variation because the term still fits.

In the interest of brevity, regardless of how often any point is mentioned, every effort has been made not to discuss any one aspect more than once. A complete definition can only be the sum of the comments about it. And consider, in a definition, the terms used as against those that might have served but were not used. The unused terms may have been partially correct but the ones used are the nearest to perfect for the intended connotation.

INTRODUCTION

GENERAL INFORMATION

Capitalization of the first letter is employed to restrict the connotation of a term to the golfer's application *only*. Which is narrower than the general application in some instances and wider in other instances. Note especially that the capitalized term may include its entire classification or only a player's Stroke Pattern. As a term is specifically defined herein, that is the basic connotation which is always a dictionary definition but not necessarily that of *Physics, Electrical,* etc. The dictionary is generally considered a standard of precision. Scientific terms in quotes denote a loose application with obvious intent, because no better term seems available. Measurements given herein are for the golf course rather than for the laboratory but the laboratory will show them well within acceptable tolerances. Clarity and usefulness are the only motive. The result is that this book provides a complete, unified golfing terminology. Even if a term offends, use it as indicated, anyway. It has ample justification, and probably much more than the term you've been applying.

INTRODUCTION

SAMENESSES

1-J. BASICS   The chapters on "Basics" are devoted to those elements that constitute the "samenesses" of Golf Strokes (Chapters 2, 7, 8, 9, 14) as differentiated from those elements that constitute the differences (Chapters 4, 5, 6, 10, 11, 12, 13). Basics, as well as Variations, are always interpreted and adjusted to the requirements of the governing Stroke Pattern (Chapter 12) as a whole.

For example — Foot Action. Whether Foot Action is the procedure, the result or the cause in shifting weight is of small importance as compared with understanding its mere involvement. Which is — *IF* the weight is shifted, it must be from one foot to the other and always for the same *reason*. That is the BASIC fact about Foot Action that stands independent of speed, degree, direction, technique, procedures or other such factors. It is not that the weight was shifted that alters a Stroke Pattern but the procedure employed to accomplish it. Learn to distinguish the "samenesses" from the "differences." The "sameness" here is — "The feet were moved because the weight was shifted." The "difference" is — "The feet were moved in a certain manner." Regardless of which manner the feet were moved. So — IF the feet were moved, they were still moved because the weight was shifted. (See 7-17.)

Now an important point for careful consideration — is, the player benefited by this fragmentation of the Golf Stroke? Undoubtedly. Not only eventually, but immediately.

The more rudimentary a player's skill, the less difference the "differences" make and the more difference the "samenesses" make. The more precise a player's skill becomes, the more this is reversed.

Considering that a player has twenty-four components of the Stroke to control, and that he seldom uses precisely the same Stroke Pattern more than once in a lifetime, the difficulties seem staggering. A "Feel" System without an "Engineering" System is a lop-sided lottery, and a "Feel" System is indispensable in such a complex action as we have in the Golf Stroke. The Engineering System isolates and coordinates the factors and components. The Feel System translates them *individually* into a describable *sensation* — describable to, and by, the individual player. This same process integrates individual components into appropriate combinations — with controllable variations — until the entire action becomes a describable whole, both as a mechanism and as a sensation. This dual process is "The Star System *of* Geometrically Oriented Linear Force." Let Mechanics produce and Feel reproduce.

INTRODUCTION

SAMENESSES

The program for solid progress is the acquisition of one factor at a time. Starting any place. But preferably at one end of the Machine or other — the clubface or the feet. Preferably the feet. At the Practice Range or Golf Course. Preferably at the Practice Range. With or without professional Authorized instruction. Preferably with. Advisedly with! Imploredly with! An Authorized Instructor.

Then the fitting, adjusting and aligning are continually checked and rechecked and refined toward "zero deviation" from the ideal, for every item listed on the selected Stroke Pattern — over and over — with steady, satisfying improvement. Basics, as well as Variations, are always interpreted and adjusted to the requirements of the governing Stroke Pattern as a whole.

INTRODUCTION

DIFFERENCES

1-K. VARIATIONS The Catalog of Component Variations (Chapters 10 and 11) is a list of the possible variations of the Twenty-Four Basic Components. It assures the elimination of unknown variables. It also assures the inclusion of those factors that will produce special effects when needed. It is devoted to the "differences" of the Golf Stroke as differentiated from the "samenesses" presented under "Basics."

Omissions may occur in some categories. It is hoped that all omissions are intentional for reasons of small usefulness, unnecessary complication, etc. It is intended that every likely variation be included in each category so that regardless of any player's procedure, the Stroke will include an item from each of the twenty-four categories. All that is necessary to develop a repeating Stroke is to identify each item and avoid deviating unintentionally.

Every faulty, pointless, misinformed or arbitrary mechanical impropriety cannot possibly be covered. Unless noted, no listed items are in themselves improper. Only their indiscriminate and haphazard misapplications, omissions and changes. Procedures that are not listed in their categories can, however, be examined and described in some manner understandable to their possessors and so become repeatable. This is the function of the "X" classification as explained in Chapter 10-0. Many variations are not listed in the Catalog simply because they are advisedly teamed with Variations that *are* listed — Proxy Variations. Applying them otherwise is a player's choice and risk, but that does not make them Catalog omissions.

Apparently there is no factor — including Clubhead Throwaway — that cannot, by proper assembly, adjustment, alignment, etc., be worked into a fairly effective Stroke Pattern for some application or other. Many things unintentionally *affect* the Stroke by affecting its *execution*. This is merely faulty execution. It cannot be classified as a mechanical variation. (Study 10-24-F.)

Otherwise — any position, motion, action or condition not listed in the Catalog Section is considered a Basic Element and not a mechanical factor that alters a Stroke Pattern. (Also, see Chapter 13.)

INTRODUCTION

THE MACHINE

1-L. THE MACHINE CONCEPT It is soon apparent that the body can duplicate a machine. Grasp the parallel and escape limiting old concepts. Develop the "Machine Feel" to where you can just turn it loose and trust it. View the Left Shoulder as a Hinge arrangement, not as a shoulder at all. The Right Arm becomes a piston — with steam or air hoses and the whole bit. The Hands become adjustable clamps with two-way power actuators — for Vertical and Rotational manipulation. The Left Wrist is merely a hinge-pin allowing Wristcock but no Wristbend. The more of this translation a player can accomplish the more understandable both golf and its Machine Equivalent become.

This Machine has Three Functions — to control: A) The Clubshaft, B) the Clubhead, and C) the Clubface. All other elements of the Golf Stroke design are concerned with facilitating and implementing these three activities (per 5-0.) But if these other elements are unintentionally omitted (Zeroed) or altered (different Variation), the Feel changes and the Stroke becomes "ungrooved" and confusion sets in. (See 2-M-2 and 7-23.)

A. The Inclined Plane is Club<u>shaft</u> Control. (See 2-F and 4-0.)
B. The Pressure Points are Club<u>head</u> Control. (See 2-K and 4-0.)
C. The Left Wrist is Club<u>face</u> Control. (See 2-G and 4-0.)

A mechanical device (as sketched 1-L) is simple and has few moving parts, but the human body as its counterpart has altogether too many (as listed in Chapter 7). Every such part requires control by some pre-selected procedure. This is done through "The Catalog" (Chapters 10 and 11).

Power and control are scientific and geometric and are proportionably and progressively dependable. Sheer determination or sheer muscular effort are helpless — except when directed at mastering the procedure which can bring acceptable results.

In every athletic activity, success seems to be unquestionably proportional to the player's sense of balance and force — whether innate or acquired. Off-balance force is notoriously erratic. The mechanical device has no balance problem but the human machine does, and mastery of the Pivot (Zone #1) is so essential for good Golf. (See 3-F-7.)

INTRODUCTION

THE MACHINE

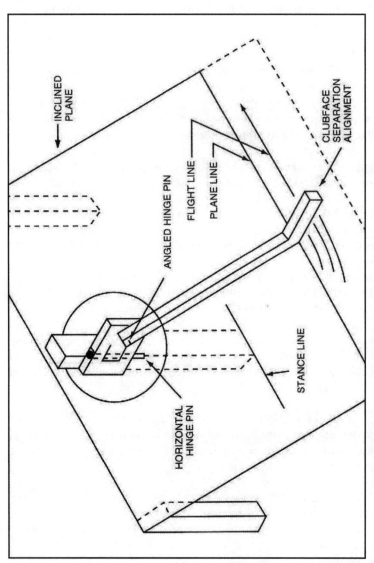

1-L. Basic Golfing Machine — to show how the Geometry and Physics of Force and Motion can be co-ordinated in any Stroke Pattern for maximum efficiency — not how it should look or feel. The above arrangement produces Dual Horizontal Hinge Action (10-10-D).

INTRODUCTION

THE MACHINE

Use Sketch 1-L — Use the Basic Golfing Machine to see and understand the following characteristics of all Mechanically and Geometrically correct Golf Strokes — from the longest Drive to the Shortest Putt, per Chapter 2. Visualize this System as based on three all-encompassing Primary Concepts on which all details can be easily attached as they surface — they are — The Hinge Action (2-G) of an Angular Motion (2-K) operating on an Inclined Plane (2-F), which must be seen as the Basic Golf Stroke. Cross check the following, throughout the book, where applicable. Actually a true gyroscope in construction and operation (10-13).

1. The Stationary Post (player's head) accurately returns the Clubhead through the ball (Centered Arc);
2. The Post may turn (Pivot) but does not "sway" or "bob."
3. There is no wobble in the Clubshaft attachment (Grip).
4. The Hinge Assembly controls the Clubface alignment.
5. The Clubshaft lies full length on a flat, tilted plane.
6. The Clubshaft always points at the Plane Line except when they are parallel to each other.
7. The Lever Assembly is driven by exerting pressure against it.
8. No *portion* of the Lever Assembly can swing *forward* independently.
9. Regardless of how the Lever Assembly is driven, it moves in a circle.
10. The Lever Assembly must be driven through Impact by an On Plane force (moving toward the Plane Line).
11. Clubhead Force and Motion is On Plane at right angles to the Longitudinal Center of Gravity (the direction of the Motion) and varies with the Speed, Mass and Swing Radius.
12. Ball Speed is dependent on both *before* Impact and *after* Impact Clubhead Speed.
13. The Clubhead travels Down-and-Out until it reaches its "Low Point."
14. Divots are taken "Down-and-Out" — not just "Down".
15. The Club starts up-and-in after "Low Point" but the *thrust* continues Down Plane during the Follow-Through.
16. The Plane Line controls the Clubhead Line-Of-Flight. Clubface alignment controls the Ball Line-Of-Flight.
17. The Clubface needs to be square to the Line-Of-Flight only at Point of Separation.
18. Changing the Plane Angle has no effect on the Plane Line.
19. Stance Line, Plane Line and Flight Line are normally parallel.
20. For any given Line Of Compression (through the ball) every Machine must produce *identical* Impact alignments.
21. The relations of all Machine positions and motions can be described by a geometric figure.

CHAPTER TWO

STATEMENT OF PRINCIPLE
INTRODUCTION TO MECHANICS

2-0. GENERAL   To Star System Golfers the letters G.O.L.F. instantly separate this system from other systems, which only teach GOLF (without the periods). It has also been given the following application:

G̲eometrically O̲riented L̲inear F̲orce

Principles are simple — their applications get complicated. The Principle of Golf is the "Line of Compression." The Mechanics of Golf is the *production and manipulation* of the "Line of Compression." The Secret of Golf is sustaining the "Line of Compression." Precision is recognizing and reconciling minute differentiations.

A precision Golf Stroke includes three Basic Essentials and three Basic Imperatives.
   A. The Three Basic Essentials are:
      1. A stationary Head
      2. Balance
      3. Rhythm
   B. The Three Basic Imperatives are:
      1. A "Flat" Left Wrist
      2. A Clubhead Lag Pressure Point
      3. A straight Plane Line

Every component of an efficient and dependable Golf Stroke has a proper relationship to every other component and that relationship is geometrical. This chapter is a brief statement of these relationships. Study 1-H in this connection.

Because this book is based on Law — the geometry and physics of Force and Motion — this chapter is included to show those who understand such things, how they are applied herein. Therefore, the terminology is that with which they can relate. So, whatever you can glean from this chapter, you are that much ahead. The Three Imperatives and Essentials operate to correct faulty procedures. So, if they seem elusive, it is *invariably* because you are trying to execute them *while you hit the ball — in your accustomed manner.* That *must* all be reversed. Learn to do those things even if you miss the ball — until you no longer miss it. *There is no successful alternative* (3-B).

STATEMENT OF PRINCIPLE

BOUNCE

2-A. RESILIENCE The response of the Ball to different applications of Force is the factor that determines how Force (LOC) must be applied to produce a desired result.

Resilience is the key factor in ball response. Neither a rock nor a spoonful of clay will act the same as a golf ball. The ball is subjected to a violent, deforming compression. The ball is actually distorted, not compressed — except for reduction of one dimension. Rubber is incompressible. Trapped air bubbles can be compressed — but not the rubber itself — it flows. It flows in two directions — but acts like a solid in the third. This third direction is the direction of the compressing force. The momentum of the violent return flow after impact also distorts the ball by exceeding the normal dimension of the compressed point. The "kick" given to the ball by this action is an important factor in ball response. Roll of the ball on the face of an inclined striker does not account for all the action produced by such an impact, especially in imparting spin to the ball. When the direction of the compressing force does not pass exactly through the center of the ball, a spin will be imparted to the ball. It will rotate on the plane of a line drawn from the line of compression to a parallel *center* line.

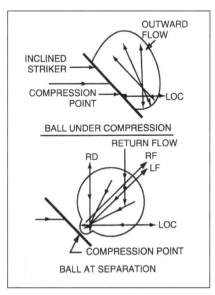

2-A. Resilience
See 2-C-1 for Symbol Legend

STATEMENT OF PRINCIPLE

HEIGHT AND DISTANCE

2-B. TRAJECTORY CONTROL   Clubface loft (2-C-1) and Hinge Action (2-D) determine altitude and backspin and are the basic elements of Ball Control. (Also study 9-3.) The sketches herein show Force Vectors as directional only, in order to depict how their interplay controls Backspin and Ball behavior.

A speeding, spinning ball is subject to the Venturi Effect, meaning that an increase in the velocity of a flow of air decreases its *cross-sectional* pressure. The air passing over (A), that portion of the ball that is turning *with* the passing air, will move faster than the air passing over (B), that portion of the ball that is turning *against* the passing air. Because the air at "A" will exert less pressure than the air at "B," the ball will be pushed in the direction of "A." If portion "A" is *above* the center, the pressure from "B" will produce a vertical lift. If "A" leans to either side of the vertical, the pressure at "B" will produce a sidewise push toward "A." If "A" is toward the player's left it will produce a hook — to his right, a slice. The action will be definite — not wavering. Predictable and controllable. The more airspeed, the more effect for any given amount of spin. Without backspin, the ball will wobble along erratically. The dimpled cover greatly magnifies this wobble control. It follows, that a Ball with "Overspin" has no "Lift" — the "Duck Hook." A truly well hit Ball (Three Dimensional Impact 2-C-0) from any Club will have a higher trajectory than otherwise, simply because the increased velocity and Backspin will lengthen the upward portion of the flight. In addition, when there is Clubface "Layback" during Impact, the additional height will be even more noticeable as the Impact Interval lengthens. ALWAYS — the more Compression Leakage, the more faulty the Angle of Separation (2-D-0) — that is, lower trajectory and less distance.

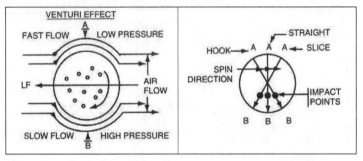

2-B. Trajectory Control. The Venturi Effect

STATEMENT OF PRINCIPLE

FORCE VECTORS

2-C-0. LINEAR FORCE The ball will respond to non-linear (angular) force exactly the same as to linear forces *only* if the application can produce forces equally linear to the ball, but not necessarily linear to anything external to the ball. Briefly stated, it is necessary to find a way to compress the ball through a particular point along a particular line, and maintain this compression through this same particular point and along this same particular straight line through the entire arc of the Impact Interval. Study 2-K and 2-N.

To maintain compression at a particular point, that *point*, then, must rotate around the same center that the rotating force does, not the physical center of the ball nor the gravitational center — just the point of compression. In other words, the original contact points of Clubface and Ball *must remain* in contact throughout the entire Impact Interval. This is possible only if the motion — or arc — is uniform. Therefore, there must be a perfectly centered action — or a compensating manipulation — during Impact. If the Swing Radius is not at Full Extension during Impact, an effect in Compression Leakage is unavoidable. Therefore, this must be habitually taken into account for distance calculations.

The Ball leaves the Clubface with a force proportional to the compression produced by Impact. Then, the ideal result of the above procedures is maximum compression. Any Clubface imprecision during Impact will permit compression to leak away. Lost compression cannot be recovered. Between the precision Impact of 2-C-1#3 and the total loss of compression in 2-C-3#3, there can be every degree of Compression Leakage. Backspin is NOT Compression Leakage but a valuable divergent Force assignment. Your main lines of defense are the Flat Left Wrist, Hinge Action, and a Three Dimensional Downstroke — that is, DOWNward (Attack Angle) AND OUTward (Plane Angle) AND FORward (Approach Angle), per 2-C-1#2A/B. (Study 2-G, 2-N and 7-3.) All Three MOTIONS are the product of the influence of the Inclined Plane on the Downstroke Forces.

Force and Motion Vectors must comply with Newton's first three laws:

1. **The Law of Inertia:** *There is no change in the motion of a body unless a resultant force is acting upon it.*
2. **Force and Acceleration:** *Whenever a net (unbalanced) force acts on a body, it produces an acceleration in the direction of the force, an acceleration that is directly proportional to the force and inversely proportional to the mass of the body.*
3. **Reacting Forces:** *For every acting force there is a reacting force that is equal in magnitude but opposite in direction.*

STATEMENT OF PRINCIPLE

SWINGERS HINGING

2-C-1. LINEAR FORCE: THE IDEAL APPLICATION IDEAL VECTOR ALIGNMENT (SHOWN WITH IMPACT INTERVAL EXTENDED TO LOW POINT).

This is designated the "Ideal Application." It produces perfect Vector alignments because the Angled Clubshaft and the Closing Clubface (the "Full Roll" of Horizontal Hinge Action — 7-10) are rotating around the same center and there is no glancing force except for backspin — 2-C-1#3 shows a Vector <u>Sum</u> instead of a <u>Resultant</u> Force.

The 2-C-1 sketches show Dual Horizontal Hinge Action (10-10).

VECTOR SYMBOL LEGEND
Herein, Vector Symbols indicate only the direction of a Force.

CF — Clubhead Force	LD — Lob Direction	M — Momentum
CL — Center Line	LF — Line of Flight	R — Rotation
CP — Compression Point	LOC — Line of Compression	RD — Rebound Direction
I — Inertia	LP — Lob Point	RF — Resultant Force

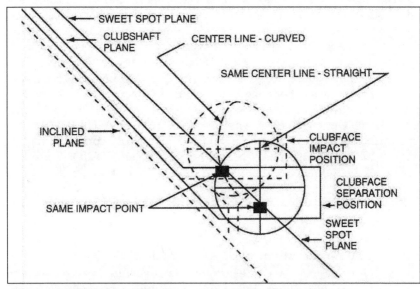

2-C-1#1 Linear Force—Ideal Application Looking Toward Target. Showing Inclined Planes per 2-F. Showing Plane Lines per 2-N.

STATEMENT OF PRINCIPLE

SWINGERS HINGING

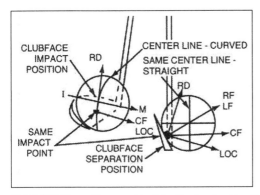

2-C-1 #2A Linear Force — Ideal Application Looking Toward Player. Showing Impact Geometry per 2-G.

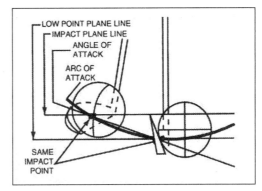

2-C-1 #2B Linear Force — Ideal Application Looking Toward Player. Showing Clubhead Path Geometry per 2-N.

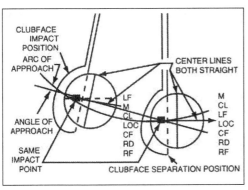

2-C-1 #3 Linear Force — Ideal Application Looking Down. Showing Impact Geometry per 2-G. Showing Clubhead Path Geometry per 2-N. Turn Book Upside Down for Player's View.

STATEMENT OF PRINCIPLE

CLUBFACE LAY-BACK

2-C-2. LINEAR FORCE: THE CUT SHOT (SHOWN WITH IMPACT INTERVAL EXTENDED TO LOW POINT).

A "Cut Shot" is any Stroke using Vertical Hinging (10-10) through Impact regardless of Plane Line (10-5) or the preceding Wrist Action (10-18). Either the Dual Vertical or Vertical (only) Hinge Action should be used for the Cut Shot to avoid weakening the Line Of Compression. It produces a higher than normal trajectory and less than normal roll—better "bite."

The 2-C-2 sketches show Dual Vertical Hinge Action (10-10).

See 2-C-1 for Vector Component Legend

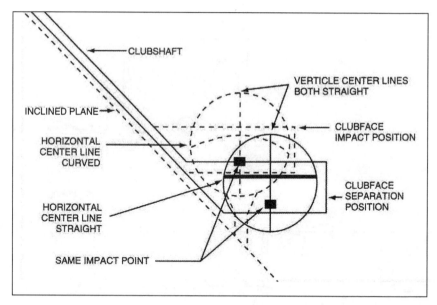

2-C-2 #1 Linear Force—The Cut Shot. Looking Toward Target

STATEMENT OF PRINCIPLE

CLUBFACE LAY-BACK

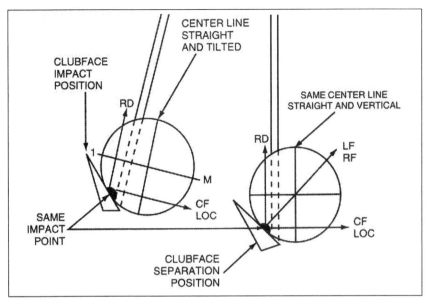

2-C-2 #2 Linear Force—The Cut Shot Looking Toward Player.

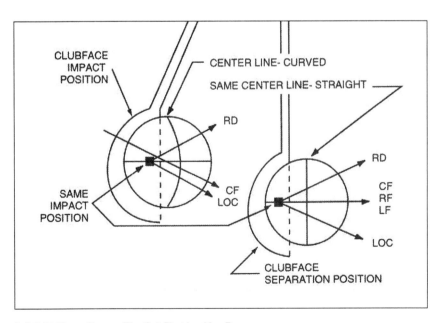

2-C-2 #3 Linear Force—The Cut Shot Looking Down.

STATEMENT OF PRINCIPLE

BALLISTIC PATH

2-C-3. LINEAR FORCE: THE LOB SHOT (SHOWN WITH IMPACT INTERVAL EXTENDED TO LOW POINT).

The Lob Shot is a special application of the Cut Shot procedure. The Club moves parallel to the ground and the "laying back" motion (typical of a Vertical Hinge Action) tilts the Clubface under the Ball, lifting the ball and releasing the Impact Compression. Distance is reduced and backspin is lost, resulting in a "Floater" that will tend to roll excessively on landing were it not for its ballistic-type trajectory. "Sweeping the Ball" describes the procedure — Come in Low and stay Low — which is an out-and-out Steering Type Throwaway with a long Low Point Line — a flat spot in the Clubhead Orbit. It MUST be a true Reverse Roll Vertical Hinge Motion, per 7-10. Very good for the Chip and Roll Shots — as well as for the Duffer's low flying "Nothing Ball." Unless Impact occurs near or at the low point of the Down-stroke arc (directly opposite the Left Shoulder — except opposite the Hands when the Left Wrist is Bending), the result may be a Duffer's low flying "nothing ball." The "Up-stroke" must not begin until Low Point is reached.(See 8-11)

The 2-C-3 sketches show Vertical (only) Hinge Action (10-10).

See 2-C-1 for Vector Component Legend.

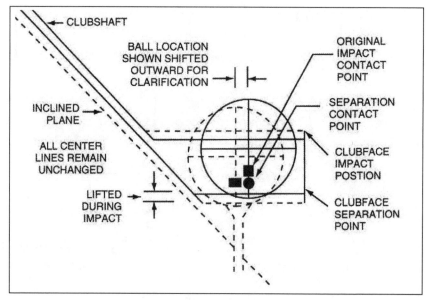

2-C-3 #1 Linear Force—The Lob Shot Looking Toward Target.

STATEMENT OF PRINCIPLE

BALLISTIC PATH

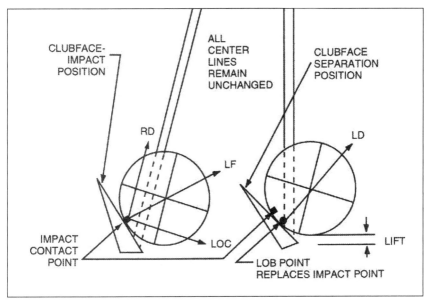

2-C-3 #2 Linear Force—The Lob Shot Looking Toward Player.

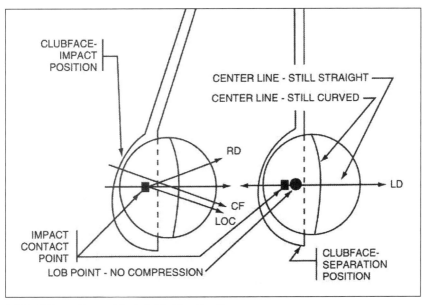

2-C-3 #3 Linear Force—The Lob Shot Looking Down.
Turn Book Upside Down for Player's View.

STATEMENT OF PRINCIPLE

PUTTING

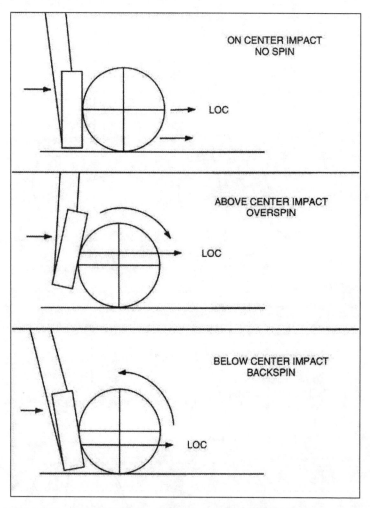

2-C-4-A. Linear Force: Putter Impact Action showing Vertical (only) Hinge Action (10-10). Inconsistent Hand-to-Ball positioning will vary the LOC location and the ball travel. (Study 2-E.)

2-C-4-B. Directional Deviation: Can be diagnostic:
    1. Shoulder Turn "Closes" the Clubface—the "Pull"
    2. Elbow Bend holds the Clubface "Open"—the "Push"
    3. Bending the Left Wrist makes the Clubface alignment erratic (Study 2-F, 2-G and 2-J-1.)

STATEMENT OF PRINCIPLE

DIRECTIONAL VECTORS

2-D-0. DIRECTIONAL FACTORS Another need for a "perfect circle" motion is for directional control. If the *Clubface* maintains a constant relationship to the radius of its rotation, whether the face is "open," "closed," or "square," then the direction imparted at any one point of the arc will always be the same for "centered" (Sweet Spot) Impact (2-F). The Lever Assembly is seldom more then an inch from Full Extension at Impact.

The direction of the ball will always be properly at right angles to the leading edge of the Clubface at separation, unless there is enough time and speed for the Venturi Effect to alter it, when scattered vectors have introduced a non-vertical spin. That is — the Flight *Line* and the Flight *Path* will always be per 2-E and the trajectory will depend on Compression Leakage per 2-B. And, Tilting the Leading Edge changes the Club*face* alignment: Up — to the left; Down — to the right, merely deviating from the Address Plane Angle will do this by tilting the Clubshaft.

The Angular Motion in a Golf Stroke is compounded by its dual Centers. One Center is for the Clubhead as a whole, and the other Center is for the Clubface position. Study 7-10 in regard to the difference between Clubhead and Clubface Hinging. Deviations in Horizontal Hinge Action during Impact can produce considerable variation in direction but little change in trajectory. Deviations in Vertical Hinge Action during Impact can produce great variation in trajectory but little change in direction. Angled Hinge Action on the flatter Planes (10-6, 10-7) approaches the Horizontal Hinge characteristics and as the Plane steepens, it moves toward Vertical Hinge characteristics. (Study 2-G.)

The direction of the ball will be the resultant of the Vectors of the forces acting on the ball, unless all the forces can be focused on one line (2-C-1#3), directional force, then, would be stabilized and, in addition, the distance of the shot would be propelled by the sum of the forces acting on it — instead of the much smaller Resultant Force of scattered Vectors. The Vector of the spin-producing force cannot be brought into the alignment or there would be a loss of altitude control as well as Spin control. But the Spin can be produced on the plane of the actual Line of Flight and, thus, exert no interference with the alignment of the other Vectors. But, the Ball leaves the Clubface at Impact Separation, not Address, nor Fix, nor Low Point, unless they were identical to Impact position. Study text and sketches in 2-B and 2-C.

STATEMENT OF PRINCIPLE

DIRECTIONAL VECTORS

The force of the Impact will hold the ball against the face of the orbiting Clubhead and so carry it along the same circular path. This places the ball under "Newton's First Law (2-C-0)," which requires that the ball leave its circular path at right angles to the radius of that path at the point at which it leaves that path. The hook-face alignment of the Clubhead, designed to give it the proper relation to the Target Line during Impact, diverts the ball from its On Plane tangential path to the Above Plane chord to its orbit.

The law of "Equal and Opposite Reaction" (2-L #3) also means that the flatter the Clubface angle (high numbers), the less the Clubhead will be slowed by Impact forces but the more it will be driven toward the ground (Divot) and vice versa with the steeper Clubface (low numbers).

Newton's Second Law (Force and Acceleration) accounts for the relationship between the Venturi Effect and Wind Direction that increases or reduces the effects of either one, a fade into the right side cross-wind can result in a straight Flight Path.

2-D-1. MAJOR DIRECTIONAL FACTORS listed below (with reference numbers) occur with uncompensated deviations from the Stroke Pattern and/or from Address configuration (3-F-5, 7-2) whether intentional or not and/or whether uncompensated or not. Changes in Component Variations or execution from Pattern (12-1, 12-2) or Address (3-F-5) configuration. Use 12-3.

1. Power Package Component Action (6-H)
2. Pivot Component Action (7-3, 7-13, 7-16)
3. Power Package Component Position (7-8)
4. Pivot Component Position (7-12)
5. Plane Line Direction (10-5)
6. Bent Plane Line (4-D)
7. Angle of Approach (2-J-3)
8. Address Position Impact (7-8)
9. Off-Center Impact (2-F)
10. Lob Shot Impact (2-C-3)
11. Lag Pressure Point (7-11)
12. Clubhead Throwaway (6-D)
13. Tilted Clubface (2-D)
14. Plane Angle (2-N)
15. Ball Location/Position (2-N)
16. Aiming Point (6-E-2)
17. Clubhead Speed (7-10)
18. Club Number (2-J-1)
19. Timing (6-F)
20. Grip Type (7-2)
21. Wrist Roll (2-G)
22. Steering (3-F-7-A)
23. Quitting (3-F-7-B)
24. Bobbing (3-F-7-C)
25. Swaying (3-F-7-D)
26. Rhythm (7-10)

STATEMENT OF PRINCIPLE

IMPACT PHYSICS

2-E. CONSERVATION OF MOMENTUM Objects in a linear collision cannot separate at a speed greater than the speed of approach.

The proportion of the separation rate to the approach rate expresses the elasticity involved, and is called the Coefficient of Restitution which is 80% for the better golf balls but drops below 70% at high speeds. Of course, Compression Leakage (2-C-0) will lower that percentage.

This means that, even with precise geometrical alignments, the ball will not separate from the club at more than 80% of its approach speed. That produces, roughly, this condition — the Clubhead approaching Impact at 100 MPH has slowed to 80 MPH at separation. The ball leaves the Club at about 70 MPH (70% of 100 MPH approach speed). To do this the ball must be travelling 150 MPH. If the Clubhead speed at separation is 40 MPH, the ball can only travel 110 MPH under this law. Notice this — the ball acquires only 70% of the Clubhead "approach" speed (so there must be speed) but 100% of the Clubhead "separation" speed (so there must be resistance to deceleration). Zero Deceleration is what would give maximum ball speed for any and all approach speeds. Speed (Centripetal Pull) and Prestress (Acceleration) stiffen the Clubshaft for consistent (minimum to maximum) resistance to Impact Deceleration. Treat that "heavy" feel of "Clubhead recovery" after Impact as though it were all Impact, even though the ball is actually long gone. (See 7-11.)

The divergent Impact and Separation Vectors (2-C-1/2/3) are always equal in Angle and Force and therefore produce a bisecting Resultant Force Vector, square to both the Clubface and the Leading Edge, and the Line of Flight Vector will be on a Center line parallel to that Vector. If the Line of Compression (LOC) is not on the Vertical Center line, the Backspin will be tilted per 2-B. This tilt, proportional to the divergence of those Impact alignments, gives the only directional manipulation available (2-D, 7-2). In fact, traction produces a Venturi Effect *action* when the spinning Ball hits the ground, and the deeper the Ball-mark (up to the point of zero rebound), the greater the traction *and* the effect which determines the amount of "Bite" the Ball will have. But a golf ball does not have sufficient Angular Momentum to sustain a non-rolling spin long enough to overcome its Linear Momentum sufficiently to produce a curving Putt.

STATEMENT OF PRINCIPLE

ON PLANE MOTION

2-F. PLANE OF MOTION All the action of the Golf Club takes place on a flat, inflexible, Inclined Plane which extends well beyond the circumference of the Stroke — in *every* direction. The full length of the Clubshaft remains unwaveringly on the face of this Inclined Plane — Waggle to Follow-through. *Every other Component of the Stroke must be adjusted to comply with that requirement.* (See Sketch 1-L.) That includes the Right Forearm. (See 5-0.) The player must hold the Forearm in the *Feel* of the same Plane per 7-3, dynamically in-line. Picture the javelin thrower with the right elbow and On Plane right forearm leading the hand toward the target (Delivery Line) all during Delivery. (See 6-B-1.) The Right Forearm of every Hacker comes into Impact too high — pointing beyond the Delivery Line during Downstroke (2-J-3, 7-3). (Study 2-G and Components 5, 6, and 7.)

Regardless of where the Clubshaft and Clubhead are joined together, it always feels as if they are joined at the Sweet Spot, the longitudinal center of gravity, the line of the pull of Centripetal Force. So, there is a "Clubshaft" Plane and a "Sweet Spot," or "Swing," Plane. But herein, unless otherwise noted, "Plane Angle" and "Plane Line" always refer to the Center of Gravity application. (Study 2-N.) Except during Impact, the Clubshaft can travel on, or to-and-from, either Plane because Clubshaft rotation must be around the Sweet Spot, not vice versa. So Clubhead "Feel" is Sweet Spot feel for #3 Pressure Point sensing functions. If Lag Pressure is lost, the Hands tend to start the hosel (instead of the Sweet Spot) toward Impact — that mysterious "Shank." When in doubt, "Turn" the Clubface so both the Clubshaft and the Sweet Spot will be on the same Plane at the Start Down. Both Planes always pass through the Lag Pressure Point. (Study 6-C-2-A.) Except for Impact, the Clubshaft is an acceptable Visual Equivalent for both Planes, especially if the Clubface is Turned "On Plane."

There are some very simple but very accurate checks for being "On Plane." Whenever the Clubshaft is parallel to the ground, it must also be parallel to the base line of the Inclined Plane, which is usually (but not always) the Line of Flight also. Otherwise, the end of the Club that is closest to the ground must be pointing at the base line of the Inclined Plane — or extensions of that line, even if they must be extended to the horizon. Precision is lost unless Start Up is a Three Directional parallel to the Three Directional Impact, i.e., the Clubhead moves Backward, Upward, and Inward, On Plane, INSTANTLY AND SIMULTANEOUSLY — the Right Forearm Takeaway. (See 3-F-5 and 7-13)

STATEMENT OF PRINCIPLE

BASIC PLANES & HINGING

2-G. HINGE MOTION Direction Control (2-D) means Clubface alignment control. The Clubface can make two <u>Motions</u> through Impact: Close and Lay-back. Except as an "Over-Swivel" Hooding the Clubface is not a Clubface <u>Motion</u> but Clubface "Position" by reason of Grip and Ball Location (2-N-0). Therefore, only the Putter can be Hooded to any advantage. Then, of the two <u>Motions,</u> we can use the one, or the other, or both, that is: "Closing" without "Lay-back" (10-10-D); "Lay-back" without "Closing" (10-10-E); and simultaneously, "Closing" and "Lay-back."

These motions actually duplicate the three possible hinge mountings: horizontal, vertical, and angled — representing all three Basic Planes (7-5). The Hands can be educated to reproduce them by holding at least one Hand vertical or parallel to the corresponding Basic Plane. Though some procedures may cause the Clubface to "Close" in relation to the Plane Line (a "Roll Feel" per 7-10), none will be an actual rolling (4-C-3) of the Hands (See 2-C and 6-B-3-0.), or a change in Grip, Grip Type, Clubface Fix positioning or anything else. Except for its orbiting, Hinge Motion is totally inert — it changes nothing. There is, however, the "Release Roll" (Swivel) which is a true rotation of the Hands into Impact alignment by Accumulator #3 (with 10-18-A only). After the selected Hinge Action has been executed, the Swivel is again useful for Snap Rolling the Hands into their On Plane Condition for the Finish (8-12). That is the Geometry of Hinging.

The Physics of Hinging is, that, Hitting or Swinging, it is actually imparted by the turning torso and/or the orbiting Arms, per 2-K and 2-K#4/#5, as described in 10-18. For a Practice drill, Educate the Left Hand (5-0) to reproduce — with Zero Pivot — the three Hinge Actions distinct and separate, while swinging continuously back and forth: First, with the Left Hand only without a Club; then with the Left Hand and a short Club; then with both Hands; lastly, with increasing Pivot motion using the Right Forearm, per 7-19. Learning only one Action isn't helpful because you won't know their differences.

The point to be learned here is that the Club, because of the Flat Left Wrist, must always travel at the same RPM as the Arms and reproduce the Hinging intended for the selected Lag Loading procedure (10-19) per 4-D, 9-2 and 9-3, *regardless of Clubhead Extension velocity.* (See 2-P and 7-18.)

STATEMENT OF PRINCIPLE

BASIC PLANES & HINGING

Steady, "squared-away" Hinge motion of the Clubface controls its alignment during Impact. Only the Putter is so constructed as to permit visual alignment. All other Clubs are angled — or hook-faced — in relation to the Clubshaft. So an alternate reference point is needed. The Left Wrist Position is a dependable standard even for Putting. If the Grip is taken in the Impact Position, with the Left Wrist Flat and Vertical, then the Clubface will be correctly aligned if the Wrist is Flat and Vertical during Impact. (Study 7-10.) Check your Hinging constantly.

Stop at the end of a short Chip Shot — the Club at about 45 degrees. With Horizontal Hinging, the toe of the Club will point along the Plane Line; with Angled Hinging, about 45 degrees across the Plane Line; with Vertical Hinging, about 90 degrees across the Plane Line with the Clubface looking squarely at the sky, and always with a Flat Left Wrist vertical to its associated Basic Plane. "Over Roll" or "Under Roll" of the Left Wrist — NOT VERTICAL — puts the Swingle out of line with the Handle (Sketch 2-K) as much as does any other form of Clubhead Throwaway. Practice these alignments until you have the same Rhythm hitting the Ball as with your Practice Swing. Their difference is *always* Rhythm.

The KEY to this Rhythm is the #3 Accumulator (6-B-3-0). As part of the above drill, hold the 45 degree Arm position while rotating the Hands and the #3 Accumulator through the three Hinging positions, over and over until you see that each position changes the LOCATION of the Clubhead. The Point to note here is that with each Hinge Action the #3 Accumulator varies the <u>relative</u> Clubhead travel — Dual Horizontal Hinging having the longest travel and Dual Vertical the shortest. This agrees with the "Roll Characteristics" discussed in 7-10 and must be so executed to produce the proper Rhythm. Doing the above drill with Zero Accumulator #3 (6-B-3-B) will show that *all* Lag Loading and Hinge Action have Angled Hinging Travel. So — intentional use of Zero Accumulator #3 can be useful while unintentional use can be hazardous. See 2-P-0 regarding PACE. Also, see 6-B-3-0 in this connection.

When Hinge Action substitutes for Wrist Action (per 7-10), Hinging may Feel like one long, slow "Swivel" from Top to Finish. On the other hand, the Release Interval may be so quick as to make even correct Hinge Action Feel like one instantaneous Swivel. Some players even intentionally execute Impact as exclusively a Swivel, making Clubface alignments extremely fleeting and erratic. (Study 3-F-7-B and 7-20.)

STATEMENT OF PRINCIPLE

ANGULAR MOTION

2-H. ON PLANE ACCELERATION The point may be made that it is impossible to inscribe perfect circles while the center — that is the turning Shoulder — is in motion. The straight line requirements of the Compression Point are satisfied as long as the Lever Assembly Center is moving in a circle during Impact and both the Vertical and the Horizontal Centers move precisely in unison. Direction control remains stable because the Centers are also moving in a circle, that is, the circumference of the Shoulder Turn.

The spine, between the shoulders, is the center of the Shoulder Turn only, not of the Left Arm, except by specific extension of the Swing Radius. Swinging from the Wrists, the Left Shoulder, the Right Elbow, the Waist or the Feet, show it to have just too many exceptions. Though the "Head" Pivot Center is recommended, it is not at all mandatory. The important thing is that the true Swing Center for ALL COMPONENTS is around a Hinge Pin with one end *at* the top of the Stationary Head and the other in the ground, precisely between the Feet, with no regard for Body *Location* or *Position* at any time. "On Plane" Right Shoulder Motion is possible only by tilting its axis, the spine. See 7-14. In this area the Left Shoulder is helpless. The geometry of Shoulder Control deals only with the Right Shoulder, there are no guide lines for Left Shoulder control of the Right Shoulder.

Being part of both the Pivot and the Power Package, the Right Shoulder must reconcile them by moving with great precision of thrust, speed, direction, and *distance* (7-13). The Right Shoulder does not flap around haphazardly — it has many responsibilities. Variations in its Impact *location* will vary the Right Elbow's Impact Bend and so may alter the Impact alignment of the Clubface. (See 6-E and 7-23.) Also, variations in Right Shoulder location will vary the Left Shoulder location at Impact and, consequently, the Lever Assembly Radius and the Low Point location as well as the Angle of Approach (2-N). The long Backstroke Shoulder Turn produces ARC of Approach procedures. The short Shoulder Turn produces ANGLE of Approach procedures (2-J-3). Therefore, if the Shoulder Turn is too great and takes the Hands inside the proper Angle of Approach (2-J-3), then you must shift to an Arc of Approach Delivery Line to "clear the Right Hip" (2-J-3), or get an unwanted Pull, OR A SHANK. Otherwise, the Three Dimensions will become uncorrelated, inducing Compression Leakage (2-C-0) and an obvious struggle. As it goes back, so it tends to come down — because of the differences in Loading Characteristics (Components 11, 19 and 22).

STATEMENT OF PRINCIPLE

CLUBFACE POSITIONING

2-J-1. IMPACT ALIGNMENTS The geometry of all alignments stems from the Impact geometry requirements. The first step in preparation for a Golf Shot is the establishment of the Impact Conditions. (See 7-8.) The Clubface must be exactly square to the Target Line (10-5) only at the Point of Separation. The Clubface alignment at Impact Fix must fit the selected Hinge Action (7-10 and 10-10). For Horizontal Hinging, it is slightly "Open" at Impact Fix to allow for "Closing" during Impact. The longer the shot, the more "Open." Angled Hinging gives the Clubface a Slice producing uncentered motion so, while the Clubface does "Close" during Impact, Clubface alignment is slightly "Open" for short shots but, for longer shots, it must be set up more and more "Closed." The alignment for Vertical Hinging and Cut Shots are the same at Impact Fix as it is intended to be at Separation because these are "No Roll" procedures. Alternative alignment procedures are presented in 7-10. The Machine (1-L) is positioned and adjusted to the Stroke — *not vice versa* (8-0). Remember — the Impact Point must become "On Line" at Separation.

Clubface alignment also includes the requirement that the center of the Clubhead arc be so located that the Clubface strikes the ball before it strikes the ground. If the Clubface is centered on the ball while soled behind it any distance whatsoever, the radius of the Clubhead arc must be shortened or the Club will meet the ground precisely where it had been soled. This procedure of shortening the radius of the stroke is popular — that is, pulling in the Hands at Impact by raising the head and shoulders a guess-timated distance, or pulling back the Left Shoulder, or bending the Left Arm, all with that same "precision." A geometrically proper procedure is to establish the correct radius with the Clubhead raised to the desired Impact relationship. Then maintain the center of the arc — that is, the Left Shoulder — as now established, and hold the Hands at the height and angle now established, then let the Club swing down from the Wrist to rest on the ground. Now apply Extensor Action (6-B-1-D) to stretch the left arm and get as "far away from the ball as possible." (Without disturbing any of the Fix Alignments.) So — "Soled," the ball is toward the Toe of the Clubface, but "on center" for Impact. All this is the geometry for a clean pick-off. Clubshaft Lean (2-J-2), #3 Accumulator Angle (6-B-3-0), Plane Angle (7-7), Grip, (7-2), Stance Line (7-5), and Ball Location/Position (2-N) are all involved in "Soling the Club" per 7-6. At this time, remember, too, that for "Open" Clubface (and/or Left Wrist) and "Open" Pivot Components, they must be rotated in opposite directions from their "Square" alignment.

STATEMENT OF PRINCIPLE

PREPARATIONS

2-J-2. LOW POINT Because the Inclined Plane **is** inclined, the Downstroke arc of the Clubhead path on this Inclined Plane moves down-and-out from inside the Plane Line until it reaches its lowest point (See sketches in 2-C), after which it moves up-and-in back inside the Plane Line. So if Impact occurs before the low point of the arc is reached, it is an inside-out Impact — or hit — and the Clubhead will still travel outward and downward *after* Impact. Though it is an "inside-out" Impact, it is not an "inside-out" *Stroke* unless the Plane Line crosses the Line Of Flight as depicted in photo 10-5-E.

If Impact occurs beyond the low point, the Clubhead travel is up-and-back inside the Plane Line and is an outside-in Impact but not an outside-in Stroke, unless the Plane Line crosses the Line Of Flight as depicted in photo 10-5-D.

When the Ball is struck at Low Point, it is an "On Line" Impact. Ball Behavior does not indicate or alter the facts of Cross Line or On Line Impact. Study 7-2.

The ball should always be struck prior to the low point of the Downstroke, even when using a Driver, except under special conditions or to produce a special effect, which is a separate area of consideration. Theoretically, Impact at any point of a perfect circle will produce the same result except for direction. The Clubshaft is never, normally, at right angles to the Plane Line through Impact — it leans forward. So, except beyond Low Point, *always be sure that it does.*

If the Ball is struck before Low Point with an *Upstroke Motion* — Hitting "up" (Starting Up after Impact) which produces Duffers and almost all Topped Shots — (most obvious with the Putter) it disrupts the Clubhead Orbit (2-C-3, 2-N and 7-23) and the Hinging (2-G), then the Ball and the Clubhead Path become circles "exterior" to each other (like two meshing gears) and the Line of Compression rotates away and produces a no-spin floater, or Lob Shot. The circle of the ball must be "interior" to the circle of the Clubface orbit and as immovable as in a spinning centrifuge.

STATEMENT OF PRINCIPLE

ARC AND ANGLE OF APPROACH

2-J-3. VISUAL EQUIVALENTS Delivery *Paths* (7-23) guide the Hands but Delivery *Lines* are needed to guide the Clubhead and the Right Forearm (5-0). The *true* geometric Plane Line is the Basic Delivery Line. But it has a very useful Visual Equivalent — the curved blur of the Clubhead path during the Address Routine and again through Release and Impact, which can be executed as a Visual ARC of Approach Delivery Line, per Sketch 2-C-1 #2B. Per Sketch 2-C-1#3, the ANGLE of Approach straight line through the Impact and Low Points is the geometric equivalent and is the Alternate Target Line as the Clubhead Path. So the two procedures are always interchangeable, but the "Arc" is the most compatible with the "On Line" Swing and the "Line" with the "Cross Line Hit" (7-23), and, herein, they are so paired.

A. The "Visual Arc of Approach" Delivery Line is the curved line of Angular Motion and actually meets the Ball on its inside-aft quadrant as it travels down to the Low Point Plane Line and back across the Impact Plane Line again. If you find this optical illusion (2-N-0) distracting, there is the alternative of "Tracing" the true Plane Line (5-0), which can be even more precise and actually not alter the Clubhead Arc in the least. (Study 2-N-0 and 4-D-0.) This is a "Wheel Rim" Procedure (7-23) and applies to both 10-23-D and 10-23-E, per 10-19-C.

B. The straight line ANGLE of Approach Delivery Line changes the Physics of Impact because the centered *Angular* Clubhead Momentum becomes an uncentered *Linear* Momentum out toward "Right Field" without ever returning to the original 10-5-A configuration during the Follow-through. This just arbitrarily requires a 10-5-E Closed Plane Line with a steeper Plane whose Angle agrees with the new Clubshaft motions so it can maintain a straight line relation to a straight line, per 2-N-0. There is no Angle of Approach to an Angle of Approach procedure because, while the Forearm "Traces" the Delivery Line, the CLUBHEAD VISUALLY COVERS IT. But remember, the new 10-5-E Plane Line is also the Angle of Approach regardless of the Right forearm alignment (7-2-3 and 7-3). Therefore, with every change in Ball position, the Plane Line changes and the Hitter has rotated *BOTH* Grip *AND* Plane Line. Per 7-23, this is the "Wheel Track" procedure. An Address procedure mentioned in 7-9 is very helpful with this Variation.

An "Outside-In" Angle of Approach sets up an Open-Open Plane Line in exactly the same *manner* as an Inside-Out Plane Line Combination, that is, with the Clubface aligned, per 2-J-1. Angled Hinging, then, will produce an action indistinguishable from the 2-C-2 Cut Shot except for a tendency to hop to the right, per 2-E.

STATEMENT OF PRINCIPLE

THE FLAIL

2-K. ENDLESS BELT VS. THE FLAIL Angular Motion is the result of at least two divergent forces. Such as, A) Centripetal Force (the Lever Assemblies 6-A) diverting Linear Force (Right Arm Thrust 6-B-1) into a rotating motion (Hitting 10-19-A); or B) Muscle tendons pulling the Body, the Arms, and/or the Wrists around their Centers to serve — singly or in combination — as the axis of the flywheel formed by the selected Lever Assemblies (Swinging 10-19-C).

The Geometry of the Circle is Plane Geometry (2 dimensional — 4-D-0) and consists of the Circumference (and Arcs), Radius, Radians, Diameter, Tangents, Chords, Plane, and Plane Line. Only the Circumference is <u>not</u> a straight line and it is described by a Radius moving around a Center producing Centripetal Force which is the basis of the Physics of Rotation.

Rotation induces a Throw-Out action, pulling the centers of gravity of every moveable component, In-Line and On Plane with its axis or center, whether or not they were originally In-Line or On Plane. With a short radius, it can accelerate easily, and quickly acquire considerable Angular Velocity. If a portion of this mass moves to a longer radius, the slowing effect (6-C-2-B) must be computed on the basis of the total mass AS LONG AS THE *PORTION* IS BEING PROPELLED BY THE *TOTAL*. That is — the slowdown would be in the same ratio that the portion has to the whole — the original central mass. This "Transfer of Momentum" process (10-19-C) eliminates Release Deceleration (6-F-0) but not Impact Deceleration (2-M-1). This Throw-Out action is termed herein as "Centrifugal Acceleration" to indicate that Centripetal Force (Centrifugal Reaction), not muscle, is propelling the Secondary Lever Assembly (the Golf Club) into Impact. Both are subject to the Endless Belt Effect, per Sketch 2-K #6 and 7-23. Swingers are totally dependent on their skill at manipulating Centripetal Force while Hitters are not. (Study 4-D, 6-B-3-0, 6-R-0 and 7-2.)

STATEMENT OF PRINCIPLE

THE FLAIL

Compare the Primary Lever Assembly (6-A-2) with the common flail. These three phases demonstrate what is termed, herein, "The Law of the Flail" — the Swinger's primary concern: (2-K)

1. THE FIRST LAW OF THE FLAIL: While the "swingle" is seeking its "in-line" (full extension) relation with the "handle" (catching up), there is "Centripetal Acceleration".
2. THE SECOND LAW OF THE FLAIL: When it becomes "in line" (caught up), this settles into "Centripetal Angular Momentum" (Full Extension).
3. THE THIRD LAW OF THE FLAIL: If it passes its "in line" relation, it again seeks its "in-line" relation (backs up) and "Centripetal Deceleration" sets in with a huge power loss.

Another very important element in the generation of Angular Motion is the Endless Belt Effect (Sketch 2-K #6) which is the Physics of the Delivery Paths (7-23). During the straight line portion of the motion (Line Delivery Path) Linear Motion give the Belt and the Clubhead identical MPH speed. When the Belt starts around the Pulley (Release) its MPH does not change (Constant Hand Speed) but the Clubhead goes into an Angular Motion and its Surface Speed becomes proportional to its: 1). Radius, 2). Belt Speed and 3). Pulley diameter. Increasing the diameter and/or the Belt Speed increases Clubhead MPH and vice versa. The Circle Delivery Path is just one big Pulley — no Belt, no Linear Motion and therefore constant Hand Speed and Clubhead Speed (RPM) but different MPH due to different Surface Speeds. It must all comply with 7-23 — which is the Geometry of the Endless Belt Action.

STATEMENT OF PRINCIPLE

THE FLAIL

If thrust is applied only to the Left Arm (Handle), the Clubshaft (Swingle) will perform more like a Rope Handle (rising Clubhead pull), but if prestressed by Clubhead Lag Pressure Point pressure, more like an Axe Handle (steady Clubhead Inertia). However, the Primary Lever Assembly is only somewhat flail-like. That is, it is bolted together as with a hinge pin, rather than tied together with a thong, so that it can only be "Cocked" and/or "Rotated," per 4-B and 4-C, and cannot pass the "Handle" (4-A-2) while moving toward full extension, per 2-P. This ensures the Imperative Flat Left Wrist (1-L, 2-0). (Study 2-F, 6-F-0 and 10-19.) As with the standard flail, the true and proper direction for its mass to move is "downward On Plane" regardless of the incidental appearance of moving "forward On Plane"—*Always from The Top*. This is indispensable for both Hitters and Swingers for inhibiting Clubhead Throwaway — study sketch 2-K and chapter 2-P, 6-E-2 and 7-18.

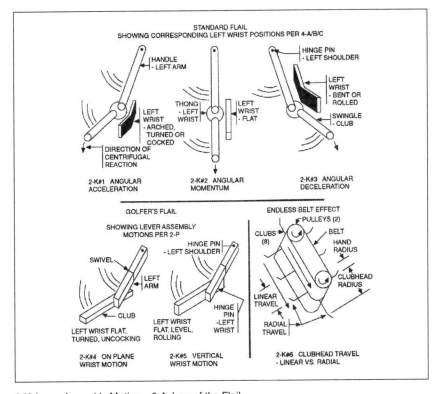

2-K. Lever Assembly Motion—6-A. Law of the Flail.

STATEMENT OF PRINCIPLE

THE LEVER

2-L. APPLICATION OF FORCE The forces generated in a Golf Stroke need to be understood before there can be any degree of genuine mastery of them. No law of force or motion can be annulled, even momentarily. The three courses that can be taken for their control are to (1) avoid, (2) harness, or (3) overpower. Engineering is the study of the application of #1 or #2 to minimize the need of #3.

Concerning #1: Centripetal Force can be avoided by moving in a straight line. (See 7-23.)

Concerning #2: A rotating motion will pass through a given point if the axis is tilted properly, instead of having to apply a compensating vector force to drive the rotating element off its normal plane toward the desired Plane Line (which is an example of Course #3 — Overpowering). (See 10-6-D. Also, study 2-N-1 and 3-F-7-E.)

Concerning #3: The "law of equal and opposite reaction" of the ball against the Clubhead can be overpowered to some degree, per 2-M-1, and so minimize Clubhead deceleration through Impact. (See 2-E.)

Of the three Lever Forms, only Form #3 is involved in the Golf Stroke as described in 6-A-2.

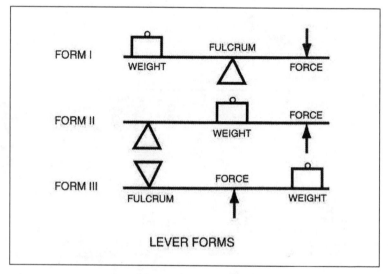

2-L. Application of Force through Lever Assemblies per 6-A.

STATEMENT OF PRINCIPLE

ENERGY—POTENTIAL AND KINETIC

2-M-1. BASIC POWER Clubhead power is directly proportional to its Kinetic Energy which is expressed as "one half the mass multiplied by the square of the Velocity ($E_{translational} = 1/2\, mv^2$ or $E_{rotational} = 1/2\, Iw^2$)." Clubhead velocity is developed by Thrust, which is an Acceleration Force, and Thrust, herein, is normally constant regardless of the velocity it has produced. (See 6-F-1.) This Thrust may be Muscular Force and/or Centripetal Force. Power is the total effective Force that is impinged on the Ball — which is related to the Angular Momentum of the Clubhead Mass, as well as to the prestressed Clubshaft (6-C-2) and the sustaining or driving actions of the above mentioned Thrusts — all of which contribute resistance to Impact Deceleration (2-E). "Centripetal Acceleration" (per 2-K) is staunchly *proportional* to the Angular Speed of its Center and reaches a maximum speed almost instantly after Release and tries to remain constant. With Drive Loading (10-19-A), the outward pull of Centrifugal Reaction tends to conceal, but cannot cancel, the considerable contribution of a prestressed (Bent) Clubshaft, though it is Bent even more at Separation. (See 7-11.) Still, always sustain the Lag through Impact <u>AS THOUGH</u> the Clubshaft were throwing the Ball off the Clubface — NO QUITTING.

2-M-2. POWER REGULATION Therefore, there are 15 variations available. Clubhead Lag Pressure Point pressure (6-C) is the Power Regulator. It meters out Power by sensing Clubhead Acceleration Rate and Direction. That is:

    To vary the Effective Clubhead Mass, vary:
      1. The Acceleration Rate (Lag Pressure 7-11)
      2. The Swing Radius (length of Primary Lever Assembly 6-B-0)
    To vary Clubhead Speed, vary:
      1. Acceleration Time (Length of Stroke 10-21)
      2. The Release Interval (Centrifugal Reaction 6-N-0)

So, it is optional to use any one, or any combination, of the four alternatives. (Also study 12-0 in this connection.)

STATEMENT OF PRINCIPLE

GENERATORS

2-M-3. MUSCLES Unless Pivot Thrust actually drives #4 Accumulator through Impact, its assignment during that interval is more clearly defined if considered as delivery, guidance and support of the Power Package, because it may or may not have contributed anything but motion during Delivery. The Pattern of the Stroke being used designates where Thrust is to originate and that is completely the player's option. (See 10-4 and 10-19.) Pivot Thrust alone (2-K), forfeits Right Arm Thrust (6-B-1). Power Package Thrust alone (6-0), forfeits Momentum Transfer (2-K). Only with the driver must you use both Pivot Thrust and Power Package Thrust for lack of a longer Club. In which case — to Pivot Thrust add a strong Pressure Point #1 thrust, per 10-19-C, or to Power Package Thrust add the Shoulder Turn, per 2-M-4. (Study 4-D-0, 6-B-2-B and 10-4-D in this connection.)

The Hands are strong, educated, adjustable Clamps attaching the Club to the Arms for control of the Clubface alignments. By themselves, they are actually able to drive the ball only a relatively short distance. Even the Wristcock is not properly an action of the Wrist muscles. So the only absolutely essential muscular contribution of the Wrists is "holding on." Study 7-20 in this connection.

The greatest hazard this Component faces is the belief that "Effort" is "Power." No amount of effort will produce more than a player's maximum turning speed. Regardless of effort, you simply cannot push anything faster than you can run. Mechanical Advantage (1-H) must be utilized, making Clubhead acceleration an "Overtaking" process (2-P and 6-M-1). However, tremendous energy can be consumed in trying to offset conflicting alignments, without ever achieving the player's full speed potential. (Study 5-0 in this connection.)

For Power Package Power, the movement of the Clubhead — via the Lever Assemblies — is assigned to the muscles of the arms, hands and upper torso. Which are —

>Biceps — they bend the elbow
>Triceps — they straighten the elbow
>Deltoids — they raise the arms
>Pectorals — they pull the shoulders and arms forward
>Latissimus Dorsi — they pull the shoulders and arms backward

STATEMENT OF PRINCIPLE

GENERATORS

First, the less the Biceps and the Latissimus Dorsi do the better. The Right Biceps are only active during the Backstroke (7-3) and neither Biceps has any Downstroke assignment — completely "passive". And the Pectorals and the Triceps should encourage that inaction — moving the Right Shoulder, especially, is a non-essential variable. And keep both arms as straight — with Extensor Action — as the Checkrein action allows.

Power Package Muscle Power is almost entirely Right Triceps thrust straightening the Right Elbow to furnish both Extensor Action and #1 Accumulator Power. The Right Triceps and Pectoral can handle the muscle requirements of the Downstroke and need no help from those on the Left, whose feeble contributions relegate Left Arm Muscle Power to a minor status, especially for Hitting.

The Deltoids lift the arms while the Latissimus Dorsi pull the arms back to produce the Backstroke and Finish Arm movement. The "passive side" supplies the Checkrein Action on the "active" side. Keep the Shoulders forward, with Pectoral action if necessary.

The only contribution of the Latissimus Dorsi is to pull back the Arms only — not the Shoulders — while the Deltoids are lifting the Arms. This obviously produces the Backstroke and Finish Arm movements. But it should also have the exclusive assignment for bending the Elbows — with their Checkrein action.

2-M-4. BODY POWER Except per 6-B-4, Left Arm for Swinging is a transfer of Body Momentum and is very considerable. As outlined in 2-K and 6-B-3-0, this does not mean an "On Plane" Left Arm. (Study 2-P and 7-13 in this connection.) Inertia can hold the Left Arm against the chest while the Body Turn is accelerating it and Momentum can then sustain it and come out with the Feel of Left Arm Muscle Power. To clear the fog, consider Pivot Thrust as Body Power blasting a Swinger's essentially inert Left Arm into orbit toward Impact, or as supplying the initial acceleration of the Hitter's loaded Power Package so the Clubhead can be endowed with Pivot speed PLUS Right Triceps Speed. (Study 6-B-4, 6-C-0 and 7-12 in this connection.)

STATEMENT OF PRINCIPLE

GEOMETRY OF THE CIRCLE

2-N-0. CLUBHEAD LINE OF FLIGHT The Line of Flight of the Clubhead and the Line of Flight of the Ball are not the same but touch momentarily during Impact. The one has a Vertical Plane of action, the other an Inclined Plane. This involves the Angles of Approach (2-J-3) established by the Left-Shoulder-to-Ball relationship of the Lever Assemblies per 2-J-2. This line cuts diagonally across the face of the Inclined Plane and passes through both the Impact Point and the Low Point. These points also locate parallel Plane Lines passing through them — that is, the Impact Plane Line and the Low Point Plane Line, each of which must use the "Sweet Spot" Plane (2-F). Herein, "Plane Line" means the Impact Plane Line and "Low Point" means Low Point Plane Line.

The Angle of Approach Line, the Delivery Paths (10-23), the Plane Lines (2-F), and their Visual Equivalents (2-J-3) are all inscribed on the face of the Inclined Plane, but appear to the player as if inscribed on a horizontal surface — that is, ON THE GROUND. This is an optical illusion that, when understood and utilized (2-P and 2-J-3), offers tremendous advantages because it furnishes very apparent equivalents to an invisible basic. (Study 2-C-1.) In Sketch #1, the Impact Points are on the Sweet Spot Plane as well as on the two parallel Plane Lines. In Sketch #2B, they are on the two parallel Plane Lines plus on the Arc *AND* Angle of Attack. In Sketch #3, they are on the Arc *AND* Angle of Approach. (Study 6-E-2.)

When the Ball is positioned at the Low Point, the two Plane Lines combine as one, but as the Ball is moved toward the Right Foot, these Lines appear farther apart and the Angle of Approach becomes wider. Then, the steeper the Plane Angle (10-6), the steeper the Angle of Attack (2-N-1), the higher the trajectory and the deeper the Divot (7-6). So, Ball Location determines the Angle of Approach (2-J-3) and the Plane Angle determines the Angle of Attack (7-3), making the Forearm motion three dimensional (2-C-0). (See 6-B-3-0.) This "Delivery Line" procedure completely replaces the geometric Plane Line (2-F) *and* the Target Line because these were established at Impact Fix (7-8) according to the intended Hinge Action (2-J-1) and Stance Line (10-5) requirements, and their control is completely automatic. Both the Lag Pressure Point and the Clubshaft must relate to the selected Plane Line OR Angle of Approach — to the geometric or the visual, but, it is impossible to Trace both at the same time, because they are equivalents but not identical so either can be used.

STATEMENT OF PRINCIPLE

GEOMETRY OF THE CIRCLE

Therefore, don't try to Monitor both at the same time because, though equally dependable, they need not be identical in execution AS LONG AS THE CLUBSHAFT HOLDS A STRAIGHT LINE RELATIONSHIP TO A STRAIGHT LINE—POINTING AT A STRAIGHT LINE. The orbiting Clubhead must maintain its visual relationship with the selected Delivery Line, per 2-F and 2-J-3, during all Twelve Sections (Chapter 8) while Turning, Cocking, Uncocking, Rolling, and Swiveling the Wrists. (See 2-P, 7-23 and 8-0.)

Proper Clubhead control is dependent on coordinating the complete Hip Turn with the selected Right Elbow Position (10-3), Motion (6-B-1), and Path (7-3) to avoid collisions as well as for Balance and Axis Tilt. (See 7-15.) To accomplish both the Backstroke and Downstroke must be executed as 7-3, 10-3 and 10-5-0 discuss that procedure. The Delivery Path is always Monitored per 6-E-2 and 10-6-0. There must be an Underhand Pitch motion and Feel. If there isn't you are "Roundhousing" — lifting the Hands (Flat Shoulder Turn) and/or the Clubhead before Steering) "Off Line" during the Start Down. This also includes the Butt of the Club. (See 10-6-0 and study 2-P.) Take time at The Top (8-6) to "draw" and "monitor" that line per 6-E-2. It is one of the Three Basic Imperatives (2-0). The position of the Club at The Finish (Station 3, 12-3) is the precision destination of the Downstroke "blast off" from The Top. It is not just Impact "fall out." Impact must be kept incidental to The Stations. Study 3-B and 8-6 regarding The Top and The Start Down.

STATEMENT OF PRINCIPLE

GEOMETRY OF THE CIRCLE

2-N-1. FORCE VECTORS Actually, the Forward Force Vector of the Clubhead (7-23) is a resultant force (2-C-1); that is, it is the product of two divergent and synchronous forces — one outward and one downward. A third force may be established, as well.

A. The Primary Outward Force Vector is produced by the action of the Shoulder Turn (2-H), and/or the Right Arm Thrust (6-B-1). Otherwise, just pushing or swinging the Lever Assemblies Outward from their Hinges (2-G) will suffice as the Outward Force Vector.

B. The Primary Downward Force Vector is produced by straightening the Right Elbow — including the Uncocking of the Left Wrist. Otherwise, just dropping, pulling, or pushing the Lever Assemblies Downward from their fulcrum (6-A) will suffice as the Downward Force Vector.

C. The "On Plane" Resultant Force Vector is established by the On Plane Shoulder Motion of the Axis Tilt as it cranks up the Clubhead Gyroscope.

These two forces Outward and Downward are "balanced out" (held On Plane 7-19) by Clubhead Lag (Hitting 10-19-A) or by Centripetal Force (Swinging 10-19-C). So, On Plane Motion (2-F) automatically duplicates — but cannot annul (and should not obscure) — those Vector Forces (2-C-1). All three are equally critical but totally independent of Clubhead Velocity.

STATEMENT OF PRINCIPLE

LEVER EXTENSION

2-P. THE WRISTCOCK The Uncocking of the Flat Left Wrist is a Perpendicular Motion — not a Horizontal Motion (as defined in 4-O). The Left Wrist (6-B-2) is Cocked and Uncocked per Stroke Pattern (Chapter 12), per 4-B and 4-D. It normally moves from "Cocked" to "Level" between Release and Impact, and from "Level" to "Uncocked" during the Follow-through. Wristcock is a Club*head* motion — not a Club*face* motion. Only with a Turned Left Wrist, such as 10-2-D, can Uncocking be both motions, that is, actually Throwing the Club*face* at the Ball.

The Wristcock shortens the Swing Radius to facilitate and synchronize the Rhythm and Acceleration of the Pivot and Power Package. This is equally applicable with the Left Wrist in its Flat, Level and Vertical Condition, per 7-2, that is, not actually fully extended, but also, not extending, as in very Short Shots and Putts. The true Angular Speed (RPM) of the Clubhead is identical to that of the Hands due to the mandatory Flat Left Wrist. (See Sketch 2-K#5.)

Uncocking the Left Wrist is Lever Assembly Extension only. Its appearance of "Overtaking" is incidental because it is actually seeking (Overtaking) its maximum MPH — of Full Extension — not its maximum RPM, which it already has by reason of the Flat Left Wrist. Therefore, it does not — and *must not* — affect the Lever Assembly RPM, (the Endless Belt Effect). The #3 Power Accumulator is the true Club*head* overtaking Action by reason of either "Maintaining" or "Returning to" its In-Line relationship (6-B-3-0) and its "Vertical-to-a-Plane" Hinge Action Alignment (2-G). The Lever Assembly Extension RATE aids the #3 Accumulator Action (6-B-3-A) and is regulated by Trigger Delay until FULL EXTENSION (per 7-18).

Full Extension (Angular Momentum 2-K) can occur at any time or exist all the time during a Stroke per Pattern, regardless of Impact Point or Low Point (2-N). Impact during Full Extension produces a "soft" Impact and is a very useful simplification. (See 2-K-2 and 2-L#2.)

Centripetal Force *alone* Uncocks the Swinger's Wrists, but Right Arm Thrust *during Release* is the Hitter's procedure. Except per 2-M-3, these procedures are not compatible (10-19-0).

STATEMENT OF PRINCIPLE

PICTURES

2-R. THE PICTURES in this book are a visual explanation of the Mechanics and go hand-in-hand with the written explanation. The captions for the pictures do not explain the pictures, but only denote the subject of the picture and includes the cross-reference number which indicates the section (having the same reference number) which discusses the subject that the picture presents.

The picture presents the subject only as noted in the written discussion and is not intended as a reference regarding any of the other aspects or subjects which the picture may include incidentally. Every Component has two aspects — its individuality (one picture) and its many relationships (many pictures). Complete understanding of it includes both aspects.

When the reference number of the picture ends in a number such as "#2," that indicates that it is one of a series of pictures on the same subject and the sequence more fully elucidates the discussion under that reference number.

Symbols used in the pictures indicate either the location of a key point, the direction of a motion or the path of a motion.

The pictures depict exactly what they are intended to depict and as near to "Zero Tolerance" as is humanly possible and then only because they were carefully and expertly posed. "Close" is important but relative in both Horseshoes and on the golf course but must be minimal in a text book. Each picture is intended to present the ideal for its subject whether or not anyone on earth has ever achieved it. They are a goal and not necessarily any individual or universal common practice.

STATEMENT OF PRINCIPLE

PICTURES

2-S. THE WHOLE PICTURE Again it must be reiterated — there is more information in this book than any golfer can *use* in many lifetimes. But it is not difficult to *know* everything in this book if the chart shown in Chapter 11 is utilized and its unity, continuity and completeness is recognized.

There may be other ways to arrange this information, but this arrangement was selected as the most useful concentration and would permit both piecemeal application and unlimited expansion without juggling the stated relationships for either — or any other — contingency. This is the distinguishing characteristic of any Principle.

The "Whole Picture" is your total visualization of all the individual visualizations of specific areas. Both the total and individual pictures must, in their beginnings, be vague and disjointed. But the paint-pots of study and experience will continually and evenly brighten, clarify and integrate your entire album. In every program some "garbage" must surface. Let today's garbage be superior to yesterday's.

Any information needed is here, either in so many words or by obvious inference, though perhaps not in the expected or preconceived context. Any attempt to relocate or reassign any factors can only produce confusion about the arrangement as a whole. But any individual can "X" up his own Stroke Pattern to his heart's content. When the limiting tendency of such procedures is finally recognized, the player can instantly turn to the book for a correct configuration.

Finally — make full use of the Index. Don't panic — Instant Simplification is right here with you all the time. Just confine your research to the subjects you need information about — as with any other encyclopedia.

CHAPTER THREE

COMPONENT TRANSLATION

3-0. GENERAL An important process for acquiring over-all skill is the process of translating the individual components from a conscious, deliberate, mechanical manipulation, to an integral part of the whole, by reducing it to a Computerized "Feel," and without losing its individuality, so vital for the selective introduction of special purpose Variations. Your game will develop — whatever your procedure — according to Chapter 9. Educate your Hands (5-0) to maintain the Flat Left Wrist (4-D-1) and they can quickly Translate Stroke Components from "Mechanics" to "Feel" for each Section of Chapter 8. Your "Basic Motion" (Preface) is simply "Up-and-Back-and-Down-and-Out", per 7-23 — from Drive to Putt. Your "Total Motion" is that Basic Motion plus its Component Variations (Chapter 10) — selected and/or otherwise (Chapter 12). Whatever you are "working on" must produce a change in Feel because it's a selected addition to your previous Total Motion Feel — your "Acquired Feel," the present stage of your Total Motion development. Deliberately select either the Crash or Relative Translation (3-C/-D) for acquiring new elements. BUT RHYTHM MUST HAVE HIGH PRIORITY WITH BOTH PROCEDURES.

3-A. TRANSLATION OF INSTRUCTION There is another type of Translation to consider also — the Translation of the instructor's instructions, including those in this book. Only the correct Translation can lead to the correct application. A procedure must make sense — geometrically and technically, else the Translation is faulty. If properly Translated and it still fails, then there is faulty execution. Never move anything unnecessarily, nor farther than necessary, but allow for psychological needs and preferences too. Variations of the Variations are unavoidable, but should fit in with the Basic function in Chapter 7.

This book presents the "uncompensated" Stroke as a goal, guide and progress report, not as the minimum entrance test. Compensation for physical limitation, personal preference or special purpose are actually specialized techniques. For ball behavior resulting from faulty execution, there is only one recommendable compensation — correction. Simply resist going out on the course until you know enough, regardless of where the Ball goes, to prefer trying to do it right rather than incur life-long penalties for bad "compensation" habits.

COMPONENT TRANSLATION

PROGRAMS

3-B. PRACTICING AND PLAYING   In one sense, there seems to be two large classes of golfers. One spends his life "practicing" without ever getting around to "playing." The other dives right into "playing" and disdains any "practice" other than "just hitting that ball." The difference is merely in where the primary attention is directed. Actually, both are half right and half incomplete. Both halves are essential and coordinate. There must be, "Practicing" practice and "Playing" practice (Study 3-F-5).

If the points of techniques under consideration are being practiced, are the primary purpose of the action and have top attention, so that Impact is sacrificed rather than disrupt the selected procedure being practiced. This is "Practice" and where the ball goes can be immaterial.

If this attitude is reversed and everything is secondary to getting the Clubhead against the ball, willy-nilly, as nearly right as "Feel" alone can manage, so that — ALL THE WAY DOWN — the attention is riding hard on the "Hands-Clubhead-Ball Relationship" with a relatively shadowy mental impression of techniques (fading off behind some particular special-purpose procedure for the situation at hand), that is "Playing." And where the ball goes is important information. Even this must be practiced diligently. Become TARGET CONSCIOUS. (Study 7-23 and 14-0.) Being Target Conscious must assume more and more importance for effective Playing Practice. (Study 7-2 and 7-4.)

So learn to "Practice" a technique into "feel" and then "Play" it into "Computer" dependability. Then go on to the next Component or Alignment needing attention and give it the same one-two punch. To develop skill at golf your "attention span" must be at least as long as your Swing (See 7-23). Take advantage of the fact that the Hands learn more quickly to "hold a position" if allowed to practice moving into and out of that position first. This is especially effective with Wrist Action (10-18) and Release Motions (4-D-0). The longer the Club, the more your errors tend to be magnified.

"Practice" is observation, selection, adjustment, etc. — the flexible "researcher" approach. "Playing" is concentration, discipline, supervision, execution, etc. — the inflexible "performer" approach. Neglect neither. For instance — the *first* **WOBBLY** point in your Total Motion (12-3), not Impact, is where you should be working. Those who work constantly — and fruitlessly — on Address, Body, and Impact actually lack Educated Hands to get them through Start Down — invariably. (See 2-N.) Inability to

COMPONENT TRANSLATION

PROGRAMS

execute a *full* Pivot Stroke at one half and one quarter speed as smoothly as at full speed indicates a flaw in the full speed procedure. Don't get trapped in the wrong "approach." Continually check your execution against 12-3.

To add or analyze a Component or Variation in a Stroke Pattern, the first step is to become acquainted with its Mechanics — the Geometry and Physics of the motion — even if only to watch it make the required motion without actually understanding the laws behind the motion. But in either case — watch closely to see that it is being done properly.

No one, especially beginners, should ever trust Feel alone. With *any* change or addition — Look, Look, Look — until you're sure you have it right. When finally it can be done properly while being watched, the next step can be taken. While still watching and checking visually, start noting mentally every detectable, distinguishable "Feel" that accompanies it, both when done properly and when done improperly. Then, add the "Closed Eyes" technique in 5-0.

Of course, the next step is to learn to execute the motion by "Feel" alone — with only occasional visual verification. These steps are all necessary also for programming or reprogramming The Computer (Chapter 14).

First, execute the Stroke as was customary before the new addition and check the new component visually and note the correct and incorrect Motions and Feels that appear. Almost invariably, some adjustments will have to be made in the Feel of the original Pattern, and the Feel of the new Component may change also under the conditions of total realignment of the Pattern. This usually requires only a tightening up of the alignment tolerances of the Stroke as a whole because of the previously loose tolerances in the area of the new Component.

The new addition may seem very important at this time, but as it is assimilated, it will slip back into the picture and display its true value. All factors will eventually seem to merit about equal attention except when giving trouble or when a situation demands a specific application of key Components. So, as the Feel is perfected, again give primary attention to Impact as a performer.

Eons of manhours are lost trying to substitute effort for technique and trying to eliminate effect instead of cause.

COMPONENT TRANSLATION

METHODS

3-C. CRASH TRANSLATION PROCEDURE There are two Translation procedures available. A "Crash" procedure and a "Relative" procedure. First the Crash Procedure. The distinguishing feature of this procedure is that Variations are adopted by practicing them individually (as outlined above) with no regard for what is happening to the rest of the Pattern in the meantime. When a Component has been mastered (more or less), it can *then* be fitted into the Pattern by adjusting alignments to accommodate it into the Total Motion (6-P).

3-D. RELATIVE TRANSLATION PROCEDURE The alternative procedure is to inspect first the Component as it is presently used. Classify it and compare it to that Variation that has been selected for adoption. It may be very nearly like what you have selected. The differences should be carefully noted and a change-over procedure laid out.

As the primary purpose, carefully avoid disturbing the other components. As the secondary purpose, supervise the change-over procedure. The change-over may include some realignment or adjustment of other Components, or a tightening of tolerances here and there. Then all these areas should be slowly shifted to the new pattern.

3-E. EXPANDED TRANSLATION During its development, it is well to keep the Stroke Pattern relatively fluid until a satisfactory selection of Components is arrived at for the entire Stroke Pattern and the Translation of each Component from Mechanics to Feel is well advanced. It is also advisable — and not too difficult — to uncover a "key factor" for a simplified Feel of a Pattern, which will produce a one or two piece Translation of the Pattern as a whole. Then everything melts into a "TOTAL MOTION" and "making the MOTION" becomes your primary concern and "making the Shot" merely its inevitable result. 2-J-3 and 7-23 present effective possibilities. (The Computer is working all the time — keep it correctly programmed for alternate procedures, new Components, etc.)

COMPONENT TRANSLATION

TEACHING AIDS

3-F-1. PRACTICE PROCEDURES Golfdom would do the game a great service if it would encourage learning to hit before learning to score. Demanding that a beginner observe all the tournament rules when he is practicing Stroke techniques, is kicking him when he's down. He should be admonished, instead, against trying to hit off the fairway grass, out of deep rough, nearly unplayable lies, rocks and traps until he has learned to hit consistently from improved lies — or even from tees.

The attitude of the more skilled players about this is understandable. If they both teed up every shot, this would not benefit those who have learned, or have frozen their technique, nearly as much as those who have not yet learned Clubhead placement — let alone ball placement.

Tournament rules are for tournaments and are fair because tournaments are scoring tests. Players should shun tournament play until they have mastered "Practicing and Playing" (3-B above).

3-F-2. CROSS REFERENCING The greatest factor for improvement is proper and perceptive practice procedures. This can be acquired by cross-referencing all subjects through the Index and/or the Reference Numbers inserted in the text. Those numbers help locate information that is essential — not merely incidental — to the subject at hand and which must be considered as replacing those numbers at those locations as though written in those locations. Where there is more than one Reference Number, they are always listed in alphanumerical order. (See 1-H.)

3-F-3. INSTANT SIMPLIFICATION The monumental complexity of choices should only indicate the futility of striking out into them unaided. This book would be unavoidably bewildering were it not that it lends itself so effortlessly to Instant Simplification through the use of the Stroke Pattern concept. Which equips the player to pinpoint instantly any one, single component in any area of the Golf Stroke mechanics. (See Chapter 12.)

COMPONENT TRANSLATION

TEACHING AIDS

3-F-4. PRACTICE RANGES Then, with the Stroke Pattern selections made, the foregoing Translation procedures should be applied. It will be found that the Indoor Practice Range is unquestionably the most effective place to perfect the assembly and adjustment of the Golfing Machine, with occasional check-out trips to an Outdoor Driving Range. There, the hypnotic effect of distance, line and hazard drawing the attention away from the Hands and inducing a compulsion to Steer the ball, can be analyzed and procedures adopted for correction. Then, take your findings back to the course for final — or semi-final — fitting. The indoor range simply is not the place for that.

So — until Feel can dependably reproduce a selected procedure, there must be a visual and conscious surveillance of each and all components previously adopted — right up to the one in process. (Study 5-0.)

COMPONENT TRANSLATION

SETTING UP

3-F-5. THE ADDRESS ROUTINE Most misshots are lost at Address — by not mentally spelling out exactly the selected Stroke Variations and their technique and Feel. The most effective check-out procedures for both Practice and Play are
1. The Practice Stroke
2. The Waggle — Address and Start Down
3. The Forward Press

And usually in that order. Repeatedly, if necessary. Actually, "Address" includes all preparations prior to Start Up. By which time the Hands completely replace the Club (5-0). Practice Swing and Waggle should be over the top of the Ball to establish the inside-out Angle of Approach, or step back. Stopping at the Ball encourages Quitting (6-D-3).

The Practice Stroke is primarily a full scale rehearsal of the Zone #1 components (the Pivot), especially the Hips and Shoulders. Even for Non-pivot Strokes. Is the "Zero Pivot" partial, relative or total? Remember also, the Plane, Hand Action and Loading elements need verification. And especially the blur of the Clubhead Path, per 2-J-3. With or without a Pivot, it's the Feel of your Total Motion (6-P). Or your "Acquired Motion." At least your "Basic Motion" (3-0) — that framework on which your Stroke Pattern Components are arranged and adjusted — the "Tie That Binds" your game together. (See 14-0.) It is an indispensable part of Imperative #3 (2-0). Through it all, check and recheck Rhythm (2-G). Even through the next two steps also.

The Address Waggle is a miniature reproduction of the action of the Zone #2 components through Impact — checking out the Power alignments. That is — the Grip and Hand action applications of the Accumulators and Pressure Points; Especially the On Plane location *and* direction of the Hands *and* Clubshaft for Impact. The "Start Down" Waggle does the same for the Top alignments and could be treated as part of the Practice Stroke. It's a "Look, Look, Look" situation (3-B) — especially for beginners — to develop Monitoring skill. It should be repeated until the motion is being satisfactorily executed. It can, and should, be taken on through the Address Waggle area. Check for On Plane Clubshaft and Right Shoulder (2-F), for the Right Forearm tracing the Delivery Line (5-0 and 10-5-0) and for "Clearing the Right Hip" (2-N-0 and 10-14). Returning to Address Position may become optional. All this gives a clear picture of the Downstroke activities — instead of the usual "Downstroke Blackout." (See 7-2 and 12-3-18.)

COMPONENT TRANSLATION

SETTING UP

The Forward Press is Fixing in mind the appearance and feel of the Zone #3 (Ball Control) Components at Impact by shifting the entire Machine, per Stroke Pattern, to the Impact position. Verify six alignments:
  A. Clubface-to-Target Line (2-J-3)
  B. Grip-to-Clubface (2-G)
  C. Hands-to-Ball (4-D)
  D. Plane Angle (2-F)
  E. Pressure Points (6-C)
  F. Right Forearm Position (2-J-3 and 6-B-3-0-1)

Normally, the Address Position is resumed, if only momentarily, before the Start Up, to retain the advantages of the Adjusted Address position. Balance, Grip (7-2) and Plane Line (10-5) must be verified before every shot as long as the game is played. After which is still to come the final Practice Swing — a <u>Target Conscious</u> check of alignments. You simply must not press that Fifth Program Routine Button (14-0) until after that Target Locating procedure (See 3-B-1).

3-F-6. EXECUTION All quick, jerky and wobbly motions are improper execution. Neither the Hands nor the Club are flipped or swished around haphazardly. The ideal — even with an Automatic Release — is to be very deliberate, positive and heavy. Never dainty. Shorten the Stroke, slow the Stroke or delay the Release until a positive Clubhead Lag can give the Hands a *heavy* Clubhead to drive (or swing) against the ball — at all speeds. (See 6-F.) Erratic execution indicates loss of Rhythm (2-G).

A flimsy Power Package structure indicates lack of Extensor Action (6-B-1-D) and/or neglect of the Flying Wedges (6-B-3-0-1). Or faulty Translation; Or it may be that you are attempting to incorporate incompatible Components as discussed in Chapters 1-K and 13. Any procedure — whether Practicing or Playing — that produces awkward or un-golf-like positions or motions, is being misapplied. Go back and get it straight immediately — starting with 3-0 and 3-B. Learning step-by-step to maintain the essential Geometry, per 5-0, under all conditions, alone leads to a MASTER'S level of execution. That is — with and without Wristcock, with and without #3 Accumulator, with any Hinging, with any Plane Line Combination (10-5) from any Ball Position, Hitting or Swinging, with Right Forearm Takeaway (7-3), and with a motionless Right Wrist. But, <u>above all</u>, learn that NONE of those things alter the #3 Pressure Point function of "Tracing" the selected Delivery Line. Run, through the entire list and <u>see that they do not alter it</u>. <u>Repeatedly</u>.

COMPONENT TRANSLATION

SNARES

3-F-7-0. MACHINE ADJUSTMENT CHECK LIST The Twenty-Four Stroke Components are those things the Machine *should* do. Then there are some indications and symptoms of maladjustment — things it sh*ould not* do. (See 4-D and 6-D.)

3-F-7-A. STEERING is the Number One malfunction — The Bent Left Wrist and Clubhead Throwaway. Any or all of the following faults during Impact *may* need to be adjusted out — holding:
1. The Club*face* square to the Target Line
2. The Club*head* on Target Line
3. The Clubhead on a level or upward path

A very successful and anti-steering therapy is an exaggerated "inside-out" Cut Shot, per 10-5-E. (Study 2-J-3, 2-N and 12-3-39.) You always Swing along the Plane Line but not always along the Flight Line. So Learn to dismiss the Flight Line. Depend on Clubface alignment for direction control (2-J). In fact, learn to execute *all* Plane Line Variations (10-5) to remove all uncertainty from your Computer (14-0).

3-F-7-B. QUITTING slows or stops the Hands during Release and is almost always a semi-conscious maneuver to change the Down-and-Out Clubhead Path (2-J-2) to an On-Line Path through Impact, on the mistaken assumption that this is the purpose of the "Wrist Roll" (2-G) and/or "Wrist Bend" (6-D-3) and that such Clubhead control is, somehow, automatic Clubface control. That is a distorted interpretation of Sequenced Release (4-D). This results in:
1. a Bent Plane Line (Steering 4-D-0);
2. a shortening of the Swing Radius (loss of effective Mass);
   AND, depending on Impact Hand Location, results in either:
3. a "Down Only" Clubhead Path (deep Divot or "Fat" Hit 1-L-14);
4. an "Up-and-In" Clubhead Path (Topped Shot 2-J-2).

Also study 2-C-3. The inherent power loss causes the player to swing even faster, aggravating the whole situation. Rhythm (2-G) is the solution — Quitting is actually impossible with proper and continuous Rhythm. So are many other faulty moves during the Stroke. During all Strokes — INCLUDING, AND ESPECIALLY, WITH PUTTING.

SUSTAIN THE LAG! That is, Hitting or Swinging, losing Lag Pressure not only produces Quitting but jeopardizes Rhythm and destroys the Basic Motion, and worst of all, dissipates the Line of Compression (2-0 and 6-C-2-0).

COMPONENT TRANSLATION

SNARES

3-F-7-C. BOBBING is raising and/or lowering the Head by faulty movement of the back or knees, and disrupts the Shoulder-to-ball radius.

3-F-7-D. SWAYING is basically incorrect weight shifting due usually to a faulty Pivot. Swaying can be in either or both directions — with the swing or in reverse. It produces abnormal trajectories, erratic timing and a teetering Balance. It is usually an attempt to replace the Pivot in working toward a Turn and a Weight Shift (7-12 and 7-14).

3-F-7-E. All these malfunctions are just different ways of disrupting the same geometrical alignment — the downward-and-outward arc of the Club*face*. The farther back toward the right foot that the ball is teed, the farther to the right of the target must be the line of the Clubhead's Down-Plane angle of approach to Impact — that is, the more pronounced must be the Clubface slide across the Line of Flight through Impact (2-J). Also — the greater that absolutely mandatory forward leaning of the Clubshaft through Impact. Off Plane execution can produce Shanked Shots. The correct concept of an "On Plane" procedure is driving the Club — not "a little downward and a little outward," — but "Down Plane." Down Plane to full extension, per 2-C-0 and 2-L#2. (Also study 2-F, 2-N and 2-P.)

Aiming a Square-Square Plane Line to the right of the target is another effect of these disruptions. Stepping to the opposite side of the ball — or reference line — will prove it isn't faulty eyesight. It is habitually, but unwittingly, allowing for Pulled Shots resulting from, among others, these three major misconceptions:

1. Clubface "Square to the Target at Impact" for all shots (2-J-1)
2. Clubhead Path "Down the Target Line" through Impact (2-J-2)
3. Flattening the Right Wrist through Release for Clubhead Velocity (4-D-1)

All of which close the Clubface with a resulting Line of Flight to the Left, causing the Computer to silently align the entire Machine to the Right as a <u>corrective</u> move. It is not really an optical illusion at all: Only one "cure" has surfaced — hit, at first, Chip Shots TO THE RIGHT OF YOUR STANCE ALIGNMENT, AS YOU SEE IT. Finally, this will reprogram the Computer away from its fixation that all shots have the same relationship to the Stance Line and you can work it back to the geometrically correct alignments you only thought you were using. Check that the Grip is per Hinge Action (2-J-1) and that the toe of the Club is not raised at Impact.

CHAPTER FOUR

WRIST POSITIONS— INDIVIDUAL

THE KEYS

4-0. GENERAL The key to the control of the Golf Club is Educated Hands. The player must acquire, and continue to develop, habitually skillful, disciplined, conscious manipulation of the Hands using the Clubhead Lag Pressure Point (6-C) as the main line of communication between Hands and Clubhead — both ways. (See 5-0.)

This chapter is the first step towards that diploma. And — every — Stroke is a test. Very few are the mistakes and troubles of a golfer that do not stem from faulty Hands. For a firm Grip and flexible Wrist action, practice all Wrist positions and motions with a firmly clenched fist as well as with the open Hand. (See 2-F, 2-M-2 and 7-1.)

The three Basic Wrist Motions can be classified as:
4-A. Horizontal   Bend and Arch (Clubshaft)   Grip Motion
4-B. Perpendicular Cock and Uncock (Clubhead)   Wrist Motion
4-C. Rotational   Turn and Roll (Clubface)   Hand Motion

The terms used to identify the separate positions were selected as the most descriptive and adaptable. The terms selected for the center position in each classification are: FLAT (-A), LEVEL (-B), AND VERTICAL (-C).

As the Vertical Wrist moves to the right during the backstroke it is **TURNING** — opening to the flight line — but is not **TURNED**. Moving to the left during the downstroke, it is **ROLLING** — closing to the flight line — but is not **ROLLED**. When the Left Wrist leaves its Vertical position with a Wrist Rotation it is SWIVELING — not Hinging (study 7-20 in this connection).

WRIST POSITIONS—INDIVIDUAL

HORIZONTAL

4-A-0. GENERAL The Horizontal Wrist Positions and Motions are FLAT (-1), BENT (-2), and ARCHED (-3). These three terms are always used with reference to the *back* of the hand only.

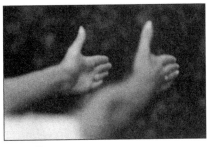

4-A-1. Flat.

4-A-2. Bent.

4-A-1. FLAT The Wrist is FLAT when the forearm and the back of the hand form a straight line.

4-A-2. BENT The Wrist is BENT when the hand is bent backward — or outward. With few exceptions, this position is not permissible for the Left Wrist. (See 10-2-D and 10-18-B.)

4-A-3. Arched.

4-A-3. ARCHED The Wrist is ARCHED when the Hand is bent forward — or inward — "rounding off" the forearm. A small amount is advisable and very useful (as insurance against 4-A-2 above and as amplification of Clubhead Lag) if its Push Shot tendency is properly compensated.

WRIST POSITIONS—INDIVIDUAL

PERPENDICULAR

4-B-0. GENERAL The Perpendicular Wrist Positions and Motions are LEVEL (-1), COCKED (-2), and UNCOCKED (-3). These three terms are always used in reference to the "Thumb Edge" of the hand only.

4-B-1. Level.

4-B-2. Cocked.

4-B-1. LEVEL The Wrist is LEVEL when the wrist-bone and the edge of the hand (to the first knuckle of the first finger) form a straight line.

4-B-2. COCKED The Wrist is COCKED when the edge of the hand forms as sharp an angle as possible with the wrist bone. The Wrist is Cocked at any point *beyond* LEVEL *toward* the maximum cocked position.

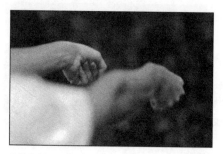
4-B-3. Uncocked.

4-B-3. UNCOCKED The Wrist is UNCOCKED when the edge of the hand forms as wide an angle as possible with the wrist bone. The Wrist is UNCOCKED at any point *from* LEVEL to the maximum UNCOCKED position. The wrist is UNCOCKED at any time it is moving away from any COCKED position. It moves per 4-D-0 and 2-P.

WRIST POSITIONS—INDIVIDUAL

ROTATIONAL

4-C-0. GENERAL The Rotational Wrist Positions and Motions are VERTICAL (-1), TURNED (to the right) (-2), and ROLLED (to the left) (-3).

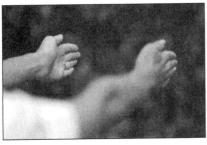

4-C-1. Vertical.

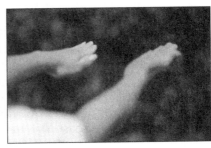

4-C-2. Turned.

4-C-1. VERTICAL The Wrist is VERTICAL when the back of the Hand would lay flat against a swinging door mounted per the selected Hinge Action (2-G), with the Shoulder at the Hinge Line.

4-C-2. TURNED The Wrist is TURNED when the hand is rotated to the right. When TURNED, the right palm faces directly *away* from the selected Plane (7-5) and/or the left palm faces directly *toward* that Plane. Whether the Wrist is TURNING or ROLLING, it is always in a TURNED position at any point between VERTICAL and TURNED.

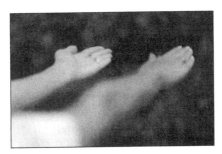

4-C-3. Rolled.

4-C-3. ROLLED The Wrist is ROLLED when it is rotated to the left. This moves the Wrist back to the VERTICAL position from the TURNED position. The Wrist should never *normally* ROLL beyond the VERTICAL position during the Release, but the Roll may be varied to suit the purpose at hand. It may begin early or late, behind or ahead of normal position, or even be left in the Turned position until after Impact. (See 4-D-0.)

WRIST POSITIONS—INDIVIDUAL

DRILLS

4-D-0. RELEASE MOTIONS This term refers to the Release of Accumulators #2 and #3. So it is not a Pattern Component in itself. Normally, it can only be either Simultaneous (Hitting) or Sequenced (Swinging), per 10-11-0-2 and 10-11-0-3. "Uncocking" (4-B-3) and "Roll" (4-C-3) are two separate motions: 1) Wrist Motion, and 2) Hand Motion — coordinate but very independent (4-0). Their execution is not a haphazard amalgamation (10-10-C and D). Normally, Uncocking is a function of the Wrists actuating the Club*head* (4-B). (See 5-0 and 7-11.) It has nothing to do with Clubface alignment at Impact — that is the function of the Hands executing the Club*face* Motion (4-C) — Accumulator #3 (2-G). Whenever the Wrist Motion (instead of Hand Motion) throws the Clubface at the ball, there will be Steering and Clubhead Throwaway. (See 2-P.) The Hitter concentrates on Hand Motion, while the Swinger concentrates on Wrist Motion. Both halves of each Release Action can be either Automatic (normally) or Non-Automatic (per Pattern). (Study 6-E.) So each must be consciously differentiated during execution (7-20).

Normally, only Swingers with their Standard Wrist Action (10-18-A) "Swivel" — that is, actually rotate the Left Wrist — through Release into its Vertical Position for Impact. That must be pre-programmed not later than The Top per 8-6. Have a clear picture of the intended Impact Hand Position all the way down — *NOT* the process of achieving it. But all players must "Swivel" — actually rotate their Wrists — into the "parallel to the Plane" position for the Finish (8-12) after the Followthrough.

It is *mandatory* that there be no break or bend in the Delivery Line direction during either half of the Release Motion. Both halves, as well as the Release and Finish Roll (2-G), must be executed on the same Delivery Line (2-J-3) — On Line or Cross Line, but not both. Construct an Inclined Plane such as shown in 10-5, or find a low bench, fence rail — or anything providing the Clubshaft with a straight edge or flat surface — and swing the Clubshaft back and forth along that edge or surface while executing the above Wrist and Hand Motions until you thoroughly understand their relation to 10-5. (Study 2-N very carefully.) That is why item 12-3-22 is capitalized (Study 2-K, 3-F-6 and 4-D-1.)

WRIST POSITIONS—INDIVIDUAL

THE GATEWAY

4-D-1. THE FLAT LEFT WRIST This section is included to stress the importance of the Flat Left Wrist during Impact. (Study 2-P and 10-18-B.) "Flat Left Wrist" and "Grip" refer to the Strong Single Action Grip Type 10-2-B. This is a highly dependable visual check for compliance with the Law of the Flail (2-K). But remember there is normally a point where Backstroke Shoulder and Wrist Motions make it difficult or even impossible to keep the Flat Left Wrist <u>vertical</u> to its Plane or the Right Forearm <u>on</u> its Plane without producing a non-golfing and Off Plane Clubshaft position or motion which is intolerable per 2-F and 3-F-6 for thinking players (1-G). (Carefully study 3-F-7.)

A Double Wristcock (10-18-B) is the Bending of the Left Wrist at the Top of the Stroke in addition to the Wristcock. All Wrist positions and motion may remain correct until the Release, where, for a variety of misconceptions, the Right Wrist is allowed to Flatten. Any loss in Impact Fix Right Wrist Bend *during Release* immediately becomes Left Wrist Bend — Clubhead Throwaway; which starts the Club swinging from the Wrists — in an "inside" and "upward" motion — the Clubface is rapidly Closing and the Clubshaft becomes "in-line" with the Right Forearm instead of with the Left Arm. Learn to <u>LOCK</u> the Left Wrist in the Flat Position at any time or at all times. However, there are times when you do not want a Flat Left Wrist. (Study 2-K, 3-F-6, 6-B-3, 6-C-2-A, 7-2 and 7-18 to become a skilled Hand Manipulator.)

Remember, a flat plane has a straight baseline. A circle is two dimensional and can lie on a flat plane. If the Plane Line loses its straightness, the Clubhead Orbit becomes three dimensional, spherical, and precision vanishes. The Gyroscope is the perfect example of the Geometry of the Circle and the Physics of Rotation.

WRIST POSITIONS—INDIVIDUAL

THE GATEWAY

Driving the Clubhead toward the *Green* (Steering), instead of toward the Ball (2-P), is the great disrupter of the Flat Left Wrist. (See 7-8 and 7-19.) Remember to take the whole Primary Lever Assembly — the Left Arm, the Hands, Clubshaft and Clubhead (2-N) — into Impact. It is the Hands AND Clubhead — not just the Club*head* — that define the Plane. (See 2-L#2.) Take a very "short" Grip and practice swinging back and forth with the top of the Clubshaft against the inside of the Left Forearm until you can hold the Wrist steady with a normal Grip. So — there must be the Flat Left Wrist. Or its equivalent (10-2-G). Or a compensation (6-D, 7-19 and 6-C-2-E).

Hitters, especially, must learn to straighten the Right Arm without flattening the Right Wrist. Practice doing just and only that — diligently — with and without a Club. Then learn to "float," from The Top through Impact, an inert, unstressed Right Wrist with its Impact Fix degree of Bend. Study 2-C-0 because deviation in any element of the Three Dimensional Downstroke is the most difficult Throwaway trigger to locate and eliminate.

CHAPTER FIVE

WRIST POSITIONS— COMBINATIONS

MONITORING

5-0. GENERAL The Wrist is *always* in one of *each* of the three INDIVIDUAL WRIST CONDITIONS (4 A-B-C). A Combination of Wrist Conditions is indicated by the use of the first letter of the term for each INDIVIDUAL WRIST CONDITION involved and, therefore, uses three letters in every Combination. With this method, every possible Wrist Condition can be readily identified for easy reference. And a complete description given by the use of just three letters. There are no duplicate letters and though always listed in the same order there can be no misapplication if listed in any order.

Though there are more possible combinations, only four pairs of combinations have much use: the -1 of each pair (A,B,C and D) is the Flat Wrist version. The -2 of each pair is the Bent Wrist version of companion combinations. Normally, the -1 combination will be the Left Wrist Condition and the -2 combination will be the Right Wrist Condition.

The Hands are the "Command Post" for all Feel processing. As the Stroke proceeds, they dictate to the Feet as certainly as they dictate to the Club. No Negative (Off Course) Feedback can get to — or from — the Clubhead except through the Hands. Regardless of the amount of technical know-how and practice, uneducated Hands can nullify it all and *never even be suspected*. Monitor all three elements of the Club (1-L) by way of the Hands — never directly. The Hands are much easier to Monitor than the Clubhead because their travel is so much more even and slower (2-K-6). The first step in this Educational Process is "Look, Look, Look", per 3-B. If you feel your game isn't reflecting your understanding of Alignments — STOP MONITORING THE CLUBFACE INSTEAD OF YOUR HANDS. Unless otherwise specified, at all times — but especially during Start Down — maintain the Clubhead Lag relationship to the Plane Line — *not to the body*. That — failure to clear the Right Hip (Roundhouse) can initiate almost every alignment disruption, including SHANKING (2-F, 3-F-7-E and 6-C-2). Constantly upgrade their information storage and retrieval — as with any other Computer.

WRIST POSITIONS—COMBINATIONS

MONITORING

"Monitoring" is awareness — through "Feel," "Feedback," sensation — of the location, condition, direction, etc., of any element for any purpose. When you watch as you reach for your cup, you are unaware of your hands. But with your eyes closed, you are acutely dependent on them. Then notice how quickly they can adapt when "monitored." Golfers have the same problem. Because your eyes must be on the Ball, they cannot watch the Club. So swing the Club with your eyes closed until you realize how consciousness of the Club, per se, is so disruptive as compared with consciousness of the Hands. Learn to SWING THE HANDS, MONITOR THE HANDS. Some players use the Club *only* to develop its TOTAL equivalent in Lag Pressure Point Feel. That is — until the Hands no longer consciously Monitor the Clubhead or the Body — only themselves, and automatically dictate total Component compliance with Delivery Path (6-E) and Delivery Line (2-J-3) requirements (7-23). Both are Monitored by the Hands but the Delivery Lines, in addition, must be "Traced" by the Right Forearm. For the ARC of Approach Delivery Line that relationship is with the true geometric Plane Line, itself. The Plane Line — being the Basic — can substitute for any of its "Visual Equivalents" at any time. In either or both directions. Because the Right Forearm and the Clubshaft are on the same Plane during Release and Impact (7-3), players actually Monitor the Clubhead Delivery Line by "Tracing" along it with the Right Forearm. This is done as though a flashlight were lashed to the Right Forearm, with the #3 Pressure Point as the lens, causing its beam to move along the Reference Line (Study 4-D and 6-J-0). But this does not mean that, because the Clubshaft is On Plane, the Right Forearm is automatically On Plane also. **BOTH MUST BE MONITORED AS BEING ON PLANE AT THE START DOWN.**

The alternative to Hand Controlled Pivot is, of course, Pivot Controlled Hands, per 10-24-F. That does not alter the Basic Geometry or Physics requirements, but assigns to Physics precedence over Geometry — Force dictating alignments. Which obviously reduces precision; but, also Clubhead Throwaway. The information for such procedure is all included herein — merely Monitor the Pivot instead of the Hands. That is, primarily, the use of The Shoulder Turn Takeaway instead of Right Forearm Takeaway. But that procedure is so inferior that detailed consideration does not appear warranted except in a transitional undertaking. However, if the Clubhead is Monitored directly instead of through the Hands, it is, as always, a chronic disaster. If the Hands are Monitored, Pivot Controlled Hands vanish.

WRIST POSITIONS—COMBINATIONS

USEFUL COMBINATIONS

5-A-1. FLV
Flat
Level
Vertical

5-A-2. BLV
Bent
Level
Vertical

5-B-1. FLT
Flat
Level
Turned

5-B-2. BLT
Bent
Level
Turned

5-C-1. FCT
Flat
Cocked
Turned

5-C-2. BLT
Bent
Level
Turned

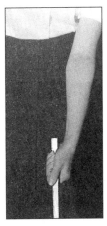

5-D-1. FLR
Flat
Level
Rolled

5-D-2. BLR
Bent
Level
Rolled

CHAPTER SIX

POWER PACKAGE

DEFINITIONS

6-0. GENERAL The Power Package concept isolates and defines the functions of the Hands and Arms in propelling the Clubhead into Impact. The Power Package consists of the Arms and the Club — as discussed herein — and includes the four Power Accumulators, the four Pressure Points, their Loading and the Clubhead Lag. There is no Stroke which does not include a Power Package Assembly and the five-step sequence of their operation — Accumulation, Load, Storage, Delivery, and Release.

STRUCTURE

6-A-1. THE TRIANGLE ASSEMBLY The Power Package is basically a Triangle and this form puts it under the Law Of The Triangle. The Straight Left Arm forms Side One, the Shoulders form the Second Side and a line from the Right Shoulder to the Hands forms the Third Side — whether the Right Arm is straight or bent. So the shape of the Triangle can be changed only by changing the length of the Third Side. (Also, regarding Structure, study 6-B-1-D and 6-B-3-0-1.)

THE TRIANGLE ASSEMBLY

6-A-1 #1. Top

6-A-1 #2. Impact

6-A-1 #3. Follow Through

POWER PACKAGE

LEVER ASSEMBLIES

6-A-2. THE PRIMARY LEVER ASSEMBLY An additional structural feature is leverage. A dual system of Form III levers. A Form III lever has the Force — or Power — between the Weight and the Fulcrum (2-L).

Consider the Left Arm and the Clubshaft together as the Primary Lever Assembly. The Left Shoulder is the Fulcrum, the Secondary Lever Assembly — Cocked or not — is the weight. This Assembly is normally propelled by the Arms, that is, Accumulators and Pressure Points #1 and/or #4, as discussed under 6-B-1 and 6-B-4. Movement of this Assembly must comply with 1-L-7 to -11 and 2-F.

6-A-2. Primary Lever Assembly

POWER PACKAGE

LEVER ASSEMBLIES

6-A-3. THE SECONDARY LEVER ASSEMBLY The Club is both a section of the Primary Lever Assembly and the entire Secondary Lever Assembly and is an additional Form III lever with the Left Wrist as its Fulcrum and the Clubhead as the Weight. This Assembly is normally propelled by the Hands. That is, Accumulators and Pressure Points #2 and/or #3 as discussed under 6-B-2, 6-B-3 and 2-P.

6-A-3. Secondary Lever Assembly

6-A-4. ARMS It is important to keep in mind this "normal" position of the Arms — that until after the Follow-through, the Left Arm is never bent, the Right Arm is never straight. The Left Arm bends if and when it is carried — NOT THROWN — closer than about 45 degrees to the Shoulder line. (See 6-B-3-0-1.)

POWER PACKAGE

STEP ONE—POWER ACCUMULATION

6-B-0. GENERAL   Force is applied to the Ball through the Lever Assemblies. Power is applied to the Lever Assemblies through Pressure Points. Power is applied to the Pressure Points by Power Accumulators. Power Accumulators are out-of-line conditions of the Power Package Components. Out-of-line simply means "not in a straight line from end to end." Releasing them to seek their in-line condition releases their stored potential. Varying the amount of out-of-line and/or the amount of muscular effort will vary the accumulation of Power that can be Released by the selected Triggering action. Accumulators are numbered in the order of their probable widest use in Stroke Type Combinations.

Clubhead Lag (6-C) is, of course, an out-of-line condition in the Power Package but is not considered an Accumulator because its "Release" is a power *loss*. Again, the Lag and Drag in the Pivot train (6-M-1) are out-of-line conditions also (but not of the Power Package) and, likewise, are not "Released." Else the Swing Radius of the Stroke would be shortened — which also is a power *loss*. Swing Radius is what makes it harder to get a balanced 20-foot board around a corner than a 5-foot board. A hanging Driver weighs less than one pound, but at arms length the deltoids (2-M-3) are supporting about four pounds — considering the arm weight as negligible. But with arm and club parallel to the ground, the Wrist is supporting close to six pounds and the deltoids about ten. From the Feet the total moment of Inertia increases proportionately to the Pivot Lag. So, the Clubhead (or primary Lever Assembly) whose Swing Radius extends to the feet is much harder to decelerate during Impact, which means better Clubhead Speed at Separation. (See 2-E.)

POWER PACKAGE

MUSCLE POWER

6-B-1-0. THE FIRST POWER ACCUMULATOR is the Bent Right Arm — the Hitter's (7-19) Muscle Power Accumulator. Even though the Right Biceps is active, per 7-3, the Backstroke (8-5) is always made with the Right Arm striving to remain straight. But the straight Left Arm restrains this continuous Extensor Action of the right triceps with an effortless Checkrein Action. Consequently, during Release (7-24), the Right Arm can straighten only as the Left Arm moves away from the Right Shoulder. (Study 2-P.) This results in a smooth, even Thrust For acceleration of the Lever Assemblies (6-A) from an otherwise unruly force. Active or Passive, the straightening Right Elbow with its Paddle-wheel Action, powers, guides and regulates the #3 Accumulator Motion (7-18) but not the actual Clubface aligning (1-F). (Study 2-M, 7-11 and Component 19.)

POWER ACCUMULATOR #1

6-B-1-0 #1.
Down Stroke

6-B-1-0 #2.
Impact

6-B-1-0 #3.
Follow Through

6-B-1-A. MAXIMUM POWER is produced by adjusting the Hand speed to permit the maximum Thrust through Impact before maximum extension is reached.

6-B-1-B. ZERO ACCUMULATION is possible only when Accumulator #4 alone actuates the Primary Lever Assembly.

6-B-1-C. MAXIMUM TRIGGER DELAY is gained by causing the Right Elbow to "Pass the Ball" — which is the Line-of-Sight-to-the-Ball — before Release. (Study 2-N, 3-F-7, 7-8 and 10-14.)

POWER PACKAGE

MUSCLE POWER

6-B-1-D. EXTENSOR ACTION is exclusively the steady effort to straighten the bent Right Arm. This *stretches,* but does *not move,* the Left Arm and produces a structural rigidity that is a strong deterrent to collapse under the stresses of Acceleration and Impact. It is in operation from Impact Fix to the end of the Follow-through. In addition, this action promotes:

1. The full extension of the Left Arm at all times
2. The full extension of the Right Arm for the Follow-through
3. The correct rate of "Clubhead Closing"
4. The proper type of support for "passive" (non-accelerating 6-C-0) Clubhead Lag Pressure involving Wristcock

Except with Zero Accumulator #3, the "stretch" *direction* is *always Below Plane.* Because of Extensor Action, the Right Triceps can never be totally "passive."

While this particular application of Power inhibits a "take-over" of the Centrifugal Reaction, it also introduces some assurance that the available Centripetal Force will not be stifled by a premature checking of that outward drive which generates it. This relieves the Wrists of considerable responsibility and gives this drive a much more massive kind of support while freeing the Wrists for a sharper focus on Ball Control. Extensor Action gives an indispensable control to all Strokes. Stretching the Left Arm through the #3 Pressure Point gives the same action as pulling on both ends of a rope; that is, it pulls both the Left Arm and the Clubshaft tautly in a straight line. That, and just moving from "Bent Left Wrist" to "Flat Left Wrist" during — and as — the Loading Action are very effective for Short Shot procedures (10-19-0). However, improperly executed, it can cause Clubhead Throwaway. In which case, use only the #1 Pressure Point and pull on the Left Thumb to then hold at least the Left Arm in-line and retain Power Package structural rigidity. Warning: the mushier the Impact, the more Compression Leakage — the more it sounds like a stone, the less Compression Leakage — especially as the Shots become shorter (even Putts). You can kid yourself, but not the Ball. The Ball <u>ALWAYS</u> tells the truth.

This action of the Extensor force can be substituted for Downstroke Acceleration of the Arms and Hands — in part or wholly — for "less than full Power" shots calling for the precision execution of a heavy, constant Hand Speed through Release and Impact. Lag Pressure then *can* be the artificial pressure of a tight right forefinger grip — which, actually, can serve the same function for Backstroke guidance (6-C-1).

POWER PACKAGE

VELOCITY POWER

6-B-2-0. THE SECOND POWER ACCUMULATOR When the Left Wrist is Cocked (in excess of the selected Clubshaft-Left Hand Angle (6-B-3) in the Address or Fix positions) it forms the Second Power Accumulator. It's the true Velocity Accumulator per 2-P (as differentiated from 6-B-3-0 and 7-20) because of the shortness of its travel time (during a Maximum Delay Release). Centripetal Force, Accumulator #1, the muscles of both forearms, any — or all — are available to actuate this Assembly. Its "in-line" condition is FULL EXTENSION (per 2-P). It is the "Downward" (Angle of Attack) Motion, per 2-C-0 and 2-N-1.

POWER ACCUMULATOR #2

6-B-2-0 #1. Down Stroke

6-B-2-0 #2. Impact Comparison—Cocked & Uncocked

6-B-2-A. MAXIMUM POWER is obtained with maximum *Controllable* Hand Speed (10-19) and/or a sharp-breaking Line Delivery (7-23) and maximum Trigger Delay (10-20). (Study 10-19 and 10-11-0-2.)

6-B-2-B. ZERO ACCUMULATION is obtained by not exceeding the selected #3 Accumulator Angle during either the Backstroke or the Downstroke.

6-B-2-C. MAXIMUM TRIGGER DELAY is achieved by using an Automatic Snap or Flip Release (10-24-E or -F).

POWER PACKAGE

TRANSFER POWER

6-B-3-0. THE THIRD POWER ACCUMULATOR Power Accumulator #3 is formed by the angle established between the Clubshaft and the Left Forearm (per 7-2-4) and is totally independent of Wristcock (except per 2-P). Accumulator #3 should never be "Out-of-Line" — instead, it seeks to MAINTAIN its radial alignment with the Left Arm and a Left Wrist vertical to its associated Plane, that is, to synchronize the Lever Assembly with the selected Hinging, to avoid compression leakage (2-C-0). So, basically, Accumulator #3 Hand Motion (4-D-0) is "Clubface Control," "Rhythm Control," "Roll Power Control" and True Clubhead Overtaking Control of the Right Elbow (7-3). Study 2-G, 2-P, 4-D-0 and 7-20.

With true Throw-out Action (no manual Clubface manipulation), Centrifugal Reaction automatically aligns the Clubshaft and Clubface for Horizontal Hinging (10-10-D), regardless of the Grip being used. Ball Position and Location (2-N) for straight-away flight must agree with the amount of "Hookface" designed into the Club (6-E-2), and is, therefore, unalterable except with manual override action or adjustment of the Plane Line. True "Throw Out" Action holds the Clubface in Impact Fix alignment (7-10) and automatically produces Angled Hinging (10-10-C). (Study 7-3 and 10-11-0-3.) Regardless of Lag Loading Procedure, Vertical Hinging (10-10-B) is a deliberate manual manipulation. Study 6-E-2.

Photos 6-B-3-0 shows the Left Forearm version — using a slow back-and-forth motion with Horizontal Hinge Action. For the Right Forearm version, do likewise, applying Angled Hinge Action. Do both alternately until you see the distinct difference in the Rhythm and Clubhead Travel of all three of the Roll procedures. The "On Plane" Right Forearm ALWAYS establishes and maintains the correct Clubshaft-Left Arm angle through Release and Impact (See 7-3).

POWER ACCUMULATOR #3

6-B-3-0 #1. Turned | 6-B-3-0 #2. Rolled. | 6-B-3-0 #3. Comparison Accumulators #2 & #3

POWER PACKAGE

TRANSFER POWER

All the above is equally true for Putting. That is, the Swinger can use a "Reverse Loft" Putter for a precision "Low Point" Impact — really a very accurate and simple procedure. One alternative would be to use something like 10-3-F (Peck) or 10-3-H (Paw). Else manipulate the Clubface per 7-2. Either way, there is no accuracy for any procedure unless the *HANDS* (5-0) execute a definite Hinge Motion (2-G) per 2-F, 2-J-3-A and 6-L-0. However, *ANY* deviating from 6-A-4 and 12-0 is — mechanically — less than ideal. Putts are miniaturized Drives (12-0).

The Accumulator #3 motion must be accommodated in the Impact alignment or it will (with great loss of Power) produce a Quitting of the Hand motion and/or a Quitting of the Overtaking action in an effort to avoid Pulled Shots. That wilted feeling of a "Blocked Out" Stroke is the tip-off of a faulty Approach Angle. (Study 2-N and 10-5-0.)

6-B-3-0-1. THE FLYING WEDGES The Clubhead may *appear* to move in an arc around and outside the Hands when related to the Left Arm — the very basic Left Arm Flying Wedge. But when related to the Right Forearm, it appears to move "On Plane" with the Right Forearm at its normal rigid angle (Bent Right Wrist) — the Right Forearm Flying Wedge. So — except in Sections 1 and 3 (Chapter 8), **the entire Left Arm,** the Clubshaft and the back of the Left Hand are ALWAYS positioned against the same flat plane — **the plane of the Left Wristcock motion.** At the same time, the **Right Forearm** and the Clubshaft are, in like manner, positioned on **the plane of the Right Wrist Bend** AT RIGHT ANGLES TO THE LEFT ARM PLANE. That is the precision assembly and alignment of the Power Package basic structure and is mandatory during the entire motion. Hitting or Swinging. Study 4-D-1 regarding "Grip" and "Flat Left Wrist." Also see 7-3. Then, ideally, the Left Wrist is always Flat and the Right Wrist is always Level (4-A-1, 4-B-1).

POWER PACKAGE

TRANSFER POWER

6-B-3-A. MAXIMUM POWER for Swingers is obtained by using the Standard Wrist Action (10-18-A) with Automatic Snap Release (10-20 and 10-24-E) and maximum Radius (6-B-0); plus the transfer of the residual Clubhead velocity of Accumulator #2 (7-18). (Study 2-P and 10-3-D.) Hitters use Single Wrist Action (10-18-C) because they use a Cocked Right Elbow and Angled Hinging, per 7-20, 10-3-K and 10-11-0-3, whether the Left Wrist is Cocked or not. So, unless it is "Zeroed Out," there must always be a definite Accumulator #3 "Overtaking" Action.

6-B-3-B. ZERO ACCUMULATION is obtained by merely reducing the Hand-Clubshaft angle to zero by dropping the Clubhead into a Reverse Wristcock condition (FVU), or by moving the Clubshaft up into the cup of the Left Hand. Placing the Clubshaft anywhere between the Heel and Cup of the Left Hand will reduce its angle accordingly but will not alter its Rhythm (2-G) until Zero position is reached.

6-B-3-C. MAXIMUM TRIGGER DELAY for Swingers is the use of Trigger Types 10-20-D or 10-20-E for a truly Automatic Snap Release (10-24-E). But the Hitter uses the Right Arm Throw 10-20-B, per 6-B-3-A above. (Study 7-20 in this connection.)

POWER PACKAGE

RADIUS POWER

6-B-4-0. THE FOURTH POWER ACCUMULATOR The angle formed by the Left Arm and the Left Shoulder forms the Fourth Power Accumulator. The In-line condition it seeks is with the Shoulders. It is not only an independent Power Accumulator, but its Triggering function as the Checkrein of the Right Elbow is also vastly important, it thus, can be the Accumulator of the Accumulators — or Master Accumulator. (Also see 2-M-4.)

As Accumulator #4, it is Pivot (Body) Power supplying the initial acceleration of the Downstroke to throw the Lever Assemblies toward Impact by the Thrust of the Shoulder Turn. (See 7-13.) Another major contribution to Impact Power is geometric — it is the first link in the Swing Radius power train between the Club and the Feet.

"Left Arm Power" in any form or amount can still be considered #4 Accumulator Action. Otherwise, it actually substitutes for the Pivot to introduce the circular motion required to produce Centripetal Force.

POWER ACCUMULATOR #4

6-B-4-0 #1.　　　　　　6-B-4-0 #2.
At Top.　　　　　　　　Follow Through

POWER PACKAGE

RADIUS POWER

6-B-4-A. MAXIMUM POWER is obtained by using maximum On Plane Shoulder Turn Thrust against Pressure Point #4 per 7-19, and maximum Swing Radius (6-B-0).

6-B-4-B. ZERO ACCUMULATION is either no Shoulder Turn or the use of Accumulator #1 alone for actuating the Primary Lever Assembly.

6-B-4-C. MAXIMUM TRIGGER DELAY is achieved by using either the Standard or the Delayed Pivot (to increase the Lag of the Downstroke Shoulder Turn) with a Snap Loading Action (per 7-19-3 and 10-22-C), followed by a Snap Release (10-24-E) with a Pitch Basic Stroke (10-3-B). For Hitters the essential difference is that Loading is per 7-19-1.

POWER PACKAGE

LAG AND THRUST
STEP TWO—POWER LOADING

6-C-0. GENERAL "Loading" means the establishment of the Lag, Drag and Thrust — at the selected Assembly Point (10-21) by the selected Loading Action (10-22) — calculated to produce the necessary Downstroke Thrust and Impact Force for the situation at hand. "Lag" defines the condition of "trailing," or "following," and can, and usually should, exist to some degree at every point in the Stroke from <u>feet</u> to Clubhead. Every Lagging Component places a Drag on its preceding Component, which is proportional to the Rate of Acceleration of the leading component.

Pivot Lag (9-1) is Body Power for Swingers (2-M-4), launching pad for Hitters (2-M-3), and for both, operates like a "gear train" to extend the Swing Radius of the Primary Lever to any point from the Shoulder Turn on down to the Feet (Zone #1). Both Inertia and the Moment Arm of the Thrust act the same in that the farther from the center the greater the authority.

Accumulator Lag (7-19) and/or Thrust (7-11) determine the amount of Power generated by the Power Package — Zone #2 (9-2).

Clubhead Lag (7-19) promotes even and steady acceleration, assuring dependable control of distance. The Power Package utilizes four types of Thrust:
1. Accelerating (Accumulators driving the Lever Assemblies)
2. Non-Accelerating (Extensor Action supplying Power Package Mass)
3. Acceleration Control (Lag Pressure Point sensing Clubhead Inertia)
4. "Centrifugal Acceleration" (Centripetal Force pulling the Clubhead toward its In-Line condition)

6-C-0 #1. Start Down

6-C-0 #2 Impact

POWER PACKAGE

THRUST

6-C-1. PRESSURE POINTS The Force to be applied for the movement of the Lever Assemblies — both ways (opposite pressures 6-B-1-D) — is exerted against the Club (7-11) through Pressure Points — of which there are four:
  #1. The heel of the Right Hand where it touches either the Left Hand thumb or the Clubshaft (as required by the Grip used).
  #2. The last three fingers of the Left Hand.
  #3. The first joint of the Right Hand index finger where it touches the Clubshaft.
  #4. Wherever the straight Left Arm contacts the left side.

6-C-1. PressurePoints
#1. Black Arrow
#2. White Arrow
#3. Striped Arrow
#4. Edged Arrow

POWER PACKAGE

THE SECRET

6-C-2-0. CLUBHEAD LAG is the "Secret of Golf" technique — without it the Line of Compression (2-0) cannot be sustained (3-F-7-B). It is simple, elusive, indispensable, without substitute or compensation, and always present (6-C-1). It *can* be any one or any combination of Pressure Points, selected to sense Clubhead Acceleration rate and direction (2-M-2), but herein, unless otherwise specified, always refers to Pressure Point #3. Establish your "normal" procedure per 2-M-2, then its "plus" and "minus" variations in five yard increments. It also has an equalizing application — that is, in minimizing swing-weight differences. Your "normal" pressure will move lighter Clubs faster and heavier Clubs slower — the change in Approach Speed being fairly well compensated by the opposite effect on Separation Speed. (Study 2-E, 2-F, 2-M-1, 2-M-2 and 3-F-7-B in this connection.)

6-C-2-0.   Clubhead Lag.

POWER PACKAGE

THE SECRET

6-C-2-A. THE ESSENCE of Clubhead Lag technique is that it is *always* both Aiming AND Thrust. Passive — it is *primarily* Aiming the Lag Pressure. Active — it is *primarily* Thrusting the Lag Pressure Point. The Orbiting Clubhead does not seek out the Ball — it seeks out the Delivery Line. But never directly — only via the Right Forearm and the #3 Pressure Point, per 2-F, 5-0 and 7-3. It is guided along that Line to the Both Arms Straight configuration by the straight line thrust of the #3 Pressure Point toward the Angle of Approach quadrant of the Ball — or Aiming Point — per 1-F, 1-L-9/10, 2-J-3 and 6-E-2.

The Clubshaft is stressed by the weight of the Clubhead resisting a change in its direction or velocity — which is Acceleration. Acceleration bends the Clubshaft during Radial Acceleration (10-19-A). Change of direction bends it during Longitudinal Acceleration (10-19-C) which may *be*, or just *include*, the Clubhead Lag Pressure Point in addition to its main function of Acceleration Control. From Putter to Driver, the Clubhead Lag technique is indispensable.

If the Pressure Point pressure that produced the initial Clubshaft flex is maintained, it will maintain the flex also. So the pressure will be a steady smooth Thrust from the entire Power Package Assembly, and will produce a constant rate of acceleration for the Primary Lever Assembly. If the Pivot moves the Right Shoulder at the same speed as the Power Package — or the Primary Lever Assembly — the Accumulators will not be Released by this action until the Right Elbow can straighten. Even then the Clubhead Lag is still maintained — it has *NO* Release Point. Establish a "normal" Right Wrist Bend for Release — either frozen at some point, or moving from Maximum to Minimum Bend as the Ball Location is moved away from Low Point and/or the Basic Stroke changes the Elbow location (10-3) — because the Right Wrist Bend, along with Ball Location and Plane Angle, determine the precise RIGHT FOREARM ANGLE OF APPROACH (7-3).

POWER PACKAGE

THE SECRET

6-C-2-B. ANGULAR ACCELERATION The Clubhead "overtaking" speed is governed by the Law of Conservation of Angular Momentum, whereby the increased Mass resulting from any extension of the Swing Radius decelerates the Hands and, unless they are supported by Power Package Thrust (6-B-1) or Throw Out Action (2-K), can result in great loss of Clubhead Speed. Rely on Clubhead Lag to meter out the necessary support for the Primary Lever Assembly. Strictly speaking, any increase in the product of Mass times Velocity is Acceleration whether or not the Speed is changed. The formula for Kinetic Energy gives Velocity the greater value. And, actually, the acceptable tolerance in the Ball-to-Clubhead weight ratio is quite small.

6-C-2-C. IMPACT CUSHION The prestressed Clubshaft will resist the added weight of the ball during Impact, instead of cushioning the Impact with an unstressed Clubshaft. (See 2-M-1.)

Clubhead Lag Pressure normally remains constant regardless of the Velocity it has produced. Both #1 and #3 Pressure Points are the product of *Accumulator* #1.

6-C-2-D. LAG LOSS The very small degree of Clubhead Lag permitted by Clubshaft Flex, makes this procedure especially susceptible to Clubhead Throwaway. The stiffer the Clubshaft, the less margin.

Over-Acceleration is the menace that stalks all Lag and Drag. Here it allows the Hands to reach maximum speed before reaching Impact and so dissipates the Lag. The length of the Stroke and the amount of Thrust should be adjusted and balanced to produce a "High Thrust-Low Speed" Impact — "heavy" rather than "quick." Daintiness is dangerous.

6-C-2-E. GRIPS AND LAG This Clubhead Lag Loading should be the first factor learned in the Zone #2 applications of the Grips. It should be introduced with the simplest Single Barrel Stroke Types, and become habitual before any other specifics are approached, to avoid the miseries of Address Position Impact. Allow nothing to alter this habit of proper Loading — even momentarily. Nothing else matters much if this is lost. Also adhere rigidly to 2-F, 7-23 and 9-2.

POWER PACKAGE

STEP THREE—POWER STORAGE

THROW AWAY

6-D-0. GENERAL After the selected Pressure Point pressures have been established, the player's prime concern is the storage of the accumulated Power. "Power Storage" sustains the Assembly Point (normally, Top-of-the-Stroke) alignments, conditions, loading, etc., of the Hands — their total Feel per 5-0 — until triggering (7-20). Until *mastered* — consciously or sub-consciously — Power Golf is impossible. Working on anything else first is wasted time. Hitters and Swingers both have the Power Storage problems listed below but cope with them differently. (See 7-19.) With "Throwaway" there can be no Rhythm — and vice versa. And an artificial Follow-through — if any. (See 2-0-B-1 and 2-G.)

6-D-1. First, at the Top, the urge to throw the Clubhead from the Wrist, always disregards the Hands. (Carefully study 5-0, 7-19 and 10-20.)

6-D-2. Secondly, surprisingly low, sustained acceleration of the Lever Assemblies produces excessive Hand Speed which irresistibly throws the Clubhead into its Release Orbit prematurely (10-19-C).

6-D-3. Thirdly, the Feel that the Uncocking of the Wrists is to align the Clubface for Impact, forces the Left Wrist to bend backwards and produces "Quitting" (3-F-7-B). This is "False Feel Wrist Action". (Study 7-8 and 10-5-0.)

CLUBHEAD THROWAWAY

6-D-1. Wrist Action   6-D-2. Over Acceleration   6-D-3. Quitting

POWER PACKAGE

STEP FOUR—POWER DELIVERY
THRUST DIRECTION

6-E-0. GENERAL "Power Package Delivery" refers to the basic requirements for transporting the Power Package Assembly of Stored Power. Steps Three and Four overlap but must be kept distinct — intact — to the Release Point. All Structure, Structural relationships, Accumulator Loadings, etc., are carefully maintained during Delivery, as specified in the pre-selected Stroke Pattern.

6-E-1. DELIVERY PURPOSE Delivery is the players MEANS (9-0) for initiating and maintaining the Geometry of Alignment and the Physics of Motion (as outlined in 1-L and Chapter 2) through the use of Educated Hands (5-0) per 12-3. The procedure presented below is essentially an indirect and automatic equivalent of the Impact Hand Location procedure in Chapter 7-8. And is mandatory for control of any Snap Release.

6-E-2. THE AIMING POINT CONCEPT The hands and the clubhead combine as Clubhead Lag (5-0, 6-C) and can be utilized to execute "Delivery". And the shorter Clubs take less time to reach the In-Line condition from a given Release Point than do the longer Clubs, due to the Law of Conservation of Angular Momentum (6-C-2-B). And the difference in travel distance per degree of Angular Motion because Impact always occurs during the "Pulley" portion of the Endless Belt travel (sketch 2-K #6); regardless of the direction of its Straight Line travel between pulleys (or of the Thrust during the Circle Path per 7-23); because both of those lines represent the True Delivery Paths and move — physically — directly at the point on the Ball through which the Angle of Approach passes even with Aiming Point procedures; because The Machine delivers the #3 Pressure Point to Impact Fix Hand Location AT IMPACT with all Delivery Paths, Delivery Lines, Pulley Sizes, etc. because its structure is designed to do just that; hence the importance of a sturdy structure around the Endless Belt machinery. That is what makes the Aiming Point procedure possible at all. The Aiming Point replaces the ball so you no longer direct the #3 Pressure Point at the Ball but at the Aiming Point just as if it were the Ball — like an explosion shot from sand. Experiment until you grasp the effects of Ball Positioning (2-N). Directing the Lag Pressure Loading (6-C-2-A) at-and through per 4-0 — an Aiming Point can be pin-pointed by experiment and experience only, because "normal" Handspeed differs among players. Increased Handspeed and/or a Sweep Release moves it aft of its "normal" Handspeed location and decreased Handspeed and/or Trigger Delay moves it forward. 10-24 presents additional detail.

THRUST DIRECTION

Now, the wide face of the shorter Clubs allow the Sweet Spot to be moved a suitable distance back from the Leading Edge with the result that Centripetal Force squares the Clubface earlier in accordance. So, with the Ball placed further back from Low Point it could produce Straightaway Flight Line for all Clubs while having the same Release Point Feel. This led to the assumption that one Release Feel would use one Ball Location resulting in a constant struggle for consistency. Actually, when in doubt, there is always the Impact Fix Hand Location procedure (7-8).

If you "Choke Down" on longer Clubs you move their Aiming Point forward. "Choke Down" to make all Clubshafts the same length means the same Aiming Point for all your Clubs — shorter radius but precise timing. Everything is a "Trade-Off".

Remember — Aiming Point concerns only:
1. Clubshaft Length
2. Handspeed
3. Release Point — regardless of Ball Location

Remember the "identities" of those elements of Release. That is — the straight line portion of the Endless Belt locates the required Aiming Point AND VICE VERSA. But it DOES NOT dictate the Endless Belt (Hand) speed AND VICE VERSA. Summing up the Right Arm action — it is always a straight line effort and/or motion and normally, is strictly Clubhead Control. In the meantime the Flat Left Wrist (Clubface Control) under every condition or situation is concerned only with arriving at Impact, Vertical to the ground in the process of executing the selected Hinge Action. So, per 1-F the Hands are correlated independent of every other factor. Practice every phase, over and over until mastered.

POWER PACKAGE

THRUST DIRECTION

Three procedures are available:
1. Move the Aiming Point forward or aft of the established Ball location. This Aiming Point procedure seems more easily acquired if introduced as a Feel. At the top of the Backstroke, even at the End (10-21-C), mentally construct a line from the #3 Pressure Point to the Aiming Point. Let a careful Downstroke direct the thrust precisely along this line. Hitting or Swinging, direct the #3 Pressure Point strongly downward, per 1-L-9, 1-L-10, 2-J-3 and 6-C-2-A, to ensure the "Downward" element of Three Dimensional Impact (2-C-0). That is: *TRY TO DRIVE THE BALL INTO THE GROUND, NOT INTO THE AIR.* If you don't KNOW that you hit down, assume that you didn't. The Hands must ALWAYS take one of the Delivery Paths (10-23), but even with the Circle Path, the Thrust is still a straight-line EFFORT toward the Aiming Point. And even "Tracing" (5-0) must not disrupt it;
2. Move the Ball forward or aft of the established Aiming Point per the previous page, using the Hand and Club guidance procedure presented for #1 above. So the Ball Location changes required for a Push or Draw per 7-2 must exceed the changes required by this procedure before Plane Line Rotation should be employed by "True" Swingers. As usual, though, Clubface manipulators have their choice of either procedure — that is the 1 or the 2;
3. "Open" or "Close" the Stance per 10-24-F.

POWER PACKAGE

TIMING

6-F-0. GENERAL   The term "Timing," as used in Golf, means to bring about Impact during the moment of the Clubhead's maximum Force. With the Rope Handle technique (2-K), this "moment" starts at Release and its "Overtaking Rate" is a very even speed, right up to Impact. Except for Clubhead Lag Pressure, it is almost exclusively the generation and utilization of Centripetal Force. With the Axe Handle technique (2-K), top speed is also established at Release but its "Overtaking Rate" tends to decelerate, making Trigger Delay and Timing much more critical. It is almost exclusively Muscular Force, totally annulling and stifling any intrusion by Centripetal Force. (See "Swingers and Hitters.") So, the Clubhead is *not picking up speed during* the Overtaking (Release) Interval, either when Hitting or Swinging (6-C-2-B, 7-19). (Carefully study 2-N and 2-P.)

6-F-1. "RIGHT" TIMING   is not a matter of a PEAK SPEED because there really isn't any — just a steady build-up of momentum. Nor is it exclusively Clubhead Control — it is also Clubface Control. That is RHYTHM, producing maximum Compression (See 2-C-0). So, "Over Roll" and "Under Roll" (2-G) can produce early and late arrival at Impact for both the Clubhead and the Clubface. Therefore, Right Timing is actually Maximum Compression, as developed by the intended Thrust, near — but prior to — Full Extension (2-P).

Acceleration ceases when the speed it has produced equals that of the Thrust, and though the Thrust is still present and able to *maintain* Velocity, it loses the flexed, stressed Clubshaft (Hitters) and the wallop of the Centrifugal Reaction (Swingers).

6-F-2. "OFF" TIMING   Timing is a basic element of Zone #2. So Zone #2 components should be reviewed first for Power loss causes. Especially for Steering, Quitting, Scooping, Off Plane, or disrupted Rhythm (3-F-7).

But Zone #1 can actually host the cause behind Zone #2 aberrations, especially the Flat Shoulder Turn. Which, in turn, can be an effect of faulty Hip control. These flaws may be uncovered by checking the selected Stroke Pattern. Or they may simply be Components not yet incorporated into the Stroke, and therefore not known and consequently erratic. Three corrective actions are available — and in the order of acceptability are — incorporation, toleration, or compensation. Compensations are like temporary taxes — seldom eliminated and soon forgotten.

POWER PACKAGE

HAND ASSIGNMENTS

6-G-0. HAND MOTION All motion is focused on driving the Hands — *NOT THE CLUB* — toward the *BALL*. This may, with habit, seem to become reversed. But this is where and how a player's game "comes apart." The cure is to return to the original primary concern — the Hands and their Clubhead Lag, Flat Left Wrist and Plane Line (2-0). Educated Hands can compensate for Off Line Hip and Shoulder Motion but only up to a point. Off Plane Clubhead Throwaway is even a very prevalent Putting and Chipping fault. It amounts to an unintentional Plane Line shift and causes direction control to become vague. (See 2-J-3.) So — learn to hit the ball with Hand manipulation rather than with Clubhead manipulation and your game is less likely to keep falling apart (4-D, 5-0).

6-H-0. CURRICULUM You can't have Educated Hands unless you know what to teach them. The following curriculum is indispensable:
    A. Avoid disturbing the Delivery Line (2-J-3)
    B. Avoid "Starting to Hit" when using a Snap Release (6-N-0)
    C. Take all Strokes to the Both Arms Straight Position (8-11)
    D. Avoid a Bent Left Wrist (4-D-1 and 6-D)
    E. Associate the following with "Hitting" (10-19-A) See 7-19:
      1. Angled Hinging (7-10)
      2. Simultaneous Release (4-D-0)
      3. Grip Rotation (7-2)
      4. Single Wrist Action (10-18-C-2)
      5. Active Right Elbow (7-20)
      6. Fixed Lag Pressure Point (10-11-0-3)
      7. Radial Acceleration (10-19-A)
      8. Axe handle technique (6-F)
      9. Slow Start Down (6-B-1)
     10. Angle of Approach (2-J-3)
    F. Associate the following with "Swinging" (10-19-C) See 7-19:
      1. Horizontal Hinging (7-10)
      2. Sequenced Release (4-D-0)
      3. Plane Line Rotation (7-2)
      4. Standard Wrist Action (10-18-A)
      5. Active Left Wrist (7-20)
      6. Rotating Lag Pressure Point (10-11-0-3)
      7. Longitudinal Acceleration (10-19-C)
      8. Rope Handle Technique (6-F)
      9. Quick Start Down (10-23-C)
     10. Arc of Approach (2-J-3)

POWER PACKAGE

STROKE DIFFERENCES

6-J-0. INTERPRETATION Power Package Delivery is presented so as to apply to the Circle Delivery Path, as well as the Straight Line types but it must be interpreted to apply to the selected Stroke Pattern.

6-K-0. PIVOT STROKE DELIVERY In a "Pivot Stroke" the Power Package is held in a fixed relationship with the Body Turn and no independent Arm motion occurs until — or unless — the requirements of the selected Pivot are met. Then Arm Motion, independently or not, continues Delivery per 10-19 until the selected Trigger occurs (10-20).

6-L-0. NON-PIVOT STROKE DELIVERY In a "Non-Pivot Stroke" the Arm motion begins immediately and proceeds toward the Release Point as independently as possible of any incidental body motion. Monitor slow shots for "Clubhead Sag," i.e. dropping Below Plane in either direction. (See 2-N.) However, for a Zero Pivot Stroke, see 10-12-D. And be sure to locate the Ball well aft of normal to avoid "running out of Right Arm."

POWER PACKAGE

STEP FIVE—POWER PACKAGE RELEASE

RELEASE DIFFERENCES

6-M-0. GENERAL The Release triggers into action all the Power Accumulators employed in the Power Package and starts the Components toward their respective pre-selected Impact Alignments. All practice is focused on mastery of this Moment of Truth. All Concentration is directed toward holding the attention to the requirements of the Total Motion during the Downstroke sequence — that it will flow smoothly through Impact from The Top directly to The Finish (at least the Follow-through) without the slightest disturbance from — or for — Impact (12-3).

6-M-1. DOWNSTROKE SEQUENCE The Downstroke sequence of the Stroke Components is dictated essentially by Centripetal Force; "Overtaking" by a lagging Component ends at the instant it achieves an "In-Line" position with its immediately preceding Component.

Centers and Accumulators can be sequenced, overlapped, omitted, emphasized, triggered, and timed as the player's understanding and skill permit; But the Club's Swing Radius (6-B-0) ends at the "non-lagging" Component nearest to the Clubhead. The "Centers" of the Stroke start with the Feet or the *employed* Component nearest to the feet in the following order: Knees, Hips, Shoulders, Arms, *Right* Elbow, Left Wristcock and/or Left Hand rotation. For maximum Power, the position must be taken that will allow Delay of the Release until all Components, except the Right Foot and the Right Shoulder, have reached, or passed, the Line-of-Sight-to-the-Ball, per 6-B-1-C. Then the Accumulators must move very rapidly toward their "In-Line" Position. None should actually arrive (lose all their Lag and Drag) until well after Impact. (See 6-H-0.)

Power Accumulator Release sequence is #4, #1, #2, #3 — regardless of which ones are being employed. Any Accumulator number may overlap or replace its preceding number but cannot precede it. Increase Overlap to increase *Thrust* — decrease Overlap to increase *Velocity*.

POWER PACKAGE

RELEASE PAIRS

6-N-0. RELEASE TYPES There are two Release Types — The Automatic and the Non-Automatic — which are paired with a Release Point, per 10-24.

The two Types differ in that:
1. The Automatic is triggered mechanically (10-20) — the Non-Automatic is a deliberate muscular manipulation.
2. The Automatic drives the Hands at the Aiming Point (6-E-2) — the Non-Automatic drives the Hands to their Impact location (visual reference point) (3-F-5).
3. There may be a "Starting to Hit" in the Non-Automatic but not with the Automatic.

These are discussed in greater detail in Chapter 10-24.

The earlier in the Downstroke the Release occurs, the larger, longer, and slower the Release Arc will be for both Clubhead and Hands. Other things being equal, this will require higher Hand Speed to produce yardage equivalent to that of the short, quick Arc of the Maximum Delay. This involves Angular Speed which is measured by the number of degrees of an Arc through which the motion moves per second. From Release to Impact is just so many degrees of travel — at the Left Shoulder and/or at the Left Wrist. Doubling the travel *time,* (for instance), halves the travel *rate.* (Also see 2-P and 7-23.) The smaller the Release Arc (Endless Belt Pulley — constant <u>Hand</u> Speed), the faster the Right Elbow must straighten and the faster there will be "Extension" (Lever Assemblies 2-P) and "Overtaking" (6-F, #3 Accumulator) until the Right Arm becomes straight. All without affecting The Travel Rate of the Endless Belt."

POWER PACKAGE

AUTOMATIC OR NON-AUTOMATIC

6-P-0. NON-AUTOMATIC RELEASE To produce a truly Non-Automatic Stroke, the selected Stroke Pattern is perfected step by step by practicing each Factor individually until a conscious mechanical control is acquired. As each Factor is mastered — more or less — it is consciously transferred to a Feel Control while still retaining the ability to return it to a Mechanical Control at will. As more and more Factors are inserted into the Stroke, the fitting, aligning and synchronizing become more difficult, delicate and demanding. This adjusting is focused in one direction — the perfection of the Release *MOTIONS* of your Machine. Never try to "make a shot." Make a "MOTION" — the Motion makes the shot. Dependable Means — dependable Results. (Study 3-A, 12-3 and 12-5.)

Your "Motion" must include its "Pace" — that is, Handspeed (RPM), strong, consistent and *RHYTHMIC* (2-G). Then, manipulating the Trigger Delay will handle most Clubhead Speed Variations. (Study 2-M-2.)

6-R-0. AUTOMATIC RELEASE When the selected Non-Automatic Stroke Pattern is mastered it can be pushed on to maximum Delay and become an Automatic Release and an entirely different set of Factors take over the attention and concentration. The Stroke — any Stroke — can be Released Automatically at any point by setting up an automatic Triggering mechanism. The Release is Automatic when any element of the Power Package is mechanically prevented from maintaining its normal place in the sequence of Structure or Motion so that it overtakes or is overtaken by other elements. So, premature Triggering of the Release indicates an unintentional mechanical or muscular derangement of the intended sequence. (Study 6-E-1 and 7-20.)

Now with an Automatic Release, the player *may* control the Clubface alignment by direct manipulation of the Hands, especially when Hitting, or indirectly by adjustment of the Plane Line or Ball placement. Or with the Aiming Point procedure (6-E-2) for maximum Trigger Delay — especially when Swinging. As always, working from a perfected MOTION, with no alteration in the Stroke itself except for special purposes. (Study 7-2.)

Chapter 10-19 shows that Automatic and Non-automatic Releases are equally available to both Hitters and Swingers and that many will find Hitting very satisfying even *if* — and maybe even *because* — it can accommodate any amount of effort one cares to expend on it.

CHAPTER SEVEN

TWENTY-FOUR BASIC COMPONENTS

PIGEON HOLES

7-0. GENERAL Basic Stroke Component classifications are based on the fact that there are twenty-four actions in the Golf Stroke that can be properly executed in more than one way, therefore twenty-four Stroke Components must have groups of Variations for each of these basic functions.

Every Stroke has these twenty-four Basics (constants — samenesses) but few Strokes have the same Variations (variables — differences). These terms are capitalized and used interchangeably throughout the book. The Basic Components are presented in this chapter almost exclusively as "areas of action" — that is, characteristics that are common to each set of Variations and/or comparisons of Variations whenever helpful. Specific details concerning variations are covered in Chapter 10, from which Stroke Patterns are assembled.

The numerical listing of these Components is the approximate order of occurrence and/or selection during the Address and the Stroke.

NUMERICAL LISTING

1. Grips — Basic
2. Grips — Types
3. Strokes — Basic
4. Strokes — Types & Variations
5. Plane Line
6. Plane Angle — Basic
7. Plane Angle — Variations
8. Fix
9. Address
10. Hinge Action
11. Pressure Point Combinations
12. Pivot
13. Shoulder Turn
14. Hip Turn
15. Hip Action
16. Knee Action
17. Foot Action
18. Left Wrist Action
19. Lag Loading
20. Trigger Types
21. Power Package Assembly Point
22. Power Package Loading Action
23. Power Package Delivery Path
24. Power Package Release

TWENTY-FOUR BASIC COMPONENTS

THE GRIP

7-1. GRIPS—BASIC Basic Grip is the term indicating the mere act of holding onto the Club and relates primarily to the proximity of the Hands. They simply are either close enough to overlap or they are not close enough to overlap. So all non-overlapping Grips are Baseball Grips.

The Grips of Hitters and Swingers must differ in tightness. But still per 1-L-3, 6-B-3-0-1, 7-3 and 10-6-B. For the Swinger, Centripetal Force Uncocks BOTH the Left Wrist and the Right Elbow, per 7-19 and 7-20. So both must remain "Passive" but *never* "Whippy." For the Hitter, The Right Triceps become "Active" and execute both Uncocking motions with a firmness that approaches the mandatory rigidity of the Right Wrist. With both procedures, the Flying Wedges' alignments, as always, never waver. Grip Types other than the Strong Single Action (10-2-B) either destroy the Wedges or produce inferior deviations. (Also study 3-F-6.)

TWENTY-FOUR BASIC COMPONENTS

THE GRIP

7-2. GRIP TYPES Each Grip Type employs a different Hand-to-Basic-Plane relationship (2-G) and can be applied to any Basic Grip. For Impact Clubface alignment control, Hitters should rotate their Grip but not their Plane Line at Address (3-F-5 and 7-8), while Swingers should rotate their Plane Line but not their Grip (7-1 and 6-B-3-0). For Swingers the results of Ball Position changes on any one Plane Line are the opposite of those for hitters. Unless, of course, there is hand manipulation — intentional or unintentional — overriding Centrifugal Reaction Alignment activity.

The Hand relationship is invariably established at Impact Fix (7-8) with:
1. The Left Arm and the Clubshaft in-line (4-D and 6-B-3-0-1).
2. The Right Forearm "On Plane" (7-3 and 6-B-3-0-1).
3. The back of the Flat Left Wrist *and* the Lag Pressure Point (6-C-2-0) BOTH facing down the Angle of Approach (Alternate Target Line 2-J-3). Otherwise, per 7-3, both must face down the Right Forearm Impact Fix Alignment regardless of the true Angle of Approach (2-J-3 and 7-5).
4. Move the Stance Line and adjust the Knee Bend, the Waist Bend and the #3 Accumulator Angle (per 6-B-3-B) until the Left Wrist is Flat, Level and Vertical (4-0, 7-8) with the Clubface "Soled" and aligned, per 2-J-1 and 7-6. The effect of Opening and Closing the Plane Line is discussed in 2-J-3-B and 6-E-2-2. (Study 6-C-2-A and 10-23-0.).

For the "True" Hitter, moving the Ball back (Hook alignment) or forward (Slice alignment) — always with the Clubface aligned to the Target Line, per 2-J-1 — gives straightaway initial direction (2-B). Opening the Clubface (Slice Grip) or Closing the Clubface (Hook Grip) at your normal Impact Fix, produces Pushed Slices and Pulled Hooks and so require a compensating Target Line adjustment to make it square to the changed Clubface alignment.

For the "True" Swinger, "Opening" the Plane Line (10-5-D) until it is square to the Clubface alignment at the new "Aft" location, will produce a "Fade." With the Ball moved Forward, "Closing" the Plane Line (10-5-E) square to the Clubface alignment at the new location, will produce a "Draw." The Curve of their paths, after the straightaway initial direction, will be proportional to the divergence of the Plane and Target Lines. Herein, "Path" terms (Ball Path, etc.) refer to total Ball behavior, *whether or not* it remains straightaway. "Line" terms ("Target Line," etc.) refer to the straightaway direction of Aim.

TWENTY-FOUR BASIC COMPONENTS

THE STROKES

7-3. STROKES—BASIC   Because of the dominant role of Accumulator #3 (6-3-B-0, 2-N and 2-P), Golf Strokes are very dependent on the Right Elbow activity deriving from its location and the nature of the subsequent Right Arm participation. The Elbow must always be someplace and as there are only three definable locations, there are three Major Basic Strokes — Punch, Pitch and Push (10-3). Minor Basic Strokes are discussed in 10-3-0.

Right Forearm Position at the Top differs for the Angle and for the Arc of Approach procedures. So their Elbow location and action differs also. For Hitting (10-19-A), the Right Forearm should be precisely in-line with — and directly opposed to — the motion of the On Plane Loading Action (7-22) of the entire Primary Lever Assembly (6-A), not just the Clubshaft, and this alignment maintained through Impact (2-J-3 and 4-D). For Swinging (10-19-C), the Right Forearm should be precisely in-line with — and directly opposed to — the motion of the On Plane Loading Action of the Secondary Lever Assembly (the Clubshaft) and this alignment maintained through Impact in compliance with both 6-B-3-0-1 and 10-11-0-3. With this "in-line" relationship of Loading and Right Forearm, it is absolutely MANDATORY that, Hitting or Swinging, it is the Right Forearm — not just the Right Hand and/or Clubshaft — that must be thrown, or driven, into Impact, per 7-2-3. (Study 7-11.) ALWAYS, for all procedures, the Right Forearm is positioned "On Plane" — pointing at the Plane Line as the Angle of Attack (2-N). The On Plane Right Forearm shows the precise up-and-down direction it and the Clubshaft must take throughout the Stroke (2-J-3). The "Angle of Approach" position of the Right Forearm shows the precise Cross-Line direction the Forearm must take through Impact. It, thereby, precisely locates the visual Impact Point — where the eye must be directing the Pressure Point #3 — the inside-aft quadrant of the Ball. Remember, the actual Angle of Approach of the Clubhead is determined by Ball Position (2-N) so, the Cross Line position of the Right Forearm is ONLY the On Plane Forearm Thrust per 1-L-9/10/11. Even with the Pitch Basic Stroke. The Right Forearm must leave — and precisely return to — its own Fix Position (7-8) "Angle of Approach" (regardless of the true Clubhead Angle of Approach). The mandatory Right Forearm Takeaway. Both approaches produce identical Clubhead Delivery Lines.

THE STROKES

Furthermore, in compliance with 6-B-3-0-1, Bending and Straightening the Right Elbow will RAISE AND LOWER the Left Arm *and/or* COCK AND UNCOCK the Left Wrist without Bending, Flattening, or Cocking the Right Wrist. Practice this first at Impact Fix. So, Right Elbow Action either powers and/or controls all three elements of Three Dimensions Impact (2-C-0) per 1-L-9. All this you will come to know as THE MAGIC OF THE RIGHT FOREARM.

7-4. STROKES—TYPES & VARIATIONS Stroke Variations are produced by the use of Power Accumulators. Combinations of these Accumulators will produce all the Variations of the Basic Strokes that are possible. (See Chapter 6-B.)

All Combinations are correct in themselves but may be limited to particular applications to be effective — they are not 100% interchangeable.

It may appear that some of the Accumulators omitted from some combinations are still actually present in the action. But their participation is negligible, incidental or minimal. Or their presence may be simply improper execution. Full understanding and skill in their application will establish the correctness and individuality of each Combination.

However, it is not at all necessary for the non-teaching player to know any more combinations than he finds useful to his own game.

TWENTY-FOUR BASIC COMPONENTS

THE INCLINED PLANE

7-5. PLANE LINE The Stroke selected under 7-4 needs two basic alignments — its direction and its angle. Most important is its direction. This is leading up to the point to be considered here which is the relationship of these three ever present elements — (1) The Base Line of the Inclined Plane; (2) the Line of the Stance; and (3) the intended Line of Flight of the Ball. (Also study 2-G, 2-J-2 and 7-2.)

The Plane Line is located where the Horizontal Plane and the Angled Plane intersect. The Vertical Plane of the Target Line intersects them as either Square, Open or Closed to the Plane Line but always along the Resultant Force Vector. (See 2-C and 10-5.) Very important additional information regarding the Inclined Plane is presented in 2-F, 2-J and 2-N, and under Component 6.

7-6. BASIC PLANE ANGLES The Clubshaft must start its journey on the Plane of its Address angle of inclination. It may or may not move to other Planes as it travels. Clubs cannot be designed to be perfectly Soled (2-J-1) and still align the Clubshaft with more than one Plane Angle Reference Point. So those aligned between the Elbow and Shoulder Planes have become the most widely accepted, because actually the Toe or Heel can be lifted enough to safely accommodate either the flatter or steeper Plane and, therefore, any listed Plane Angle reference Point also (2-D-0). Even on hardpan, the Ball, normally, is gone before the ground is touched. Then, too, there is always the true Clubshaft Angle with 8-6 and/or 10-6-E. The ideal solution is a slightly rounded Toe and Heel for all Clubs. (Also study 10-24-F.)

This category does not determine which Shifts can be made but only identifies several Basic Reference Points. Five such settings are offered here — three fixed, one moving and one movable — each named for its particular reference point. Any Plane Angle not conflicting with other Components is acceptable. No Plane is technically too flat or too steep unless it allows the Heel or Toe of the Club to touch the ground before Separation or without compensating per 2-D and 2-F. Ball location and Plane Angle are closely associated. As the Plane Angle steepens, the Ball must be moved forward to control Divot depth and Pick-off. Never *TRY* to "take" — or "not take" — a Divot. It must be the automatic result of Ball Position *AND* Plane Angle. (Study 2-J and 2-N for more Ball positioning information.)

THE INCLINED PLANE

7-7. PLANE ANGLE VARIATIONS Due to personal preference, natural inclination or the pressure of conditions, it is not always possible or advisable to adhere to a single Inclined Plane classification throughout the entire Stroke. Players often — consciously or subconsciously — employ more than one of the "natural" Planes. The Shoulder Planes are the more consciously employed — the Elbow Plane the more — almost totally — subconsciously used. Vaguely or incorrectly defined Planes and Variations must be eliminated. The list is restricted to those of fairly common usage — good and bad. Other than the Right Shoulder positions, only the Elbow reference point has any great general usefulness. The "Hand Angle" is an emergency or special purpose application. Wrist Action and the selected Inclined Plane must be compatible — watch especially with "No Wristcock" Strokes.

During any Shift of Planes the Clubshaft is held On Plane with the Plane Line as though the Plane itself were moving to the new location. Other *controlled* procedures that achieve On Plane Impact may be more difficult but need not be deemed improper. Such as, positioning the Clubshaft at The Top to the Plane Angle intended for Release. (Study 2-N and 10-6-B in this connection).

Always view the Plane as rectangular (with four 90-degree corners), so, depending on the terrain and the situation at hand, the lower edge may be downhill, uphill, level, partially underground or above ground but always with both Plane Lines (Impact and Low Point) parallel to the upper and lower edges. But tilted, rotated or whatever, always have an Inclined Plane and a straight Plane Line. Remember, you must always adjust the Plane Angle and the Ball Location to bring the Right Forearm positioning into agreement with the intended purpose — the one Forearm MUST represent both Alignments. (Study 2-J-1 and 2-J-3 in this connection.)

TWENTY-FOUR BASIC COMPONENTS

MACHINE PREPARATION

7-8. THE FIX There is one mechanical fundamental in the Golf Stroke, it is CORRECT IMPACT ALIGNMENTS. There is no advantage in leaving these to chance if they can be consciously defined and selected by a preliminary positioning. (See 3-F-5, 8-0 and 8-2.)

There is one indispensible definition — except with 10-9-B, Impact conditions are *not* the same as in the Address except for Clubshaft angle. The most important single difference is that the Left Wrist is Bent at Address but not at Impact. Therefore precision alignment of the Grip can be taken *only* in the Impact position. Secondly, the Left Shoulder is higher at Impact so the player must be positioned accordingly for proper Shoulder-to-ball distance.

A further advantage of a separate and clearly defined Impact position is that the players have presented, right before them exactly what they will be striving to achieve at Impact. Not merely a vague approximation of the Clubface alignment, but the exact relationship of *every single Component*. And the opportunity to familiarize themselves with the correct appearance and the correct Feel. And *Fix* them in mind with more and more precision, especially regarding the Hands. They must *appear* to be near, or covering, the Left Toe—nowhere near the ball. That will, except as required in 10-8 and 10-9, change their relationship with the Ball and the Feet but they will still be in mid-body location. Move back and forth between Address and Fix until you see that. That difference separates Pro and Hacker. Much effort and poor results is the giveaway. Without exception. In-put Out-put Power Ratio also is utterly dependent on Hand Location at Impact (The Flat Left Wrist—2-G and 9-2). (Study 4-D-1 and 6-E in this connection.)

Besides the conditions mentioned under each Fix classification, The Fix as a whole is the composite of the Selected Stroke Pattern Components and must be so assembled.

TWENTY-FOUR BASIC COMPONENTS

MACHINE POSITIONING

7-9. THE ADDRESS Strictly speaking, The Address position is any position from which a player may elect to start the Backstroke. Like The Fix, The Address is a composite of all the selected Stroke Pattern Components and must be so assembled. Classically, the Left Wrist is Bent, the Right Wrist Flat (Chapter 4), the Clubface and Clubshaft square (putting the Hands at a mid-body location), and the weight evenly distributed (2-J) with the back straight from the neck down — not rounded at the waist. It is easier to control the rotation of a straight rod than a bent one. Ball relationships with the Stance (10-5) are dictated by the Plane Line, Plane Angle, and Flight Path (7-10) and may vary from Pattern to Pattern and for special purposes but not otherwise (2-N). Whether using Address or Impact Position (10-9), the Swinger must set up a "Swinging" motion; the Hitter, a "carrying" motion (10-19) to comply with the Lag Loading procedures 7-19-1/2/3.

Except for special purposes, Address Position is NEVER Impact Position. (See 4-D-1.) Address is a fluid position midway between the directions of weight shifting and makes it easier to keep both the Clubshaft and the Right Forearm "On Plane" because both can be pointing at nearly the same point along the Plane Line during the Start Up. (Study 2-G, 2-J, 3-F-5 and 9-2.)

TWENTY-FOUR BASIC COMPONENTS

BALL BEHAVIOR

7-10. HINGE ACTIONS "Hinge Actions" describe and control the manipulation of the Hands through the Impact Interval. This Hand manipulation in turn controls the Clubface MOTIONS. Study 2-G with the purpose of seeing that all Hinge Actions have identical relationships to their Associated Plane and that, actually, their differences amount, essentially, to moving the Basic Plane **with its already installed Hinge** to one of the other two possible positions. The next step is to understand that all the Hinge Actions in G.O.L.F. **are executed on an Inclined Plane** without altering their TRUE relations to their TRUE Basic Plane. For a very basic drill, practice *all* Hinge Motions — by moving the Left Arm — (only) — back and forth — on their normal Plane AND on the Inclined Plane, without a Club and with the Wrist Flat and Vertical to learn the Feel of the Rhythmic motion required through Impact per 2-G.

Besides the coverage in 2-D, 2-G and 10-10, "Basic Hinging" has the following characteristics of appearance and feel: **Between the "Full Roll" of Horizontal Hinging and the "No Roll" of Vertical Hinging, Angled Hinging takes on a "Half Roll" motion.** While Horizontal Hinging retains the "Feel" of a "Roll", Angled Hinging takes on a "No Roll" Feel, and Vertical Hinging is executed as a "Reverse Roll."

All these types can also be duplicated (exactly) with Wrists only, Arms only or Body only manipulations using Minor Basic Strokes. But all must produce Rhythm, per 2-G. Use the "Turn" Feel to determine the "Roll" Feel. For special purposes a selected Impact Hinge Action might also be applied to the entire Stroke (becoming Stroke Pattern Component #18 also). Or initiated at *ANY* point prior to Impact. With either procedure, precision is unattainable without — among other requirements — correct Rhythm **in both directions.** Experimentation with all three Rhythms, per 2-G, is about the best drill for understanding the results of excessive or inadequate Turn and/or Roll of the Hands during the Stroke in order to avoid doing either unintentionally. Chronic Fades and Pushes *can* mean insufficient Roll. Chronic Draws and Pulls *can* mean excessive Roll. Both can be induced by unregulated Turn Clubhead Travel (2-G). All of which can also be the cause or effect of Steering. (See 3-F-7-A. Study 6-B-3-0-1.) However, Centripetal Force, by bending the Clubshaft, can tilt the Clubhead down (2-D). So, the faster the intended Swing, the more the Clubhead must be raised at Address and Fix. Centrifugal "Throw Out Action" also affects Clubface alignment for Swinging. (Study 6-B-3-0.)

TWENTY-FOUR BASIC COMPONENTS

BALL BEHAVIOR

The importance of taking the Grip in the Impact Fix Position is discussed in Chapter 7-8. Normally, in the precision position, per 2-G, the Left Wrist becomes Vertical to the ground at Low Point for all Hinge Actions but "Vertical-to-the-ground-at-Impact" gives a very desirable sameness for all Ball locations — easily compensated by Clubface adjustment without disturbing the prescribed Hand Motion (4-D-1 and 10-10). Both procedures are completely optional. However, without realizing it a major disturbance to Hand Motion are "Reminder Grips." The only required Left Hand alignment (4-D-1) is the Plane, and not the Clubshaft per se.

Always starting from that same Wrist Position, one Hinge Action is as easy to apply as another. Also, if the Clubface is always aligned square to the Plane Line, Angled Hinging will give an Open-Open Target Line, Horizontal Hinging will give a Closed-Closed Target Line, and, Vertical Hinging will give a Square-Square Target Line.

The Left Shoulder, the Right Elbow and/or the Wrists supply the Club<u>head</u> Hinging because it does not require more control than that of Swivel type Hinging; However, The Flat Left Wrist supplies the precision Hinge Motion Control required for the Club<u>face</u>. The Flat Left Wrist rides The Lever Assemblies and its relationship is constant. But also independent by reason of its required relationship to the Basic Planes per (2-G). Per sketch 1-L, Hinge Action is inseparable from Angular Motion and so it can only go <u>aright</u> or <u>awry</u> but <u>not away</u>.

The "Hinges" are actually mounted at the Left Shoulder but the real control comes with moving or holding the Left Wrist in the positions called for by the respective Hinge arrangements. This means that the Flat Vertical Left Wrist is held IN LINE WITH THE HINGE — the BLADE of the Hinge — independent of the Left Arm alignment. Only this alignment can assure Rhythm (2-G). The Hinge Action Control is required only from Impact to the end of the Follow-through. Except, of course, when the Stroke Pattern Wrist Action dictates otherwise. In which case, the "Left Wrist — Hinge Blade" alignment is — usually — maintained throughout the entire Stroke. There are actually five Hinge Action procedures (10-10). Some procedures are more difficult but all have equal precision in producing the Rhythm of a consistent Clubface motion for minimum Three Directional Impact Compression Leakage (2-C-0).

TWENTY-FOUR BASIC COMPONENTS

APPLICATION OF THRUST

7-11. PRESSURE POINT COMBINATIONS Fundamentally, Power must flow from its source (the Accumulators) and must be exerted against something (Pressure Points) that will directly or indirectly drive the Club through Impact. The "indirect" drive is exerted against the "Clubhead Lag." So in every Stroke, Clubhead Lag must be assigned to some Pressure Point. The "direct" drive normally uses the remaining employed Pressure Points. (See 6-A and 6-C.)

There are only four Pressure Points but they can be used in any desired combination — using one, two, three, or all four Points. As with Power Accumulators, this produces 15 different combinations. Each Power Accumulator normally actuates its "same numbered" Pressure Point and each Accumulator has its own Loading procedure, as explained in Chapter 10-11.

The "On Plane" Pressure Point Thrust of the Power Accumulators translates their Potential Energy into Clubhead "On Plane" Kinetic Energy — *always at Right Angles to the Clubshaft* (1-L-11). However, it is Clubhead Lag Pressure (10-11-0-2 and 10-11-0-3), educated, per 5-0, that enables the player to comply with Delivery Line and Delivery Path requirements (2-J-3 and 7-23). Clubhead Lag (Pressure Points 1, 2, and/ or 3) deals exclusively with the Sweet Spot Plane (2-F and 7-5) and *is always driven directly into Impact* — through a point, normally, on the inside-aft quadrant of the Ball per 7-3. Ball Positioning — as the Ball is moved toward the Right Foot, the Fix alignment of the Clubface becomes more and more "Closed" to THE DELIVERY LINE, DELIVERY PATH, AND THE LAG PRESSURE POINT (for the straightaway Flight Line) while the Left Wrist and the Right Forearm relationships become more and more "Open." (Study 6-E-2 and 7-3.)

TWENTY-FOUR BASIC COMPONENTS

POWER PACKAGE TRANSPORT

7-12. PIVOT—SWING CENTER TRIPOD The Pivot is the utilization of multiple centers to produce a circular motion for generating Centripetal Force on an adjustable Plane. Plus the maintenance of balance throughout the weight shifts that accompany the turning and bending necessary for the two Line Delivery Paths. A Pivot is only superficially correct that fails to maintain alignments or allows the player to get "out of alignment."

It is the massive vehicle which transports the Power Package Assembly to the launching pad and back-up support for the Hitter's driving Right Arm (6-B-1). It is the massive rotor, supplying Angular Momentum for the Throw Out power transfer to the Swinger's orbiting Left Arm (6-B-3). The Pivot along with the Arms and Hands, supply the Basic Hinging which The Flat Vertical Left Wrist individualizes into the Three Hinge Motions of the Clubface.

It is the sequencing and spacing of the Zone #1 Stroke Components. It consists of — as separate and distinct elements — the motions and actions of the Shoulders, Hips, Knees and Feet. The term Pivot is relative in that it can be classified as anything between Full motion and Zero motion and may include all, part or none of the possible Component Motions and actions. It defines their participation (6-M-1), *including the requirements of Plane Angle and Stance Line Variations* (10-12 and 10-15-0). It is Zone #1, the first and foundational of the three Zones in Chapter 9. (Study 2-0, 9-0 and items 1 and 2 under Sketch 1-L.)

As a Stroke Component, the term PIVOT refers only to the degree and direction of its own motion as the framework or pattern within which all the Pivot Components must be arranged and adjusted. The relative participation of the individual Pivot Components is always determined under their own Pattern references. *ALL* motion — Pivot *and* Power Package — move parallel to the selected Delivery Line. That is, prior to the Downstroke Turn, a Slide parallel with either the Angle of Approach or the Plane Line, per 2-J-3; Because, starting down with a Hip Turn tends to bring the Right Shoulder and Elbow too close to the Ball, which delays the straightening of the Right Arm and leaves the Clubface too open at Impact.

TWENTY-FOUR BASIC COMPONENTS

DUAL AGENT

7-13. SHOULDER TURN The Shoulder Turn Component is controlled by establishing the Planes on which the Right Shoulder can be rotated — which, in turn, is regulated by the Axis Tilt. The Shoulder is the fastest and farthest moving component of the Pivot and actually transmits the Pivot motion to the Arms. (Study 2-H.) Being part of the Power Package, as well as the Pivot, the Shoulder motion does not necessarily violate a Zero Pivot requirement.

When the Shoulder moves on the same Downstroke Plane as the Hands, it provides its greatest support and its best guidance to the Stroke.

However, it can also turn "Off Plane" and still impart rotation, and it can turn not at all and reassign this function to the swinging Arms. The Arms will always seek to move to — and on — the Plane of the Shoulder Turn, requiring compensation by Pressure Point #3, per 2-L#2 and 10-11-0-3. This, with inadequate Backstroke Shoulder Turn and/or inadequate Downstroke Shoulder Lag, will always produce an "Outside-In" Impact, with its stifling of the Clubhead orbit (4-D-0). Keep that Right Shoulder not only "back" but also "down" (On Plane) or you will "run out of Right Arm" before the Hands reach Impact Position—an automatic Throwaway (7-14, 8-6 and 10-6-D). The number one cause of Shoulder Turn Spin-out is the failure to clear the Right Hip. It is actually essential in BOTH directions in order to forestall a Pivot Controlled Stroke.

Incidentally, with a Zero Accumulator #3 there is, theoretically, a Left Shoulder Inclined Plane Angle. Therefore, being synonymous terms, it is far better to consider it as Zero Accumulator #3. (See 6-B-3-B.)

TWENTY-FOUR BASIC COMPONENTS

HULA HULA

7-14. HIP TURN The Hip Turn as a Stroke Component is, per 10-14, the product of the Knee Bend and the Waist Bend. Not otherwise could the weight be shifted and the Shoulder Turn Axis be tilted without moving the Head. A Hula Hula flexibility allows the Hips and Shoulders to be independent but coordinate and so avoid Right Elbow-and-Hip interference and its "Roundhousing" Throwaway (4-D-0) during the Start Down — the Delivery Line *ROLL PREPARATION* (12-3-22).

Except for its being, in itself, the Weight Shift, the Hip Turn is a motion permitting — rather than causing — the other effects, actions, and motions of the Pivot. Weight Shift is strictly a HIP MOTION; Substituting a Head Motion and/or a Knee Motion will make Swaying inevitable.

The Hip Turn can be used to control or modify Hip Action Variations and prevent Zone #1 (9-1) exaggerations. (See 2-N and 7-16.)

7-15. HIP ACTION The Hip Action Category is included to separate the "motion" of the Hips from any work they may accomplish.

The work the Hip Action does, is to lead and pull the Shoulders back and down in varying combinations. This has very valuable applications. Forgetting to shift the weight or clear the Right Hip is difficult if the Hips are initiating the Downstroke Shoulder Turn — in either direction. Study 2-N and 7-3. With Swingers using the Arc of Approach (2-J-3), this actuation may be executed as a "throwing" of the Right Shoulder by the Hips, as in 10-19-C.

Hip Action must not be haphazard. It is a Pivot Component that must be carefully timed and sequenced to sustain the continuity and spacing of the Pivot Train (of Components). Omitting the Hip Action unintentionally will disrupt the Feel as well as the continuity of the entire Pivot (See 6-B-3-0 regarding Pivot Rhythm).

TWENTY-FOUR BASIC COMPONENTS

THE LEGS

7-16. KNEE ACTION Knee Action is classified on the basis of (1) combinations of bent and straight conditions and (2) the Reference Points selected at which these combinations occur. The combination and the Reference Points selected will determine the slanting of the Hips during the Pivot. The slant is up in the direction of a straightened Knee. The slant of the Hips affects the degree of the Hip Turn. Actually, the primary function of Knee Action — as with Waist Bend — is to maintain a motionless Head during the Stroke.

The proper amount of Knee Bend is determined at Impact Fix (7-8) by the distance the Hips must move to allow the Right Forearm to point at the selected Plane Line per 2-J-3 and 7-3. The amount of Bend will also determine the amount of Backstroke Turn and Downstroke Slide. The less Bend, the more the Pivot and Hip Slide will be restricted in both directions and the more upright the Plane tends to be.

If the straightened Knee is allowed to lock "beyond center" the subsequent unlocking is disruptive.

The unloaded Knee should not sag into an extreme position. That weakens the strong in-line structure of the normal knee and ankle alignment.

When the Address or Fix Knee Bend of either Knee is maintained throughout the Stroke, it feels and acts like the Body has a solid anchor to the ground and, therefore, it is so designated. The "anchor" designation still allows the Knees to rotate through the Sit-Down Position as the Strokes lengthen. So, seldom does Impact occur during the true Sit-Down Position.

THE LEGS

7-17. FOOT ACTION Foot Action accommodates the Knee Action resulting from the motion of the Weight Shift, and accepts the changes in the loading of the Feet. The loading can shift between the inner and the outer edge of the Foot but shouldn't roll the Foot over on its edge. The majority of the weight should be on the heel and it is better to turn on one's heel than to roll excessively. Address Position loading of the Feet is even distribution between both Feet but with enough on the heels to allow the toes to be lifted up momentarily without altering the distribution between the toe and heel.

The heel should not be *lifted* off the ground, but *pulled* off — and then no more than necessary. Merely lifting the heel accomplishes nothing.

Halting the Backstroke motion with the Feet and letting this same tension pull the Downstroke through Impact is "swinging from the Feet" and gives the Stroke maximum Swing Radius.

TWENTY-FOUR BASIC COMPONENTS

TURN AND ROLL

7-18. LEFT WRIST ACTION Left Wrist Action is classified according to changes in Left Wrist Condition prior to Impact. The Downstroke changes are the opposite of the Backstroke changes but do not necessarily occur at the same Points in the Stroke so long as Impact condition is reached at Impact where Hinge Action joins the procession (per 2-P and 4-D-0). These changes may be incidental or deliberate, per 10-18-C, without changing their classification as "The Wristcock" (2-P and 4-B). Hinge Action (2-G) and the Grip (Components 1 and 2) are separate but interlocking areas of this complex activity, (as is specialization of the Hand assignments 1-F, 4-D), and are acquired and applied per 3-B and 5-0. Normally, between the two Hands every Wrist Position in Chapter 4 may come into play. (Study 9-0 and 9-2.)

Then, understanding and executing the Left Wrist Action per 2-N-1, synchronizes the entire procedure. Trigger Delay alters little geometrically but magnifies the physics. The Paddlewheel Action of the straightening Right Elbow (10-10-C) initiates and sustains the #3 Accumulator Hand Motion (4-D-0) until the Both-Arms-Straight and Zero Accumulator #3 position of Full Extension — smoothly, steadily, with no change in the straightening or the Paddlewheel rate of Clubface Closing as set up AT RELEASE. Variations in Trigger Delay are possible ONLY because the Cocked Left Wrist allows the Right Elbow to straighten faster than the Left Arm would otherwise allow (6-B-1). The greater the Delay, the more rapid the Paddlewheel Action and the more Swivel-like it becomes without increasing the actual Endless Belt speed of the Left Hand.

Accumulator #3 Action is not Lever Assembly Extension. (See 2-P.) With the Endless Belt Effect, the Belt (Hands) and the Clubhead have the same RPM, but the Surface factor sets in and gives the Clubhead greater MPH — in reverse proportion to the size of the Pulley (the smaller, the faster). That is, raised Hand Position — reducing the Accumulator #3 Travel — plus Trigger Delay. Conversely — a larger Pulley (lowered Hands) requires a higher Handspeed and an early Trigger. (See 6-B-3-A, 6-F and 6-N-0.)

Herein, the use of the terms "Single," "Double," etc. only means there are that number of actions or positions so indicated, to identify and differentiate the Variations in that category. This applies to Grip Type Variations also and refers to an entirely different set of actions and positions than the Left Wrist Action category.

TWENTY-FOUR BASIC COMPONENTS

HIT OR SWING

7-19. LAG LOADING This category recognizes the over-all control by the Clubhead Lag Pressure Point (6-C-2) and that manipulation of its Loading Procedure determines the Physics of both Hitting and Swinging (Preface). (Study 6-H-0, 7-3 and 7-20.)

The correct Clubhead Lag Pressure "Feel" is a deadweight inertia—exactly like dragging a wet mop through Impact—constant Loading, constant direction. A careful nursing of the Clubhead Feel. Clubhead Lag can be established in three different ways:
 1. by resisting the Backstroke motion for Drive Loading
 2. with the Start Down motion for Float Loading; and
 3. by "throwing" the Club against the Lag Pressure Point at The Top for Drag Loading

Properly manipulated, Clubhead Inertia can withstand all the Lag Pressure anyone can generate, including Extensor Action (6-B-1-D).

Incorrect Clubhead Lag Pressure "Feel" does not set up a steady driving pressure but a convulsive, impatient *THROWING* pressure, guaranteeing Clubhead Throwaway. Rolling and/or Uncocking have the assignment of doing any throwing of the Clubhead. Lag Pressure is totally inert. The slightest "pushing away" will produce Clubhead Throwaway. When you find yourself swinging fast whether you want to or not, you are contending with Clubhead Throwaway and it could be induced by improper Clubhead Lag Pressure Point action. Instead of "driving" the Club, you find yourself "chasing" it — and never catching up with it. Obviously, if the thrown Clubhead doesn't pass the Hands until after Impact Fix Position (7-8) is reached, it still complies with the Law of the Flail (2-K), but precision Timing and Clubface alignment becomes difficult and, however widely used, is still an essentially perilous deviation. (Also see 6-B-0 and 7-17 regarding Swing Radius.)

The "Right Arm Swing" is simply 10-3-K with loosened Wrists (7-1) and longitudinal acceleration using 7-19-3 above. Only with this "Rope Handle" procedure can the Right Arm be said to "Swing" per 1-L-9 and -10. But with the Axe Handle procedures there must be a straight line piston action to avoid injury to the right elbow ligaments. So, if there is a twinge in the elbow, you are Swinging your Right Arm.

TWENTY-FOUR BASIC COMPONENTS

PLAN AHEAD

7-20. TRIGGER TYPES The term "Trigger" is used to denote that action which initiates the Release of the Power Package Assembly of Power Accumulators (6-B) to develop and apply force to the ball. It is the lengthening of the third side of the Triangle Assembly which moves the Lever Assemblies toward and through Impact per Pattern. (See 6-M-0.)

The procedures are termed "Throws" whether they "throw" or are "thrown." They may be used individually or in combinations. The standard combinations are listed only in Chapter 11-20. Trigger Types are selected according to Release Type and Release Point as defined in 10-20 and 10-24 — that is, Sweep with Sweep, Snap with Snap, etc. For Hitters that means that Triggering (7-20), Assembly (7-21), Loading (7-22), Delivery (7-23) and Release (7-24) require an Active Right Elbow and an inactive Left Wrist. For Swingers — vice versa. But "Active" or "Passive" their "Motions" and "relationships" are not visibly altered and per 6-B-3-0 the Right Elbow is still and always the Key (6-N-0). Remember — only Right Elbow Feel — neither the Triceps or Lag Pressure — can safely Monitor the Paddlewheel Motion of the straightening of the Right Arm for proper Clubface Closing motion (6-B-1-D-3). With the Flat Left Wrist in line with the Right Forearm (7-2-3) the #3 Accumulator "Closes" only as the straightening Right Elbow — active or passive — provides the Basic Paddlewheel Motion for the Left Arm Flying Wedge (6-B-3-0-1) and for the Hand Motion per 4-D-0. This is the true "Overtaking" Action (6-F) of the Lagging Clubhead as differentiated from Lever Assembly Extension in 2-P. So with Downstroke Waggles, verify — through the hands only — that the Right Elbow will be On Plane before Triggering to assure accurate Tracing (5-0) for the Follow-Through. Especially with Delayed Release this will rotate the Left Hand in a Swiveling Action as required for Rhythm (2-C-0, 2-G, 6-J-0). Study 2-G regarding the Swivel and Rhythm.

Maximum Trigger Delay noticeably restricts maximum Handspeed (6-N-0). Every player has a maximum Handspeed and no amount of violent effort will change it much. However, that violent effort can, per 7-19, cause the Clubhead to fly out into its own orbit prematurely with typical Throwaway results.

AT THE TOP

7-21. POWER PACKAGE ASSEMBLY POINT This Component concerns itself with the "where" of the Assembly, the definable Hand location to develop and direct the Impact Force as calculated for the situation at hand — Loaded and ready for Delivery. Different types of Strokes, conditions, purposes and personal preferences tend to change this point around. But it does not change the fact that it must be accomplished some place or other. To attempt variations on the basis of just one "Feel" produces improper alignments and relationships. So conscious differentiation must be practiced. (See 6-D and 10-19.)

7-22. POWER PACKAGE LOADING ACTION An important element in the Power Package is the load that is put on the Power Accumulators for them to propel toward Impact. The amount of Loading can be controlled by either the speed of the entire motion, or by the sharpness of the specific procedure, or both. The use of speed actually only modifies whichever procedure is employed. So, when the Assembly Point and Accumulator Loading procedures are selected, you can know the point where the Action must be initiated to comply and therefore this "Where" becomes the basis for this category.

Though the Action is infinite in variety, all fall into three simple Alternatives — as sharply as possible, as gradually as possible, and somewhere in between — noting the approximate fraction of the full arc.

The Inertia of the Clubhead is magnified or attenuated by speed, changes in direction, etc. This adjusted Clubhead weight (Clubhead Lag 6-C and 7-19) must neither collapse nor derange the structure of the Power Package — nor leave all the Accumulators empty.

TWENTY-FOUR BASIC COMPONENTS

FROM THE TOP

7-23. POWER PACKAGE DELIVERY PATH The three possible paths of the Hands down the Inclined Plane (10-23) are the Basic Delivery Procedures and the Delivery Line Equivalents (2-J-3) must comply with them. Per 2-J-3, the *LINE* Delivery Paths are "*Cross* Line" procedures and the *CIRCLE* Delivery Path is "*On* Line" in their relation to *the* geometric Plane Line. For a Circle "Equivalent," the Hands sense (5-0) a flat gyroscopic circular "orbit" path from Takeaway (8-4) to The Top (8-6) AND BACK AGAIN. The player envisions — is *consciously* aware of — a turning wheel RIM motion of the Hands, Clubshaft and Clubhead toward *and on through* the Ball. For a Line "Equivalent," the Hands, from Takeaway to The Top AND BACK AGAIN, sense the Clubshaft as a wheel SPOKE tracing a straight line extension of the selected Delivery Path. The player envisions — is consciously aware of—a straight line wheel TRACK motion (rather than its rotation) toward and on through the Ball, or THROUGH THE AIMING POINT. (See 6-E-2-1.)

Normally, Delivery "ACTION (Thrust)" is "*Cross* Line" — Delivery "MOTION" is "*On* Line," even at Low Point, because the Delivery Path Angle (direction) is ALWAYS the Right Forearm Angle of Approach (7-3) even with the Circle Delivery Path (1-L-9 and -10). (Study 6-E-2, 7-11 and 7-19).

The Straight Line Path is a simpler procedure than the Angled Line Path. In fact, the Elbow Plane is normally a "Pivot Controlled Hands" Component, as discussed in 10-6-B and 10-24-F. The sharpness of the arcs at either end of "Line" Paths determines how much of that "Line" can remain and how much the change from Linear Speed (Downstroke) to Angular Speed (Release) will increase Clubhead Speed without changing Hand Speed — the "Endless Belt Effect," (per 2-K#6 and 6-E-2 and 7-18. 6-B-3-B.)

The Circle Path of the Hands is mandatory for all Non-Pivot Strokes (6-L-0), whether Hitting or Swinging (7-19). The "Axis Tilt" (2-H) allows a Line Delivery Path but does not require it.

TWENTY-FOUR BASIC COMPONENTS

FROM THE TOP

7-24. POWER PACKAGE RELEASE The Loaded Power Package enroute with its Accumulators full of stored Power must, at some selected point and in some selected manner, start applying its energy. That is — be Released. (Study 7-19 and 8-7.)

The Release must sufficiently precede Impact to develop the calculated Velocity, Thrust and Direction for the Impact requirements.

The Release includes two inseparable but variable elements — The Release "Type" and the Release "Point."

There are only two Release Types — Automatic and Non-Automatic. Then, like the Loading Action (7-22), it has the same three points for the Unloading action — as early as possible, as late as possible, and somewhere in between, noting, again, the approximate fraction of the full arc, as with 7-22.

The term "Release" can well be considered a continuing action including Impact and Follow-through and could be so used when that grouping is intended for — what is sometimes referred to as, "Through the Ball." Otherwise, adhere to Chapter 8 usage.

CHAPTER EIGHT

TWELVE SECTIONS

ITINERARY AND PREPARATIONS

8-0. GENERAL This Twelve Section arrangement presents a chain of Basic Positions and Motions through which every Stroke must pass. Throughout the book, positions and motions are located according to the Section in which they occur. This chapter defines those Sections. The Section *areas* are specific but the Section *boundaries* need not be. Boundaries are tailored to the particular procedures under consideration as specified during their presentation in the book. Every Stroke Component should be tracked through all Twelve Sections — independently — to give it its full recognition, application and continuity. And also through the Three Zones (Chapter 9) to define relationships. (Study 12-3-0.)

The Stroke moves from one Basic Position to the next with a precision and smoothness in exact proportion to its completeness and the player's mastery of each element, whether it be consciously or subconsciously acquired. Every move is coldly deliberate, calculated and disciplined. Starting with a watchful eye on the Address Routine (3-F-5) in preparation for the Fifth Programming Routine (14-0):

1. Visualize the intended Path of the Ball (Preliminary Address)
2. Visualize the Machine adjustments (Impact Fix)
3. Visualize the PATH OF THE CLUBHEAD THROUGH *AND BEYOND* IMPACT (Adjusted Address)

Then, be sure you actually see the proper blur of the Clubhead passage through Release. Be sure to Look, Look, Look, per 3-B. This is a precision system and is dependent on precision execution.

TWELVE SECTIONS

ADDRESS

8-1. SECTION 1—PRELIMINARY ADDRESS This Section covers the interval of preliminary assessment of the situation at hand (Chapter 14), including all surveying, housekeeping, discussion, etc.

8-2. SECTION 2—IMPACT FIX This Section starts with the final club selection and includes the time needed for calibrating — and recalibrating — Target Line, trajectory, Ball behavior, etc., until a satisfactory procedure is selected.

8-3. SECTION 3—ADJUSTED ADDRESS This Section is a dress rehearsal of the selected Pattern (Chapter 12) and includes the time needed for the Practice Swing (9-1), Waggle (9-2) and Forward Press (9-3), and ends with assuming the selected Address Position (2-J, 10-9). (Also study 2-0, 2-F and 3-F-5.)

8-1. Preliminary Address.   8-2. Impact Fix.   8-3. Adjusted Address.

TWELVE SECTIONS

TO THE TOP

8-4. SECTION 4—START UP This Section starts with the initial Takeaway motion and continues until it settles into its Backstroke path. Catch the Clubhead Path from the corner of the eye to confirm its "Angle of Approach" Path to be identical in both directions (2-J-3).

8-5. SECTION 5—BACKSTROKE This Section starts with the Stroke safely on its way and continues until arrival at the Top (7-19).

8-6. SECTION 6—THE TOP This Section starts when the Backstroke motion of the Hands ends, and continues through a static period of alignment and relationship corrections, until a deliberate aiming of the Lag Pressure Point (6-E). (Study 6-D-0.) The Hands must have time to define and visualize compliance with the Section 6 requirements in 12-3 before Start Down — the "Start Down Waggle" (3-F-5).

8-4. Start Up.   8-5. Backstroke.   8-6. Top.

TWELVE SECTIONS

FROM THE TOP

8-7. SECTION 7—START DOWN Strictly speaking, the next six Sections are all just divisions of the Downstroke for pinpointing interim locations. This Section starts with the initial move toward Impact — the period of Shoulder Acceleration (or its equivalent — 2-H) and continues until the motion settles into its Delivery Line Path (7-23).

8-8. SECTION 8—DOWNSTROKE This Section covers the interval between completion of the Start Down, with the Stroke settled into its Delivery Line course, until "Release" point. This is the period of Hand Acceleration.

8-9. SECTION 9—RELEASE This Section starts at the point of Release "Trigger" and continues until Impact — the period of Clubhead Acceleration. (See 8-8 above.)

8-7. Start Down.   8-8. Down Stroke.   8-9. Release.

TWELVE SECTIONS

FROM IMPACT

8-10. SECTION 10—IMPACT This Section covers only the interval between Impact and Separation — the period of Ball Acceleration.

8-11. SECTION 11—FOLLOW-THROUGH This Section covers the interval between Separation (of Ball and Clubface) and the Both Arms Straight Position as determined by the Shoulder position at Impact. (See 2-C-3.)

8-12. SECTION 12—FINISH This Section starts at the Both Arms Straight position and continues until the end of the Stroke. If it does not continue, then the Follow-through is also the Finish per 12-3.

8-10. Impact   8-11. End of Follow Through   8-12. Finish

CHAPTER NINE

THREE ZONES

THREE LANE FREEWAY

9-0. GENERAL The Basic Motions that constitute the Golf Stroke are divided among three separate — but simultaneous and synchronous — Zones of the action that is occurring throughout the Twelve Sections listed in Chapter 8. It must be recognized that, in reality, these motions are neither cause nor effect. Law is cause. Ball behavior — intended or unintended — is effect. Procedures, Swings and Strokes are — "Means" only. That is, the player's choice of a Means for applying law so that it will produce a desired effect.

The following four sets of terms should be considered interchangeable and synonymous. Use that set of terms that best brings out the points under consideration:

Zone #1. Body Control: 1. Pivot   1. Body   1. Balance
Zone #2. Club Control: 2. Power   2. Arms   2. Force
Zone #3. Ball Control: 3. Purpose   3. Hands   3. Direction

Each of the Three Zones concerns certain of the Twenty-Four Basic Components listed in Chapter 7. Therefore, the Basic Motions of the Golf Stroke are the Three Zones of Action and their accompanying Basic Components, as listed below — in the suggested order to follow for a complete course. The individual Components in the Three Zones are governed by Stroke Pattern regardless of Zones, which only maintain and coordinate the individuality as well as the interaction of these Components, as pre-packaged cargo to assure that malfunction in other Zones stay in their own package and not foist unnoticed Compensations on each other to plague The Machine.

The Three Zones are a natural division of the action. Their identities must be maintained in teaching, practice and playing. And unless developed in sequence, a very weak "compensated" game is inevitable. Consider Putting. Zero Pivot (10-12-D) IS Body Control (Zone #1). One Accumulator (10-11-A) IS Club Control (Zone #2). And, any Hinge Action 10-10) IS Ball Control (Zone #3). Educated Hands (5-0) ARE exactly as mandatory here as with any other Pattern.

THREE ZONES

ZONE #1

THE "BODY" LANE

9-1. ZONE #1 includes all the elements of BODY MOTION, movement and balance, and defines the geometrical alignments and relationships of the Body Components. These motions are to be completely uncompromised by Arm and Club motions. Execution of a Preselected Pivot should be identical with or without Arms and Club to avoid any awkward "hitch" in the Turn when actually playing. Emphatically, Hands are not educated unless they control the Pivot. That does not abolish, neglect, or replace the Pivot, but it does revise its role per 2-M-3, 5-0, 10-6-B and 10-24-F. Those two roles are mutually exclusive and the hands Monitor delivery of the cargo per its manifest.

Zone #1 includes the following Basic Components:
- #12. Pivot
- #13. Shoulder Turn
- #14. Hip Turn
- #15. Hip Action
- #16. Knee Action
- #17. Foot Action

PRELIMINARY ADDRESS

9-1-1 #1. Medium Shots.

9-1-1 #2. Short Shots.

9-1-1 #3. Long Shots.

THREE ZONES

9-1-2. Impact Fix.

9-1-3. Address.

9-1-4. Start Up.

9-1-5. Back Stroke.

9-1-6. Top.

9-1-7. Start Down.

THREE ZONES

9-1-8. Down Stroke.

9-1-9. Release.

9-1-10. Impact.

9-1-11. Follow Through.

9-1-12. Finish.

ZONE #2
THE "ARMS" LANE

9-2. ZONE #2 adds the Arms and the Club to the circular motion of the Pivot just for generation of Clubhead Power (10-19-0). Zone #2 includes all the elements of the Force and Motion of the Arms and Club action — the Power Package — strictly the development of Clubhead power rather than Ball manipulation. Execution of a Preselected Stroke should be identical with or without Pivot and/or Ball to avoid "throwing away" the Clubhead power when actually playing — per 2-G, 3-F-6, 6-B-1-D and 6-E-2, especially. Zone #2 is the Club<u>head</u> and NOT the Club<u>face</u> (Zone #3) activity. It defines the geometric alignments and relationships that will produce precision Impact at ALL speeds. So mastery of "Release Motions" (4-D-0) is essential, indispensable, mandatory and imperative.

The choice must be made here between "Mop Swinging" (Drive Loading), "Towel Snapping" (Downstroke Loading) and "Whipcracking" (Drag Loading) — (See 7-19.) Zone #2 Components are Power Components. Good Golf is Power Golf — don't be mislead by "Accuracy" problems. As you master Clubhead Control (Power), you will gain a basic Clubface Control (Accuracy) — Zone #3 can never be any better than its Zone #1 and #2 support. Remove all pressures against "Power First." Power techniques are Power Control. (See 2-M-3.)

Study 3-B carefully: look, *look,* LOOK. Monitoring rejects any unintentional compensation for malfunctions in the relationships and maintains the relationships of the Power Package AS A WHOLE with Zones #1 and #3. It also rejects attempts of lazy or wobbly execution to lean on Zone #3 finesse backup. If the Flat Left Wrist (4-D), Lag Pressure (6-C) and/or the Delivery Line (2-J-3) become lost or even vague, stop immediately and find them before that becomes a subconscious addiction. (Study 6-M.) Do NOT worry about specific direction control in this Zone. As "Power" is acquired, "Direction" will improve until Zone #3 becomes mostly "Finesse" control. Do not delay moving on — Zones #2 and #3 must be coordinated as soon as feasible.

Zone #2 includes the following Basic Components:

- #1. Basic Grips
- #2. Grip Types
- #3. Basic Strokes
- #4. Stroke Types & Variations
- #8. Fix
- #9. Address
- #10. Hinge Action
- #11. Pressure Point Combinations
- #18. Left Wrist Action
- #19. Lag Loading
- #20. Trigger Types
- #21. Power Package Assembly Point
- #22. Power Package Loading Action

THREE ZONES

PRELIMINARY ADDRESS

9-2-1. #1.

9-2-1 #2.

IMPACT FIX

9-2-2 #1.

9-2-2 #2.

THREE ZONES

ADJUSTED ADDRESS

9-2-3 #1.

9-2-3 #2. Waggle Back Stroke.

9-2-3 #3. Waggle Down Stroke.

START UP

9-2-4.

BACKSTROKE

9-2-5 #1.

9-2-5 #2.

THREE ZONES

9-2-6. Top.

9-2-7. Start Down.

9-2-8. Down Stroke.

9-2-9. Release.

THREE ZONES

IMPACT

9-2-10 #1.

9-2-10 #2.

9-2-10 #3.

FOLLOW-THROUGH

9-2-11 #1.

9-2-11 #2.

THREE ZONES

FINISH

9-2-12 #1.

9-2-12 #2.

ZONE #3

THE "HANDS" LANE

9-3. ZONE #3 includes all the elements of Ball Control Variations. The execution of a Preselected Impact should be identical with or without Pivot and/or Ball to avoid "Steering" (3-F-7-A) when actually Playing. Finesse, <u>normally</u>, should not be practiced as Clubface Manipulation through Impact, but as Impact Fix adjustments and per 2-M-3; Avoid any procedure that requires any change in your Basic or Total Motion. It may yet claim squatters' rights at the Computer.

Monitoring repels the urge for Zone #3 to take over any Zone #2 "Power" functions of basic Direction Control. Keep it on a "finesse" basis to reduce unnecessary Monitoring duties. But its contents stand ready for any corrective action the Hands call for.

These Components should all first be practiced without a ball until a reasonable skill and understanding are evident. Then practice should concentrate on perfecting one's TOTAL MOTION. Boil your Pattern down to The Star System Triad (Preface).

Zone #3 includes the following Basic Components:
#5. Plane Line   #23. Power Package Delivery Path
#6. Plane Angle — Basic   #24. Power Package Release
#7. Plane Angle — Variations

THREE ZONES

9-3-1. Preliminary Address.

9-3-2. Impact Fix.

9-3-3. Adjusted Address.

9-3-4. Start Up.

9-3-5. Back Stroke.

9-3-6. Top.

THREE ZONES

9-3-7. Start Down.

9-3-8. Down Stroke.

9-3-9. Release.

9-3-10. Impact.

9-3-11. Follow Through.

9-3-12. Finish.

CHAPTER TEN

CATALOG OF BASIC COMPONENT VARIATIONS

10-0. GENERAL This chapter lists and briefly analyzes each Variation of each Basic Stroke Component using the same order and the same designations as in Chapters 7, 9, 11 and 12, and should be studied in conjunction with them. All Variations in this chapter are "possible" and unless otherwise noted are geometrically acceptable but may still have only limited special purpose usage by the highly skilled. The Star System does not advocate teaching "unorthodox" procedures, but does make provision for them. Except for the alphabetical listing below, the Twenty Four Basic Stroke Components are always listed in numerical order. Regardless of the Variation called for, it's "-0," or "General" section must also be studied as part of it.

In addition, for use in the Stroke Pattern Forms (12-4) is the omnibus term of "Modified" using the Alphabetical Designation of "X," which will indicate an aberration, of some sort, from the accepted listings under each respective category and can be accompanied by an appropriate term to describe the action so designated.

The aim of every player should be an Uncompensated Stroke — no faulty elements needing to be counteracted or offset.

ALPHABETICAL LISTING

Address	9	Plane Angle — Basic	6
Fix	8	Plane Angle Variations	7
Foot Action	17	Plane Line	5
Grips — Basic	1	Power Package Assembly Point	21
Grips — Types	2	Power Package Delivery Path	23
Hinge Action	10	Power Package Loading Action	22
Hip Action	15	Power Package Release	24
Hip Turn	14	Pressure Point Combinations	11
Knee Action	16	Shoulder Turn	13
Lag Loading	19	Strokes — Basic	3
Left Wrist Action	18	Strokes — Types & Variations	4
Pivot	12	Trigger Types	20

CATALOG OF BASIC COMPONENT VARIATIONS

BASIC GRIPS

HAND TO HAND

10-1-0. GENERAL Basic Grips are classified according to the amount of Hand Overlap — including no Overlap. All the fingers that encircle the Clubshaft "grip the Club" except, to some degree, the right hand forefinger, to keep it sensitive to Clubhead Lag pressure. (See 6-B-1-D.)

10-1-A. OVERLAPPING Any number of the last fingers of the Right Hand may overlap any number of the first fingers of the Left Hand. Increasing the amount of overlap further diminishes the leverage of the Right Hand.

TYPICAL OVERLAPPING GRIP

10-1-A. #1.   10-1-A #2.   10-1-A #3.

CATALOG OF BASIC COMPONENT VARIATIONS

HAND TO HAND

10-1-B. BASEBALL Increasing the distance between the hands increases the Right Hand support of the Clubhead Loading during Impact but dampens Clubhead acceleration. Very effective for the execution of a strong, deliberate Stroke — low Speed and high Thrust.

10-1-C. REVERSE OVERLAP Any number of the first fingers of the Left Hand may overlap the last fingers of the Right Hand. Increasing the amount of overlap further reduces the control of the Left Hand.

BASEBALL GRIP   **REVERSE OVERLAP**

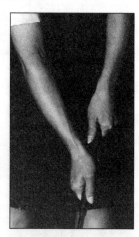

10-1-B #1. Normal.   10-1-B #2. Exaggerated.   10-1-C.

CATALOG OF BASIC COMPONENT VARIATIONS

HAND TO HAND

10-1-D. INTERLOCKING The last finger of the Right Hand interlocks with the first finger of the Left Hand and there are no adjustments or variations available without disturbing the "interlock."

10-1-E. CROSS HAND The Cross Hand GRIP requires a completely different set of procedures and its shortcomings make that appear an unwarranted expenditure. The Hand positions are reversed — the Right above the Left — and its main feature is that the Right Arm Action cannot overpower the Flat Left Wrist. Everything applies to this grip that applies the normal Overlap, including Variations B, C, and D. There are NO recommended exceptions.

INTERLOCKING   **CROSS HAND GRIP**

10-1-D.   10-1-E. #1.   10-1-E #2.

CATALOG OF BASIC COMPONENT VARIATIONS

GRIPS — TYPES

HANDS TO PLANE

10-2-0. GENERAL Grip Types are classified at Impact Fix according to:
1. Whether the Hands are at right angles or parallel with:
   A. Each other, or B. the Ground
2. The location of the #3 Pressure Point
3. The extent of certain Wrist Actions per 10-18-0. Two Motions — A. Horizontal (4-A) and B. Perpendicular (4-B), disregarding incidental Rotational Positions (4-C). Two separate actions involving two separate Wrists can produce four possible combinations of Actions — Single, Double, Triple and Quadruple.

These conditions are established at Impact Fix by assuming the Individual Wrist Conditions and the Pressure Point location indicated for each Hand. Usually, the only real difference between the Right and Left Hand Grip is that the Clubshaft lies somewhere between Under-the-Heel and In-the-Cup of the Left Hand (6-B-3-B).

Besides the alphabetical designation of "A" through "G," each Grip type also has a descriptive name plus the code letters for the Rotational Wrist Condition (4-C) of, first, the Left Wrist, next, the Right Wrist, and third, the location of #3 Pressure Point. For example — V/V/A — Vertical/Vertical/Aft. When Pressure Point #3 is On Plane during Impact, it is a "strong" Grip. Otherwise, it is termed a "weak" Grip and usually implies a Pull Minor Basic Stroke. Basically, there are three Grip Types with a "weak" and a "strong" version of each. Plus two Variable arrangements acceptable for a "True Swing" (6-B-3-0) and frequently adopted for non-geometric reasons — habit, preference, pseudo-mechanics, etc. Normally Educated Hands position and move each Hand either parallel or at right angles to one of the Basic Planes; Or from one classification to another. (See 2-G and 7-18.)

Unless otherwise indicated, the left thumb is always placed on the same line as Pressure Point #3, and covered with the cup of the right hand palm. With strong Grips, this places the Thrust of both the #1 and the #3 Pressure Points On Plane so that the Clubhead Lag alignments are established and can be verified by the Waggle and the Forward Press. The Thumb position encourages the ideal Right Wrist Bend - identical to the Accumulator #3 Angle - which avoids the disruptive Feel of an Off Plane Follow-through Swivel. Don't hesitate to adjust your Grip for better direction. (Study 2-P, 6-B-3-0 and 7-2.)

CATALOG OF BASIC COMPONENT VARIATIONS

HANDS TO PLANE

10-2-A. WEAK SINGLE ACTION V/V/T Both Wrists are Vertical and both the Left Thumb and the #3 Pressure Point as far toward the "Top-of-the-Clubshaft" location as possible without losing the essentially Vertical Right Wrist. Wristcock only — Single Action.

10-2-B. STRONG SINGLE ACTION V/V/A The #3 Pressure Point and the Left Thumb are now on the Aft Side of the Clubshaft in an On Plane Location for Impact support. Wristcock only — Single Action.

10-2-C. WEAK DOUBLE ACTION V/R/T The Left Wrist is Vertical and the Right Wrist is Rolled to the top of the Clubshaft so that the Right Wrist Bend will be on the same line as the Left Wrist Cocking motion. The Pressure Point and the left thumb are also on the line of the Left Wrist Cocking motion. This Grip Type satisfies the urge for the maximum Wristcock Feel and gives stronger support to Wrist Motion than to Hand Motion (4-D-0). Left Wristcock, Right Wrist Bend — Double Action.

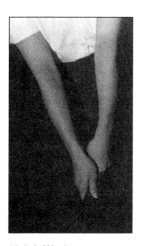
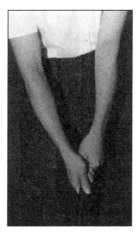
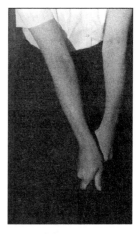

10-2-A. Weak Single Action.   10-2-B. Strong Single Action.   10-2-C. Weak Double Action.

CATALOG OF BASIC COMPONENT VARIATIONS

HANDS TO PLANE

10-2-D. STRONG DOUBLE ACTION T/V/A The Right Wrist is Vertical and the Left Wrist is *Turned* to the top of the Clubshaft so that the Left Wristcocking motion will be on the same line as the Right Wrist Bend. The #3 Pressure Point and the left thumb are also on the same line as the Right Wrist Bend — Double Action — same as 10-2-C.

Very compatible with Cut Shot procedures. Any Left Wrist Bend at Impact Fix should be maintained throughout the Stroke.

This Grip Type features maximum Wristcocking action and strong support for *both* Acceleration and Impact loads. The palm of the Right Hand moves toward Impact exactly like a paddle-wheel rotating On Plane — no separate Rolling Motion until after Impact. (See 10-10-C.)

10-2-E. WEAK DOUBLE ACTION UNDERHAND V/T/U The Left Wrist is Vertical and the Right Wrist is Turned On Plane and "Arches" (or even "Rotates") with the Left Wristcock motion. The #3 Pressure Point being "under" the Clubshaft, resists Below Plane Clubhead sag tendencies during shorter shots. Left Wrist "Cocks," Right Wrist "Arches" — Double Action.

10-2-D. Strong Double Action.

10-2-E. Weak Double Underhand Action

CATALOG OF BASIC COMPONENT VARIATIONS

HANDS TO PLANE

10-2-F. STRONG SINGLE ACTION UNDERHAND T/T/U This Grip differs from 2-E above only in that *both* wrists are Turned — positioned to lay, move and Cock On Plane — no Turn or Roll; Wristcock only — Single Action.

10-2-G. TRIPLE OR QUADRUPLE ACTION By rotating the Hands with any of the above Grip Types so that either or both Wrists cannot Cock On Plane without also Bending — Feel loses its geometric basis. Also the natural Wrist motions conflict. A bit of Left Wrist Turn properly becomes exactly the same amount of Double Wristcock to keep the Clubshaft On Plane and to maintain Impact Wrist Position. Except with a "True" Swing (6-B-3-0) where Centripetal Force will produce the "geometric" *Flat* Left Wrist when there is actually a "visual" *Bent* Left Wrist. That is, the Clubshaft and the Left Arm are in a straight line, per 6-B-3-0 and 2-K, regardless of the Left Wrist Position. These procedures may be either "Weak" or "Strong" but either or both Wrist are Double Cocked per 10-18-B.

10-2-F. Strong Single Underhand Action.

10-2-G. Triple Action.

CATALOG OF BASIC COMPONENT VARIATIONS

STROKES — BASIC

ELBOW POSITIONS

10-3-0 GENERAL Major Basic Strokes are classified according to Elbow Position during the Stroke (7-3) and every Stroke must use one of the three. Minor Basic Strokes are classified according to Arm Motion during (normally) less than full Strokes. The recommended combinations of Stroke Types are listed in 11-3.

MAJOR BASIC STROKES

10-3-A. PUNCH From a "down-and-at-the-side" Elbow Position, whether the Elbow is touching the Body or not, a straight-line Right Hand Punch is delivered through Impact (6-E). (Per 6-C-2-A and 7-19.) Except with 10-3-C (Push), the Right Forearm must have a "Fanning" type of motion, not a "Linear" Push Stroke type of motion (10-3-C). Trigger Delay (7-20) of the Right Elbow can be augmented only through Hip Slide or Hip Turn, per 10-14.

10-3-A. Punch.

CATALOG OF BASIC COMPONENT VARIATIONS

ELBOW POSITIONS

10-3-B. PITCH (or Slap) From a "down-and-in-the-front" Elbow Position, whether the Elbow is touching the Body or not, a Right Forearm underhand Pitch is delivered at the Aiming Point with a stiff-wrist slapping motion.

The only real difference from 10-3-A is that the Right Elbow can lead the Hands into Release much farther with the same amount of Hip travel (6-B-1-C) and is therefore conducive to greater Trigger Delay (10-20) for Snap Releases (10-24).

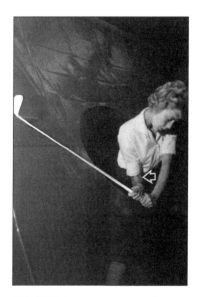

10-3-B. Pitch.

CATALOG OF BASIC COMPONENT VARIATIONS

ELBOW POSITIONS

10-3-C. PUSH From an "up-and-out" Elbow Position, which keeps the Hands always between the Elbow and the Ball (or the Plane Line), the Right Arm is Triggered into a heavy pushing action through Impact. Large differences in applied power produce relatively small differences in distance with the Push.

This is essentially a Hitting procedure for less than full power. It is fairly independent of Hip motion and location. Moved "On Line" (7-23), it produces an automatic Vertical Clubface Hinging. Moved "Cross Line" it produces an automatic Angled Clubface Hinging. (See 10-10.)

10-3-C. Push.

MINOR BASIC STROKES

ARM MOTIONS

10-3-D. PULL The term "Pull" indicates that the Club is being accelerated by either Arm (1-F) but *always* with a Rope Handle procedure, per 2-K, 6-B-4 and 10-11-0. It is always a "Swing," per 10-19-C. (Study 7-1.) When used with a Major Basic Stroke, it can produce Full Power (10-11-0).

10-3-E. PUTT This term specifies a completely motionless body — especially the Right Shoulder — as opposed to 10-3-H.

10-3-D. The Pull.   10-3-E. The Putt.

CATALOG OF BASIC COMPONENT VARIATIONS

ARM MOTIONS

10-3-F. PECK This term refers to any "Wrist-Action-Only" type of Stroke using Grip Type 10-2-D for Angled or Vertical Hinging and 10-2-B for Horizontal Hinging.

10-3-G. PICK A "pick-axe" motion indicating both elbows are bent with both Forearms kept On Plane. This offers a strong, heavy "Yip" free Arms only procedure.

10-3-F #1. The Peck. (At Top)

10-3-F #2. The Peck. (At Finish)

10-3-G. The Pick.

CATALOG OF BASIC COMPONENT VARIATIONS

ARM MOTIONS

10-3-H. PAW This term describes a Stroke made with both arms "frozen" either straight or bent. The Power Package is "Zeroed Out" to make it a rocking "Body Only" Stroke. Shoulder Motion must impart either Angled or Vertical Hinge Action per 10-13-C.

10-3-J. PAUSE This term indicates a pecking motion of the Hands toward the ball causing the Left Hand to stop and become the center of the Clubhead Impact arc with the Right Arm driving hard against the stationary left Wrist Fulcrum but with almost no Follow-through.

10-3-H. The Paw.   10-3-J. The Pause.

CATALOG OF BASIC COMPONENT VARIATIONS

ARM MOTIONS

10-3-K. BAT   The term "Bat" indicates that the Club is being accelerated by the Right Arm (1-F) but *always* with an Axe Handle procedure per 2-K. It is always a "Hit" and when used with any Major Basic Stroke can produce Full Power.

For the "basic" execution of this procedure, "freeze" the Right Wrist in its Impact Fix Position — Bent and Level. (Chapter 4.) Then the Checkrein Action (6-B-1-0) bends the Right Elbow only until it cocks the Left Wrist (10-2-0 and 10-18-0). Straightening the Right Elbow (10-20-B) for Release Action (4-D-0) can be manipulated for any Release Type (10-24). The proper execution must comply with the Right Arm activity as discussed in 7-3.

It is a quite uncomplicated procedure — The Club is an angled but rigid extension of the Right Forearm and the advisability of keeping both On Plane is the same as with the Left Arm version but is much more obvious. The "Bat" guarantees simultaneous Release Motions (4-D-0).

10-3-K. The Bat.

CATALOG OF BASIC COMPONENT VARIATIONS

STROKE TYPES AND VARIATIONS

ACCUMULATOR COMBINATIONS

10-4-0 GENERAL Stroke Types are classified according to the number of Power Accumulators used and are termed Single, Double, Triple or Four Barrel Strokes. Variations are classified according to possible combinations within each Type — which produces fifteen combinations (Variations).

10-4-A. SINGLE BARREL Immobilizing all Accumulators but one — any one — will produce a Stroke very limited in power and variables — comparatively delicate and readily controlled — ideal for use on and around the green with either 12-1 or 12-2 Basic Patterns.

1. 1st Accumulator Only (right elbow)
2. 2nd Accumulator Only (left wrist)
3. 3rd Accumulator Only (left hand)
4. 4th Accumulator Only (left arm)

10-4-A-1. Power Accumulator #1.

10-4-A-2. Power Accumulator #2.

10-4-A-3. Power Accumulator #3.

10-4-A-4. Power Accumulator #4.

CATALOG OF BASIC COMPONENT VARIATIONS

ACCUMULATOR COMBINATIONS

10-4-B. DOUBLE BARREL The Double Barrel Combinations — utilize any two Accumulators — produce a wide variation of force, but, theoretically, less than all that is available. A very satisfactory game can be developed without ever using more than a Double Barrel Power Package. Variations 3, 4 and 6 have quite limited applications.

1. 1st & 2nd Accumulators
2. 1st & 3rd Accumulators
3. 1st & 4th Accumulators
4. 2nd & 3rd Accumulators
5. 2nd & 4th Accumulators
6. 3rd & 4th Accumulators

10-4-C. TRIPLE BARREL Controlled application of three Accumulators in the Power Package requires increased skill, but there is a very profitable increase in power and versatility.

1. 1st, 2nd & 3rd Accumulators
2. 1st, 2nd & 4th Accumulators
3. 1st, 3rd & 4th Accumulators
4. 2nd, 3rd & 4th Accumulators

10-4-D. FOUR BARREL This high performance Four Accumulator Combination can produce many problems during its mastery by the player. But it can make the difference in top competition. Well controlled Double or Triple Barrel Combinations have little to fear from the Four Barrel Combination that is less than fully mastered.

CATALOG OF BASIC COMPONENT VARIATIONS

THE PLANE LINE

THE GUIDELINE

10-5-0. GENERAL These classifications are based on the combinations of positions described by the identifying dual-term names. The first term in each combination refers to the Plane Line — the second term refers to the Stance Line (Feet only) and denotes the relation of each Line to the Line Of Flight. Three possible Plane Lines are presented but the three possible Stance Lines for each are discussed with the Square Plane Line only, because parallel Stance and Plane Lines are the basic Variation of each group of positions. Any "Line" rotated — even slightly — to the left of parallel to the Target Line (CCW), is in its "Open" position — rotated to the right (CW), it is in its "Closed" position. Use the appropriate dual-term names in the Stroke Pattern for Variations not listed herein. No Plane Line Combination is restricted to Clubs of any length. (Study 2-F, 2-N, 7-2, 7-10 and 8-3.)

The relations among Plane Line, Angle of Approach and Ball Location are constant per 2-N. Changing one changes all three and usually, Plane Angle as well, but not necessarily the Clubface alignment (2-J-1). All can be synchronized by "Laying the Clubshaft on the Line" (the selected Plane Line) during the "Parallel to the Ground" (2-F) portions of the Stroke. For additional information, see 2-G for Basic Clubface Action, 2-F for Basic Clubshaft Action and 2-N for Basic Clubhead Action.

CATALOG OF BASIC COMPONENT VARIATIONS

THE GUIDELINE

10-5-A. SQUARE-SQUARE This "Basic" combination sets up the Plane Line and the Stance Line parallel to each other and to the Target Line — the classic "Square Stance". (See 10-12-A.)

10-5-B. SQUARE-OPEN This combination differs from 10-5-A above, only in that the Stance Line is now Open to both the Plane Line and the Target Line — the classic "Open Stance." (See 10-12-C.)

10-5-C. SQUARE-CLOSED This combination differs from 10-5-A above only in that the Stance Line is now Closed to both the Plane Line and the Target Line — the classic "Closed Stance." (See 10-12-B.)

10-5-A. Square-Square.   10-5-B. Square-Open.   10-5-C. Square-Closed.

CATALOG OF BASIC COMPONENT VARIATIONS

THE GUIDE LINE

10-5-D. OPEN-OPEN This is a group of combinations based on a Plane Line "Open" to the Target Line with three possible Stance Line Variations to complete the group just as with the "Square-Square" Plane Line group above.

10-5-E. CLOSED-CLOSED This is a group of combinations based on a Plane Line "Closed" to the Target Line with three possible Stance Line Variations to complete the group just as with the "Square-Square" Plane Line Group above.

10-5-D. Open-Open.   10-5-E. Closed-Closed.

CATALOG OF BASIC COMPONENT VARIATIONS

BASIC PLANE ANGLES

CLUBSHAFT CONTROL

10-6-0 GENERAL Basic Plane Angles are classified on the basis of reference points on which the Inclined Plane can be set. Five such settings are considered here — three fixed, one moving, one moveable — each named for its particular reference point.

10-6-A. ELBOW Where the Right Elbow touches the waist is the reference point used for this Plane Angle. It is the "flattest" normal Plane that will still allow the Right Forearm to be On Plane during Impact. This produces a very flat Angle of Attack (2-B) with reduced Backspin and should be avoided for Short Shots unless it is also part of your Full Stroke Pattern. The Elbow Plane allows maximum #3 Accumulator requiring earlier Release per 6-N-0.

ELBOW BASIC PLANE

10-6-A. #1. At Address.

10-6-A #2. At Top.

CATALOG OF BASIC COMPONENT VARIATIONS

CLUBSHAFT CONTROL

10-6-B. TURNED SHOULDER This reference point is primarily the point reached by the Right Shoulder after a Flat Backstroke Shoulder Turn. So with whatever Body Position (9-1-1) the Plane passes through, the Right Shoulder and the Hands are always precisely AT the Right Shoulder level at "THE TOP" (10-13 and 10-21-0), regardless of Plane Angle or Shoulder Turn. But any other Shoulder Turn can also provide the acceptable reference point. (See 10-13-0.) This Plane Angle has far better performance characteristics than any other because any Plane Angle Shift is very hazardous. This procedure does not refer to the disruptive Shoulder Turn Takeaway — which is always too "Flat" and/or too "Low," making a Plane Angle Shift mandatory and usually unintentional and unsuspected. (Study 7-3 and 10-24-F.)

TURNED SHOULDER BASIC PLANE

10-6-B #1. At Address.

10-6-B #2. At Top.

CATALOG OF BASIC COMPONENT VARIATIONS

CLUBSHAFT CONTROL

10-6-C. SQUARED SHOULDER The reference point for this Plane Angle is the point occupied by the Right Shoulder (or Left — for putting) at the Address. With this steep Plane, Angled Hinge Action becomes almost Vertical Hinge Action (2-D). Accumulator #3 can be Zeroed out.

SQUARED SHOULDER BASIC PLANE

10-6-C #1. Address   10-6-C #2. Top.

CATALOG OF BASIC COMPONENT VARIATIONS

CLUBSHAFT CONTROL

10-6-D. TURNING SHOULDER The basic "Turning Shoulder Plane" procedure — "A" below — has been undoubtedly the most widely used Basic Plane. The Player who takes the Clubhead "straight *back* from the ball" is using this Plane Angle. The Clubhead is also brought "straight *down* through the ball" for Impact. This is a dependable explanation of the "Feel" of this procedure. And this procedure brings the Club into the Loaded condition on a vertical Plane instead of on the Inclined Plane. With a full Wristcock Stroke, the Hands are "under the Club." This calls for Single Wrist Action (10-18-C). Its most obvious feature is the vertical line of the muscular effort — an inclined plane with a vertical force. It is extremely effective and dynamically correct. (Study 2-L#2, 2-N-1 and 2-P.) As a matter of fact, that characteristic could be incorporated in any Pattern to great advantage for Three Dimensional Impact insurance.

    A- The Arms are simply raised and lowered vertically and the Wrists are Cocked and Uncocked with the Left Wrist vertical to the ground at all times in a true Single Wrist Action — no Turn or Roll (10-18-C). All this, while the Pivot is imparting the On Plane motion to the Hands and Arms in both directions. It brings the Hands directly to the Top on the selected Plane. Its Off Plane (Vertical) Loading motion tends to feel like Clubhead Throwaway but it is the Vertical Wrist application of the Golfer's Flail, as shown in Sketch 2-K#5, which ensures a positive Downward motion for an effective Three Dimensional Impact.

CATALOG OF BASIC COMPONENT VARIATIONS

CLUBSHAFT CONTROL

B- By a semi-reversal of the roles of the Arms and Clubshaft, a related similar procedure is possible. The Clubshaft moves on the selected Plane Angle while the Arms take over the vertical element — pointing at and along a line on the ground parallel to the Target Line. The Arms hang at Address and move in a simple back-and-forth up-and-down straight line path while utilizing the Throw-Out Action of Accumulator #3 (2-K and 6-B-3-0) to "flip" the Club "On Plane" past the Hands at The Top and "in-line" with the Hands at Impact (2-P). So, there are actually two Turning Shoulder Planes: A) The Vertical Wristcock version and B) The Vertical Left Arm Swing Plane version.

TURNING SHOULDER BASIC PLANE

10-6-D #1. Address.

10-6-D #2. Half Way Up.

10-6-D #3. Top.

CATALOG OF BASIC COMPONENT VARIATIONS

CLUBSHAFT CONTROL

10-6-E. HANDS ONLY The Hands must always be On Plane but in situations where only an adjustable reference point is suitable, the intended Impact *location* of the Hands serves very well — especially with the "Peck" Basic Stroke.

HANDS ONLY BASIC PLANE

10-6-E #1. Address. 10-6-E #2. Top.

CATALOG OF BASIC COMPONENT VARIATIONS

PLANE ANGLE VARIATIONS

CUSTOMIZED PLANES

10-7-0. GENERAL Plane Angle Variations are classified according to the shifts in the Plane Angle of the Stroke path. A shift may be made (1) during the Backstroke, (2) during the Downstroke, or (3) at the Top of the Stroke.

10-7-A. ZERO This classification is included so it can be indicated in a player's prepared Stroke Pattern that one Basic Plane Angle is to be used throughout the stroke without a "Variation" — that is, *No Shift*.

10-7-B. SINGLE SHIFT This Shift relates only to the shift from the Elbow Plane Angle to the Turned Shoulder Plane Angle during the Backstroke, with a Downstroke on the Turned Shoulder Plane Angle.

10-7-C. DOUBLE SHIFT This involves the return of the Stroke to the Elbow Plane Angle after a Single Shift during the Backstroke.

10-7-D. THE TRIPLE SHIFT This Backstroke is the same as for -B and -C above. It starts out on the Elbow Plane Angle and finishes on the Turned Shoulder Plane Angle. It then shifts immediately to the Vertical Downstroke motion of the Turning Shoulder Plane Angle.

10-7-B. Single Shift.   10-7-C. Double Shift.   10-7-D. Triple Shift.

CATALOG OF BASIC COMPONENT VARIATIONS

CUSTOMIZED PLANES

10-7-E. REVERSE SHIFT As its name implies, it is the exact reverse of the Single Shift. That is, the Shift is from a Turned Shoulder Plane Angle Backstroke to an Elbow Plane Angle Downstroke.

10-7-F. THE LOOP The Loop is similar to the Single Shift except that the Shift is made *to* the *Squared* Shoulder Plane Angle and is done with a looping motion of the Clubhead. Knowing how to stay On Plane, per 2-F, will correct for the Flat Shoulder Turn "Shift" to this steeper Plane — intentional or not. But the *cure* is Pivot Correction. (See 9-1.)

10-7-G. THE REVERSE LOOP This is similar to the Reverse Shift except that the Shift is made from the Squared Shoulder Plane Angle but also is done with a looping motion of the Clubhead. Handled with skill, this Shift can be very effective.

10-7-H. THE TWIST Here the Backstroke is on the Turning Shoulder Plane Angle but the Downstroke shifts directly to the Squared Shoulder Plane Angle by an immediate Flat Shoulder Turn with its obvious looping action.

10-7-E. Reverse Shift. 10-7-F. The Loop Shift. 10-7-G. Reverse Loop Shift. 10-7-H. The Twist Shift.

CATALOG OF BASIC COMPONENT VARIATIONS

THE FIX

ADDRESS ENGINEERING

10-8-0. GENERAL The three IMPACT FIX POSITIONS are classified according to combinations of Impact and Address positions for the *hands* and *body*. That is one or the other or both are in the Impact Fix location.

10-8-A. STANDARD The identifying features of this position are:
1. Body at Impact Fix, per 3-F-5-3
2. Hands in Impact Location and Condition, per 7-8

10-8-B. SPECIAL The identifying features of this position are:
1. Body at Impact Fix (10-8-A)
2. Hands remain in Address Position Location and Condition, per 7-9

10-8-C. HALF AND HALF The identifying features of this position are:
1. Body in the Standard Address Position, per 7-9
2. Hands at Impact Fix Location and Condition, per 7-8

10-8-A. Standard Fix.

10-8-B. Special Fix.

10-8-C. Half & Half Fix.

CATALOG OF BASIC COMPONENT VARIATIONS

ADDRESS

ADDRESS POSITIONING

10-9-0. GENERAL The four ADDRESS POSITIONS are classified according to combinations of Impact and Address positions for the *hands* and the *body*.
1. Both at Standard Address
2. Both at Selected Impact
3. Body at Selected Impact with the Hands at Standard Address
4. One combination Impact-Address *body* position

10-9-A. STANDARD The identifying features of this position are:
1. Body Standard in Address Position, per 7-9
2. Hands at Address Position Location and Condition, per 7-9
3. The Standard Address position condition of the Wrists — left B/L/V, right F/L/V.

This arrangement encourages a Lagging Clubhead Takeaway for Lag Loading per 7-19-3 and 7-20.

10-9-A. Standard Address.

CATALOG OF BASIC COMPONENT VARIATIONS

ADDRESS POSITIONING

10-9-B. IMPACT The identifying features of this position are:
1. The Body remains in Standard Impact Fix Position
2. The Hands remain in Impact Fix Location and Condition

This arrangement encourages a Non-Lagging Clubhead Takeaway for Lag Loading per 7-19-1 and 7-20.

10-9-B. Impact Address.

CATALOG OF BASIC COMPONENT VARIATIONS

ADDRESS POSITIONING

10-9-C. HALF AND HALF The identifying features of this position are:
1. The Body in Standard Impact position
2. The Hands in Address Position and Condition

This arrangement encourages the Extensor Action Takeaway for Short Shot Lag Loading per 10-19-0.

10-9-D. SPECIAL The identifying features of this position are:
1. The Body moves to an "Open" Fix Position, including the Stance Line
2. The Hands remain in Standard Address Location and Condition

This arrangement encourages restricted Lag Loading and unrestricted Follow-through with Push Basic Stroke.

10-9-C. Half &Half Address.   10-9-D. Special Address.

CATALOG OF BASIC COMPONENT VARIATIONS

HINGE ACTIONS (HINGING)

BALL CONTROL

10-10-0. GENERAL   HINGE ACTIONS are classified according to the Plane of MOTION they impart. An ordinary door is an example of HORIZONTAL HINGE ACTION. A pendulum is an example of VERTICAL HINGE ACTION. The action of a canoeist's paddle approximates ANGLED HINGE ACTION. (See 2-F, 2-G, 4-D-0.)

10-10-A. HORIZONTAL (ONLY) HINGE ACTION   This "Closing Only" procedure must be per 2-G but is possible only by moving the Clubhead on a Vertical Plane, or around a cone that tilts slightly toward the Plane Line. The Flat Left Wrist is always <u>Vertical</u> to the <u>Ground</u> and imparts a motion that is <u>Parallel</u> to a Horizontal Plane (the ground).

10-10-A. Horizontal Hinge.

CATALOG OF BASIC COMPONENT VARIATIONS

BALL CONTROL

10-10-B. VERTICAL (ONLY) HINGE ACTION This "laying back only" procedure is usually limited to shorter shots because its vertical Plane Angle tends toward better "line" control and low power but is also the basis for 10-10-E. In both cases, the Left Hand is "palm up" *before* Low Point (2-N) — especially at Impact Fix (7-8) — and "palm down" *after* Low Point. Always vertical to a Vertical Basic Plane (2-G).

10-10-B. Vertical Hinge.

CATALOG OF BASIC COMPONENT VARIATIONS

BALL CONTROL

10-10-C. ANGLED HINGE ACTION This simultaneous "Closing and Layback" procedure holds the Flat Left Wrist vertical to the Inclined Plane (2-D, 2-G). This is identical to the paddle-Wheel motion of the straightening Right Arm but is a superior procedure (1-F). It greatly simplifies Hitting (10-19-A). The Shoulder Turn changes the appearance of this 10-18-C Wrist Action but not its *Feel* (See 7-10). Its Slice tendency must be compensated per 2-J-1. The "Laying Back" action makes Ball location very critical for Trajectory Control. (Study 4-D-0.)

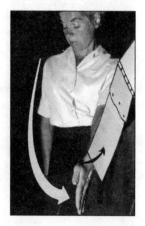

10-10-C. Angle Hinge.

CATALOG OF BASIC COMPONENT VARIATIONS

BALL CONTROL

10-10-D. DUAL HORIZONTAL With this arrangement the Angle Mounted Hinge maintains the Clubshaft on the Inclined Plane while the Horizontally Mounted Hinge keeps the Clubface turning (closing) throughout the Impact and Follow-through intervals by holding the Left Wrist vertical to the ground per 2-G and 6-B-3.

10-10-E. DUAL VERTICAL With this arrangement the Angle Mounted Hinge maintains the Clubshaft on the Inclined Plane while the Vertically Mounted Hinge is tilting (Laying Back) the Clubface during Impact and Follow-through. (See 10-10-B above.)

10-10-D. Dual Horizontal Hinge.   10-10-E. Dual Vertical Hinge.

CATALOG OF BASIC COMPONENT VARIATIONS

PRESSURE POINT COMBINATIONS

THRUST

10-11-0. GENERAL Pressure Point Combinations are classified according to the number of Pressure Points being used and the possible combinations thereof. They constitute Clubhead control per 1-L-B.

Each Point, Point Combination or Variation must be reconciled to the Accumulator Combinations being employed in the same Stroke. For instance — if only Accumulator #1 and Pressure Point #3 are used, then Pressure Point #3 drives both Lever Assemblies *and* Clubhead Lag, funneling all Right Arm Thrust against the Clubhead. This is a Hitting procedure with Axe Handle characteristics (2-K, 10-19).

Again — any time Accumulators #2 and #3 (the Hands) are employed, but only Pressure Points #1 and/or #4 (the Arms) are used to actuate the Primary Lever Assembly, so that Centripetal Force alone actuates the Secondary Lever Assembly, this would be the classic golf "Swing" and the Clubshaft would exhibit the "Rope Handle" characteristics mentioned in 2-K and 10-19. (Study 6-C-0.)

PRESSURE POINT LOCATIONS

10-11-0-1 & 2.
Pressure Point #1—Black Arrow.
Pressure Point #2—White Arrow.

10-11-0-3 & 4.
Pressure Point #3—White Arrow.
Pressure Point #4—Black Arrow.

CATALOG OF BASIC COMPONENT VARIATIONS

THRUST

10-11-0-1. PRESSURE POINT #1 (Photo) is active Power Package "direct drive" (7-11) of Accumulator #1 for actuating the Primary Lever Assembly (6-A-2) for Hitting (10-19-A) as well as Extensor Action (6-B-1-D). It is Loaded (7-22) per 6-B-1-0 and 7-19-1. It is only a passive "direct drive" with any *true* Swing procedure — Right Arm (7-19) or Left (6-B-3-0) — except per 2-M-3.

10-11-0-2. PRESSURE POINT #2 (Photo) actuates the Secondary Lever Assembly (6-B-2), normally, only as "Passive Clubhead Lag" (6-C-2-A). It is Loaded (7-22) per 6-B-2 and 7-19-3 and is a Swinger's Rope Handle application (2-K, 2-M-3).

10-11-0-3. PRESSURE POINT #3 (Photo) can be either active or passive (6-C-2-A) Accumulator #1 indirect drive (7-11) of the Secondary Lever Assembly (6-A-3) (2-K). That is, actively as Accumulators #2 and #3 (Axe Handle) application for Hitting (10-3-K, 10-19-A) but passively as Accumulator #3 (6-B-3-0, 10-19-C) or with a Right Arm Swing (7-19). This Pressure Point is used for sensing and guidance for all swing procedures (7-19) and is located and manipulated per Grip Type (10-2), Lag Loading (10-19) and Delivery Line (2-J-3) requirements. It is Loaded (10-22) per 7-19 as required by Component 19 application being employed (7-20). (Study 2-G and 6-C.)

Remember, with Swinging, Pressure Point #3 *must* have a *Feel* of being rotated a quarter turn at The Top with Standard Wrist Action (10-18-A), just and only because of the Loading Action *direction* — *no actual movement of anything*. So from The Top to Release, the Loading puts the top side of the Clubshaft against the first knuckle of the forefinger. With Hitting there *must* be NO change whatever.

When the Wrists "Swivel" back to the Vertical Position (4-C-3) during Standard Wrist Action (10-18-A) per 6-B-3, Pressure Point #3 *may* — but *need not* — return to its "strong" position (Aft side of the Clubshaft). That is — if left in "Top-of-the-Clubshaft" position, it becomes a Weak Single Action Grip (10-2-A) and the interchangeable equivalent to 10-2-C for Swingers. Both are improper for Hitters using Single Wrist Action (10-18-C).

CATALOG OF BASIC COMPONENT VARIATIONS

THRUST

10-11-0-4. PRESSURE POINT #4 (Photo) is normally active direct drive (7-11) of Accumulator #4 for actuating the Primary Lever Assembly (6-A-2) for Swinging (10-19-C) per 6-B-3-0 and for Hitting (10-19-A) per 2-M-4. It is Loaded (7-22) per 6-B-4 and 7-19-3.

10-11-0-5. INTERCHANGEABILITY in this category is limited strictly to the Pressure Points. An Accumulator cannot properly be separated from its Loading procedure. This means, as an example, that #3 Pressure Point may drive the #2 Accumulator in place of Pressure Point #2. But the motion, construction, identity and application of Accumulator #2 is unchanged. Only what actuates it is changed — #3 Pressure Point is used instead of #2.

This amounts to four Pressure Point Combinations having altogether fifteen Variations, some with perhaps small — but possible — utility. The variations are readily applied once the four Basic Pressure Point functions are grasped, so no attempt will be made to give them in any greater detail than the accompanying list.

CATALOG OF BASIC COMPONENT VARIATIONS

THRUST REGULATION

10-11-A. ONE POINT VARIATIONS There can be only four single Point applications:

Des.	Point No.	Des.	Point No.
1.	#1	3.	#3
2.	#2	4.	#4

10-11-B. TWO POINT COMBINATIONS There are six possible two Point Combinations:

Des.	Point Nos.	Des.	Point Nos.
1.	#1-#2	4.	#2-#3
2.	#1-#3	5.	#2-#4
3.	#1-#4	6.	#3-#4

10-11-C. THREE POINT COMBINATIONS There are four possible three Point Combinations:

Des.	Point Nos.	Des.	Point Nos.
1.	#1-#2-#3	3.	#1-#3-#4
2.	#1-#2-#4	4.	#2-#3-#4

10-11-D. FOUR POINT COMBINATION Here all four Points are used and in their normal application.

CATALOG OF BASIC COMPONENT VARIATIONS

BODY CONTROL

PIVOT

10-12-0. GENERAL Pivot Variations are classified according to the degree of MOTION produced — in either or both directions as determined by the Stance alignment being used.

10-12-A. STANDARD PIVOT This Pivot is a free turn in both directions — used when the Stance Line and the Plane Line are parallel (10-5-A, -D, and -E).

10-12-B. SHORT PIVOT The Short Pivot is a free Backstroke Turn with a restricted Follow-Through. Used when the Stance Line is Closed in respect to the Plane Line. (See Chapter 10-5-C.)

STANDARD PIVOT

10-12-A #1. Top.   10-12-A #2. End of Follow Through.

SHORT PIVOT

10-12-B #1. Top.   10-12-B #2. End of Follow Through.

CATALOG OF BASIC COMPONENT VARIATIONS

PIVOT

10-12-C. DELAYED PIVOT The Delayed Pivot is a restricted Backstroke turn with a free Follow-Through. Use when the Stance Line is Open with respect to the Plane Line (10-5-B).

10-12-D. ZERO PIVOT The Zero Pivot is the zero participation of all the Pivot Components. Use with all Plane Line combinations.

DELAYED PIVOT

ZERO PIVOT

10-12-C #1. Top.   10-12-C #2. End of Follow Through.   10-12-D #1. Top.   10-12-D #2. End of Follow Through.

CATALOG OF BASIC COMPONENT VARIATIONS

SHOULDER TURN

10-13-0 GENERAL The five Shoulder Turn types are classified according to the relationship of the Right Shoulder motion to the Inclined Plane Angles used during the Stroke. The "flatter" the Plane Angle, the more Shoulder Turn is required to put — and keep — the Right Shoulder On Plane. And vice versa.

10-13-A. STANDARD This is a dual application of the Flat (-B below) Backstroke and On Plane (-D below) Downstroke Shoulder Turn.

10-13-B. FLAT This is a relatively flat Backstroke Shoulder Turn which places the Shoulder "On Plane" for any Plane Angle with a flatter angle than the Rotated Shoulder Angle. A Flat Downstroke Shoulder Turn can serve only to impart the circular motion to the Stroke, but almost irresistibly "Off Plane."

10-13-B #1. Address.   10-13-B #2. Top.   10-13-B #3. 3/4 Down.

CATALOG OF BASIC COMPONENT VARIATIONS

SHOULDER TURN

10-13-C. ROTATED The Rotated Shoulder Turn moves the Shoulder in a "normal" path — at right angles to the spine. The Rotated Backstroke Shoulder Turn *can* locate a Turned Shoulder Plane Angle. The Downstroke Turn may shift to On Plane for whatever Plane Angle or Variation is used. Or it may continue in its "Rotated" pattern simply as transportation for the Power Package, as in -B above. "Axis Tilt" moves the Plane Line and Angle so, use the Shiftless Hip Turn. If the Waist Bend is exactly right, a Rotated Shoulder Turn may also be "On Plane" — in both directions — a simplified equivalent to 10-13-A.

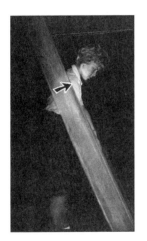

10-13-C #1. Address.

10-13-C #2. Top.

10-13-C #3. End of Follow Through.

CATALOG OF BASIC COMPONENT VARIATIONS

SHOULDER TURN

10-13-D. "ON PLANE" After a 13-B or 13-C Backstroke Shoulder Turn, the Right Shoulder moves toward Impact precisely on the preselected Downstroke Clubshaft Plane, establishing and supporting the Power Package Delivery alignments. When the Shoulder can't quite reach the Plane, it is better to use a steeper Plane.

10-13-D #1. Address.

10-13-D #2. Top.

10-13-D #3. End of Follow Through.

CATALOG OF BASIC COMPONENT VARIATIONS

SHOULDER TURN

10-13-E. ZERO The term Zero is applied here as either relative or absolute. Only on the very short Strokes is absolute Zero Shoulder Turn either possible or necessary. Absolute Zero is important whenever the geometry of the Stroke is based on Body position rather than Ball position.

10-13-E #1. Top.

10-13-E #2. End of Follow Through.

CATALOG OF BASIC COMPONENT VARIATIONS

HIP TURN

10-14-0. GENERAL Hip Turn Variations are classified according to the type of motion imparted — if any — and the manner of the Weight Shift — if any — to separate it from the Hip Action classification.

10-14-A. STANDARD The Standard Hip Turn (of any length) is a free turn in both directions with a weight shift in both directions. During Circle Path Delivery (7-23) use the Turning Hip to carry the Right Elbow around into Release position for a Trigger Delay Control procedure (7-20) with shorter strokes where the Elbow does not leave the Right Side and "Clearing the Right Hip" is not feasible. But only with a Delayed Pivot under strict Hand Control.

STANDARD

10-14-A #1. Top.   10-14-A #2. Finish.

CATALOG OF BASIC COMPONENT VARIATIONS

HIP TURN

10-14-B. SLIDE The Slide Hip Turn (of any length) is a free motion in both directions by the sliding of the Hips with a weight shift in both directions and a delayed turn. With exactly the same restrictions as required for 10-14-A.

10-14-C. SHIFTLESS The Shiftless Hip Turn is a free turn in both directions but with no weight shift in either direction. It tends toward a "soft" stroke with emphasis on accuracy. It can produce an On Plane Downstroke Shoulder Turn only with the Rotated Shoulder Plane Angle (10-13-C). Only the Pitch Basic Stroke is available to carry the Right Elbow into Release position for a Trigger Delay Control procedure.

SLIDE　　　　　　　　　**SHIFTLESS**

10-14-B #1. Top.　　10-14-B #2. Finish.　　10-14-C #1. Top.　　10-14-C #2. Finish.

CATALOG OF BASIC COMPONENT VARIATIONS

HIP TURN

10-14-D. REVERSE The Reverse Hip Turn is essentially a sliding motion back to Fix Position during the *Backstroke*. This will not affect the Backstroke Shoulder Turn *in relation to the body,* but will sharply restrict it *in relation to the ball* — On Plane, well back and well down.

This is extremely useful for all short Strokes. As a substitute for Impact Fix Address, it encourages moving into Impact Position habitually with all Strokes and discourages Address Wrist Condition (B/L/V) tendencies during Impact. Very compatible with Grip Types "E" and "F."

10-14-E. ZERO The Zero Hip Turn has no turn, slide or weight shift, and consequently, no knee or foot action. Most effective from the Half and Half Fix (10-8-C).

REVERSE   **ZERO**

10-14-D #1. Top.   10-14-D #2. Finish.   10-14-E #1. Top.   10-14-E #2. Finish.

CATALOG OF BASIC COMPONENT VARIATIONS

HIP ACTION

10-15-0. GENERAL Hip Action classifications are based on the directions in which Hip Action — if any — actuates the Shoulder Turn.

10-15-A. STANDARD The Hips initiate and lead throughout — pulling the Shoulders in both directions.

10-15-B. DELAYED The Shoulders lead and power the Backstroke Hip Turn — or at least lead. The Hips then take over and lead and power the Downstroke Shoulder Turn. Use this Hip Turn to prevent overswinging. Turn the Hips a predetermined amount — or none at all — and then "semi-lock" them at that point before starting back with either the Shoulders or the Club. Delayed Hip Action is the only Variation that assures "Clearing of the Right Hip" in both directions (2-N-0). So Hip Action is delayed until Start Down.

STANDARD   **DELAYED**

10-15-A #1. Start Up. 10-15-A #2. Start Down. 10-15-B #1. Start Up. 10-15-B #2. Start Down.

CATALOG OF BASIC COMPONENT VARIATIONS

HIP ACTION

10-15-C. SHORT   This is the opposite of the Delayed Hip Action — It powers the Backstroke Shoulder Turn but lets the Shoulders take over the Downstroke action.

10-15-D. ZERO   Except with Zero Hip Turn, this can resemble -A above (Standard) but there is usually a perceptible slackness in the Hip and Shoulder relationship in both directions. The motion is a Hip *Turn* only — not a "true" action in either direction.

SHORT **ZERO**

10-15-C #1. Start Up.   10-15-C #2. Start Down.   10-15-D #1. Start Up.   10-15-D #2. Start Down.

CATALOG OF BASIC COMPONENT VARIATIONS

KNEE ACTION

10-16-0. GENERAL Knee Action is classified on the basis of (1) combinations of bent and straight conditions and (2) the Reference Points at which these combinations occur.

10-16-A. STANDARD This method involves extremes of action in both directions. That is, the Right Knee straight and the Left Knee bent at the Top Position and passing through a double Knee Bend (Sit-Down Position) on to the reversed condition of Left Knee straight and Right Knee bent for the Finish. This sequence produces the maximum Hip slant at each end of the Stroke.

10-16-B. LEFT ANCHOR The action here is identical to -A above (Standard), except that there is no straightening of the Left Knee after passing the Sit Down Position. This method holds the Hips to a flatter turn through Impact and Follow-Through.

STANDARD   **LEFT ANCHOR**

10-16-A #1. Top.   10-16-A #2. Finish.   10-16-B #1. Top.   10-16-B #2. Finish.

CATALOG OF BASIC COMPONENT VARIATIONS

KNEE ACTION

10-16-C. RIGHT ANCHOR This method is the exact reverse of -B above (LEFT ANCHOR). Here both Knees *remain* bent until the Sit Down Position is passed. Then the Left Knee begins to straighten. This keeps all pre-Impact motion flat but the Follow-Through tends to rise quicker with the straightening of the Left Knee.

10-16-D. DOUBLE ANCHOR Here both Knees are held at Address Position bend throughout the entire Stroke, producing a very flat Hip motion.

RIGHT ANCHOR   **DOUBLE ANCHOR**

10-16-C #1. Top.   10-16-C #2. Finish.   10-16-D #1. Top.   10-16-D #2. Finish.

CATALOG OF BASIC COMPONENT VARIATIONS

KNEE ACTION

10-16-E. ZERO Here the Knee Action is Zero or minimal. No action occurs because this method is used only with the Zero Pivot or the Zero Hip Turn and with Zero Foot Action.

ZERO

10-16-E #1. Top.   10-16-E #2. Finish.

CATALOG OF BASIC COMPONENT VARIATIONS

FOOT ACTION

10-17-0. GENERAL Foot Action is classified according to combinations of three Foot Positions (considering each foot separately):
    1. Flat   2. Rolled   3. Lifted (Heel)
And in conjunction with three Reference Points in the Stroke;
    A. Top   B. Sit Down   C. Finish
"Rolling" and "Lifting" are restricted to the "unloaded" Foot.

10-17-A. STANDARD This procedure produces the maximum Foot Action. The Left Foot is Rolled and Lifted at the Top and the Right Foot is "Rolled" and "Lifted" at the Finish after passing through the Sit-Down Point with both feet Flat.

STANDARD

  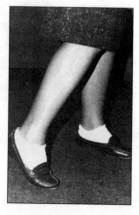

10-17-A #1. Top.   10-17-A #2. Sit Down.   10-17-A #3. Finish.

CATALOG OF BASIC COMPONENT VARIATIONS

FOOT ACTION

10-17-B. FLAT This procedure keeps both feet Flat throughout the Stroke but allows the normal Roll of the feet.

10-17-B #1. Top.

10-17-B #2. Finish.

10-17-C. FLAT LEFT This procedure differs from -A above (Standard) only in that the *Left* heel is not Lifted at any time.

10-17-C #1. Top.

10-17-C #2. Finish.

CATALOG OF BASIC COMPONENT VARIATIONS

FOOT ACTION

10-17-D. FLAT RIGHT This procedure differs from -A above (Standard) only in that the *Right* heel is not Lifted at any time.

10-17-D #1. Top.

10-17-D #2. Finish.

10-17-E. ZERO Here "Roll" and "Lift" are minimal as this method is used only with Zero Pivot or Zero Hip Turn.

10-17-E #1. Top.

10-17-E #2. Finish.

CATALOG OF BASIC COMPONENT VARIATIONS

CLUBHEAD CONTROL

LEFT WRIST ACTION

10-18-0. GENERAL Wrist Action is classified according to changes in Left Wrist Position prior to Impact. The Backstroke Positions are "Turned" and/or "Cocked." The Downstroke Positions are "Rolled" and/or "Uncocked" (Chapter 4). But never "Bent" or "Arched" except with 10-2-C, 10-2-D or Variation "B" below. So the possible Positions — in both directions — can be — the one — or the other — or both — or neither of the alternatives. Seven Actions are listed below. Comply with 6-B-3-0-1 and 6-C-2-A. All Wrist Action is subject to the requirements of Loading and of Grip Types.

10-18-A. STANDARD With this procedure the Wrist is Turned *and* Cocked (FCT) during the Backstroke which requires that it be Rolled and Uncocked during the Release. Only where this procedure is used, do the Hands "Swivel" into Hinge Action Position. (Study 4-D-0.)

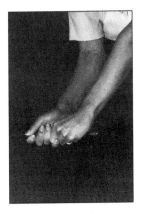

10-18-A. Standard

CATALOG OF BASIC COMPONENT VARIATIONS

LEFT WRIST ACTION

10-18-B. DOUBLE This procedure is identical to -A above (Standard) except that the Left Wrist is in a Double Cocked position (Cocked and Bent). It is restricted to true Centripetal Force Swings, as explained in 2-K and 6-B-3-0. Because though it increases Elbow Bend and Release Travel it destroys the Left Arm Flying Wedge and leaves Clubface Alignment to Centrifugal Reaction (7-2) or to the mandatory Frozen Right Wrist (7-3).

10-18-C. SINGLE Here, the Left Wrist is Cocked but not Turned. The Action has three alternative procedures:
1. Let the Pivot bring Horizontal Hinging to a normal On Plane "Top" position.
2. Let the Pivot bring Angled Hinging to a normal On Plane "Top" position.
3. Hold the Wrist "Vertical" throughout for a True Single Action "Top" position.

Because there is actually NO HAND MOVEMENT during the Stroke, Clubhead Fix alignment remains undisturbed.

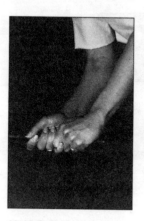 

10-18-B. Double.   10-18-C. Single.

CATALOG OF BASIC COMPONENT VARIATIONS

LEFT WRIST ACTION

10-18-D. HALF Here, the Wrist is "Turned" then "Rolled" but not Cocked — emphasizing the #3 Accumulator.

10-18-E. CUT SHOT Here, regardless of Plane Line Combination (10-5) or Pre-Release Wrist Action, there is no "Roll" through Impact. (See 4-C-3, 10-2-D and 10-10-B and -C.)

10-18-D. Half.   10-18-E. Cut Shot.

10-18-F. SPECIAL Here, Single Wrist Action Backstroke is given a Standard Wrist Action Downstroke.

10-18-G. ZERO Use the selected Hinging throughout the Stroke with no additional Turning, Rolling or Cocking.

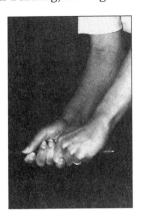 

10-18-F. Special.   10-18-G. Zero.

CATALOG OF BASIC COMPONENT VARIATIONS

LAG LOADING

HITTING OR SWINGING

10-19-0. GENERAL Lag Loading (Clubhead Feel) is classified according to difference in the procedures for accelerating the Secondary Lever Assembly (the Club). That is Radially or Longitudinally — which are mutually exclusive. That is — both cannot be applied at the same time. All of which also determines the nature of their execution — that is, Drive the one (10-19-A), Drag the other (10-19-C) or Flick either one (10-19-B) into Release. (Study 7-3.) This affects the Feel and emphasis of the entire motion. Especially Clubhead Lag Pressure Point participation. All must comply with the Law of the Flail in 2-K.

Drive Loading tends toward minimum Lag [the short, (Compact) Stroke] — meaning *contracted* muscles (muscle pull). Drag Loading tends toward maximum Lag [the full (Long) Stroke] — meaning *stretched* muscles (tendon pull). Float Loading can be either one. (See 7-20.) Study 2-J-3 for Delivery Line procedures.

The above characteristics apply to Strokes of any length. If you cannot handle both Short and Full Shots with the same Lag Loading procedure, you really do not understand either Hitting or Swinging. Master first the Short Shots — where you have time for careful Monitoring, per 3-F-6. Two Procedures — presented in 6-B-1-D — will help reduce excessive Arm Motion in the search for the Feel of Lag Pressure: For Hitters — substituting Extensor Action for Acceleration in both directions. For Swingers — the "Bending Right Wrist" and/or "Extensor Action Takeaway" will — more or less, as desired — snap the Clubshaft into its In-Line condition (with the Left Arm) with little or no Arm Motion except what results (intentionally) from Clubhead momentum. Then, use a normal Flat Left Wrist Downstroke per Pattern for both procedures — distinctly 12-1 OR 12-2. That is — PUSH or PULL.

Hinge Action does *NOT* differentiate Hitting and Swinging. All are interchangeable — with reservations. Hitters using Horizontal Hinging must consciously resist the tendency of Right Arm Paddlewheel Action toward Angled Hinging. Swingers using Angled Hinging must consciously resist the tendency of Centripetal Force toward Horizontal Hinging. Both procedures require skill in Clubface manipulation, per 7-2. Clubface MANIPULATION for Swinging requires the same Grip Type as for Hitters (10-2-B) because 10-2-G offers no such precision.

CATALOG OF BASIC COMPONENT VARIATIONS

HITTING

10-19-A. DRIVE LOADING Drive Loading is the "Axe Handle" technique of the "Hitter" — an out-and-out Right Arm Thrust against Clubhead Lag (Angular Inertia) striving to accelerate (radially) a Pre-stressed (Bent) Clubshaft, from a *slow Start Down* through Impact per 7-19-1. (See 2-N.)

All Short Shots can be short, strong Strokes, eliminating all unnecessary motion by using only one Accumulator (until greater distance is needed). But always — PUSH a lagging Clubhead through Impact.

Clubhead Throwaway here is due usually to over-acceleration. Use shorter Strokes and/or lower Thrust. The Stroke can be shortened per 10-15-B or by taking advantage of the fact that the Backstroke will stop when the Right Elbow becomes fully bent.

DRIVE

10-19-A #1. Top of $^3/_4$ Stroke (Zero Wrist Action).   10-19-A #2. Impact.

CATALOG OF BASIC COMPONENT VARIATIONS

HIT OR SWING

10-19-B. DOWNSTROKE (OR FLOAT) LOADING This procedure delays the Wristcock until the Start Down and completes it as specified by the Stroke Pattern Assembly Point Component. "Float Loading" also describes this procedure — especially the sensation, because the Cocking motion should not be at all sharp, but gentle, or even lazy. With a "Frozen Wrist" procedure (10-3-K), the Downstroke Cocking Action is limited to increasing the Right Elbow Bend only.

Assembly, Loading and Release are usually accomplished simultaneously, then with a Flicking action — automatic or non-automatic — continues as either Drive or Drag Loading, designating it as either 19-B/A or 19-B/C. And use corresponding Short Shot recommendations.

Downstroke Loading (7-19-2) must set up either Radial Acceleration per 10-19-A, or Longitudinal Acceleration, per 10-19-C for the corresponding Release procedure.

Quitting and/or collapse of the Wrist alignments and structure need special attention here for Clubhead Throwaway prevention.

DOWNSTROKE

10-19-B #1. Top of ³/₄ Stroke (Standard Wrist Action)

10-19-B #2. Release.

CATALOG OF BASIC COMPONENT VARIATIONS

SWINGING

10-19-C. DRAG LOADING Drag Loading is the Rope Handle Technique of the "Swinger," an out-and-out PULL, striving to accelerate the Clubshaft lengthwise, from a *quick Start Down* to Release. Start the Club down as though it were being drawn from a quiver like an arrow — feathered end first. Maintain this motion until the Release switches ends. This is possible only if, and for as long as, Inertia can hold the Clubhead inside the arc of the Hands or hold to a Line Delivery Path (2-L). Centrifugal Reaction will set in when the Clubhead crosses to the outside and it will begin to pull into its own incidental orbit per 2-P and 2-K#5. Then further acceleration can be applied only at Pressure Point #1 to support the Pull on the Clubshaft — especially for Short Shot Power.

Develop an "Instant Acceleration" Hip Action (to the desired Handspeed, per 10-15-B) so that the Throw Out Action (6-B-3) can immediately set up the Rhythm and take over the rest of the Downstroke sequence (6-M-1). (See 2-K and 6-F-0.) With or without Wristcock, always Drag (or Pull 10-3-D) a swinging Club Down Plane — even with only Centripetal Force (Angular Momentum) (2-K). (See 10-23-C.)

For Clubhead Throwaway prevention, monitor the pull of Centripetal Force and the Drag of the Lagging Clubhead.

DRAG

10-19-C #1. Top
(Standard Wrist Action).

10-19-C #2 Automatic
Snap Release (Standard
Wrist Action)

CATALOG OF BASIC COMPONENT VARIATIONS

TRIGGER TYPES

THE THROW

10-20-0. GENERAL Trigger Types are classified according to the point of origin of the action. Five basic procedures are listed for Triggering the Release of the Power Package. Unlisted procedures adopted by players should be noted under the "X" classification for the Stroke Pattern selections. The five basic procedures are listed in approximately the same order as the Power Package Releases (11-24) to keep these closely related categories parallel. Variations MUST comply with 4-D-0. (Study 6-B-0.)

10-20-A. THE HAND THROW The *Hands* swing the Club right from The Top. This is very hazardous except for well Educated Hands. Accumulator Release is very gradual so they won't all become empty at — or before — Impact. This classification includes any "Hands Only" Putting Stroke, such as 10-3-E.

10-20-B. THE RIGHT ARM THROW The Right Arm (6-B-1) simply pushes the Lever Assemblies (6-A) toward Impact with either early or late Release. Usually restricted to Hitting (10-19-A). (See 2-M-4.)

10-20-C. SHOULDER TURN THROW Sharp initial acceleration of the Shoulder Turn against the #4 Pressure Point Loading motion of the Left Arm (10-11) Automatically throws the Left Arm off the chest when the Pivot acceleration subsides, per 10-19-C. (See 2-M-4.)

10-20-A. During Start Down.   10-20-B. Release.   10-20-C. During Down Stroke.

CATALOG OF BASIC COMPONENT VARIATIONS

THE THROW

10-20-D. DELIVERY PATH THROW Wherever the bottom arc of the Delivery Line begins (10-23) — a long arc or short (7-23) — it triggers this Throw automatically. Usually used in combination with 10-20-B for Hitting or with 10-20-C for Swinging.

By deliberately Triggering the Release before the end of the Delivery Path Line, a Non-Automatic version can be produced. This will normally require an adjustment of the Aiming Point also.

10-20-E. WRIST THROW Here, the Right Hand remains palm-up to the Plane until Release to produce a Sequenced Release, per 2-G and 4-D-0. By deliberately initiating the Wrist Roll at any point before reaching the end of the Delivery Path Line, the Non-Automatic version can be produced. If you find this procedure too difficult, stay with 10-20-D, above. Only compatible with Swinging. (See 6-H-0-F.)

10-20-D. At Release.   10-20-E. At Release.

CATALOG OF BASIC COMPONENT VARIATIONS

POWER PACKAGE CONTROL

POWER PACKAGE ASSEMBLY POINTS

10-21-0. GENERAL Power Package Assembly Points are classified according to the reference points along the Delivery Paths where Assembly is completed. Three reference points produce five Variations:
1. The Top of either Line Path
2. Any Point along any Delivery Path
3. Any Point beyond the Top (End)

Assembly is not completed until the #3 Pressure Point Downstroke has been established.

"Top" as used in #1. above, means the Hands are Shoulder High and On Plane. The Club, Plane Angle or Body Position do not alter this relationship. Otherwise, "Top" is the end of any Backstroke.

10-21-A. TOP Here the Package Assembly is completed at the Top *before* the Hands actually start on the Downstroke.

10-21-B. SIDE This procedure is identical to "A" above (Top) except that any point *along* the Path can be the end of the Backstroke — or the Top of that particular Stroke at hand.

10-21-C. END When the Backstroke arches on beyond the Top, the Assembly can occur at the End of the Backstroke travel, regardless of which of the Paths to the ball will be used on the Downstroke.

10-21-A. Top of the Line.

10-21-B. Side.

10-21-C. End.

CATALOG OF BASIC COMPONENT VARIATIONS

ASSEMBLY POINTS

10-21-D. DOWNSTROKE TOP This procedure is identical with 10-21-C above (End) except that the Hands do not wait for the Assembly to be completed at the End of the Arc but move back toward the Top so that Assembly is actually completed at the Top while the Hands are moving strongly along the Downstroke Path.

10-21-E. DOWNSTROKE SIDE This procedure is a shortened version of 10-21-D above (Downstroke Top). It is identical to 10-21-A (Top) except that the Hands do not wait for the Assembly to be completed at the Top but move back toward the ball so that Assembly is actually completed at some pre-determined Point along the Line (up to and including the Release Point) while the Hands are moving along the Downstroke Path.

10-21-D #1. At End.   10-21-D #2 Top.   10-21-E #1. Top.   10-21-E #2. Side.

201

CATALOG OF BASIC COMPONENT VARIATIONS

POWER PACKAGE LOADING ACTION

10-22-0. GENERAL Loading Actions are classified on the basis of Three reference points where the action can be initiated. Though the Action is infinite in variety, all fall into three simple alternatives — as sharply as possible, as gradually as possible, and somewhere in between — noting the approximate fraction of the full arc.

10-22-A. FULL SWEEP This pattern starts the Loading Action at the beginning of the Backstroke and smoothly and evenly accelerates the Lever Assemblies so they arrive in position at the intended Assembly Point.

10-22-B. RANDOM SWEEP This pattern starts the Loading Action at any pre-determined Point between the extremes of the Snap and the Sweep and arrives in Position at the intended Assembly Point.

10-22-C. SNAP This pattern places the Loading on the Power Package at the last instant with a delayed Snap of the Lever Assemblies into position.

10-22-A. $^3/_4$ Up.   10-22-B. $^3/_4$ Up.   10-22-C. $^3/_4$ Up.

CATALOG OF BASIC COMPONENT VARIATIONS

POWER PACKAGE DELIVERY PATHS

10-23-0. GENERAL Power Package Delivery Paths are classified on the basis of three possible TYPES of paths the Hands can take toward impact. This results in five definable Paths. These Paths are actually the paths taken by the *Hands* — NOT the *Clubhead*. (See 2-J-3.) The five Downstroke Paths are all valid for equivalent Backstroke shifts, also.

10-23-A. STRAIGHT LINE This pattern holds the Hands on a Delivery Path that is a Straight Line leading from the Top-of-the-line hand position directly at *and through* the Aiming Point (2-J-3) when there is no Plane Shift (10-7).

10-23-A #1. Top.   10-23-A #2. ³/₄ Down.

CATALOG OF BASIC COMPONENT VARIATIONS

BASIC DELIVERY PATHS

10-23-B. ANGLED LINE This pattern is used with the Plane Angle Variations that include a shift to (or back to) the Elbow Plane Angle during the Downstroke (10-7).

From the Top-of-the-Straight-Line hand position the Hands take a nearly vertical path to the Plane of the Elbow Plane Angle before they start their drive directly at *and through* the Aiming Point (2-J-3).

10-23-B #1. Top.   10-23-B #2. At Angle.   10-23-B #3. Release.

CATALOG OF BASIC COMPONENT VARIATIONS

BASIC DELIVERY PATHS

10-23-C. TOP ARC AND STRAIGHT LINE This pattern takes the Hands beyond the Top-of-the-Line point, up and back along an Arc that is *retraced* when the Hands return to the Top-of-the-Line point. This "retracing" is ideal for longitudinal acceleration with 10-19-C.

10-23-D. TOP ARC AND ANGLED LINE This path is the same as "C" above except that from the Top-of-the-Line position the Hands take the Angled Line Delivery Path ("B" above).

10-23-E. CIRCLE Here, no straight Line Path is attempted. The Hands swing along on a continuation of the Top Arc formed below or above the Top-of-the-Line because any portion of the Path can be the Top Arc regardless of having reached a Top-of-the-Line position or not. So — from any Assembly Point the Path to the ball in this case is circular and is used, normally but not necessarily, only with "No Axis Tilt" (2-H) and Arc of Approach Delivery Line (2-J-3). (See 7-23.)

10-23-C. End.   10-23-D. End.   10-23-E #1. $\frac{1}{2}$ Down.   10-23-E #2. Release.

CATALOG OF BASIC COMPONENT VARIATIONS

POWER PACKAGE RELEASE

10-24-0. GENERAL Power Package Releases are classified on the basis of Combinations of Release Types and Release Points. The Three Release Points (Sweep, Random, and Snap) and the two Release Types (Automatic and Non-Automatic) produce six combinations. All Release Variations are valid for both Hitting and Swinging (10-19). All releases are subject to the same Angle of Approach requirements per 2-N. Snap Releases can be either, or both, Release Motions (Study 4-D-0.)

10-24-A. FULL SWEEP RELEASE This procedure Triggers the Release at the Start Down by either the Hand Throw or the Right Arm Throw (10-20) Non-Automatic Trigger Types. All the employed Accumulators slowly and evenly straighten and the Clubhead slowly and evenly accelerates through Impact, per 2-N. (See 6-C-2-B.)

FULL SWEEP RELEASE

10-24-A #1. Top.   10-24-A #2. Down Stroke.   10-24-A #3. During Release.

CATALOG OF BASIC COMPONENT VARIATIONS

RELEASE

10-24-B. NON-AUTOMATIC RANDOM SWEEP This procedure is identical with "A" above except that the deliberate manipulation of the Release (Non-Automatic Trigger) is delayed until some preselected point in the Downstroke is reached.

10-24-C. AUTOMATIC RANDOM SWEEP This procedure differs from "B" above *only* in that an Automatic Trigger Type or Combination is employed in place of the deliberate muscular manipulation of a Non-Automatic Trigger. Usually, by Aiming Point Manipulation (6-E-2).

10-24-B #1. At Side Release Point.   10-24-B #2. During Release.   10-24-C #1. At Side Release Point.   10-24-C #2. During Release.

CATALOG OF BASIC COMPONENT VARIATIONS

RELEASE

10-24-D. NON-AUTOMATIC SNAP RELEASE This procedure delays the Triggering of the Release as long as possible and still allows sufficient time to execute the deliberate maneuvering of a Non-Automatic Trigger Type so that the Hands will still arrive in Impact location and position at Impact. A strong, deliberate whiplash type of motion.

10-24-E. AUTOMATIC SNAP RELEASE This procedure drives the Lag Pressure Point through a Snap Release (6-N-0) as if there were to be no Release at all. This action is possible only through the use of the Aiming Point Concept (6-E-2). So is precision Impact control. A strong automatic whiplash type of motion is very effective in understanding this procedure (Study 2-P, 6-B-2-0 and 10-11-3-0).

10-24-D #1. During Down Stroke.   10-24-D #2. At Release Point.   10-24-E #1. During Down Stroke.   10-24-E #2. At Release Point.

CATALOG OF BASIC COMPONENT VARIATIONS

RELEASE

10-24-F. FLIP RELEASE This Pivot Controlled procedure causes *Release* (with all Clubs) to occur by an automatic "Flip" — quick or lazy — when the Hands reach a certain point in relation to the body, on the basis of Feel. This need not be a subconscious procedure, because the Hands can consciously sense and manipulate the Rhythm of Centripetal Force (5-0) and, with only this, be able to move the Clubshaft "On Plane." Release is Triggered (7-20) by allowing the Arm Swing and/or the Shoulder Turn to Swing the Hands per 10-20-E — automatically or deliberately — and move the Clubhead to an Off Plane relation to the Arms so Centripetal Force can accelerate the "Throw Out" action thus initiated (6-B-3-0). Proper Impact is the result of the Hands timing the sequence of these actions. That means, basically, keeping the Left Arm (with or without Momentum Transfer (2-K) or Right Arm aid) pulling strongly throughout, because the Throw-Out Action inhibits Throwaway except from Quitting (6-D-3).

The Aiming Point (6-E) equivalent for this procedure is the "Open" and "Closed" Stance Line (10-5) which varies the Ball location in its relation to the body for any given Release Type (10-20 and 10-24), to compensate for different Clubshaft lengths and must be worked out by experiment (See 9-1-1) because the player's habitual Pivot procedure will bring the Hands very dependably into Release Position at the same point in relation to the body. So then, of course, errors in the Pivot affect the results adversely. As with any Swing Release (10-19-0), Ball placement (2-N) depends on Clubface alignment design (6-B-3-0) as well as Hinge Action (2-G). Right Arm participation must be per 2-K and 2-M-3.

CATALOG OF BASIC COMPONENT VARIATIONS

RELEASE

The Flip Release procedure always uses the Shoulder Turn "Takeaway" (10-6-B) which produces a curved Plane Shift by both the Hands and Clubhead. This is part of its Body related (not Ball related) execution as "Pivot Controlled Hands" referred to in 5-0. The Pivot may be educated to produce geometric Hand and Club alignments and relationships with some degree of precision which would definitely improve control. Expanding this infiltration could serve as your "Relative Translation" procedure (3-B) to true "Hand Controlled Pivot" procedures which must start with a Right Forearm Takeaway (2-M-3 and 7-3). But — except as a temporary Band-Aid, any mandatory Component position or location can only be disruptive and carries a prohibitive price tag. (See 1-K.)

10-24-F #1. Impact Stance (Short Club).   10-24-F #2. Impact Stance (Long Club).

CHAPTER ELEVEN

SUMMARY OF CHAPTER 10

11-A. GRAPHIC SUMMARY This chart is a map of the road to good golfing and shows the continuity of the routing.

Chapters 1-12

Basic Golf Stroke
(Chapters 1-6)

Twenty-Four Basic Components
(Chapter 7)

144 Component Variations
(Chapter 10)

Twelve Sections
(Chapter 8)

Three Zones
(Chapter 9)

Zone #1	Zone #2	Zone #3
Body Control	Club Control	Ball Control
6 Components	13 Components	5 Components
28 Variations	87 Variations	29 Variations

Stroke Pattern
1 to 24 Components
(Chapter 12)

Players Basic Stroke Pattern

SUMMARY OF CHAPTER 10

11-0. A SUMMARY OF CHAPTER 10 This Chapter summarizes the information presented in Chapter 10. It covers the following subjects used in Stroke Patterns in the same numerical order in capsulated column format.

1. Grips — Basic
2. Grips — Types
3. Strokes — Basic
4. Strokes — Types and Variations
5. Plane Line
6. Plane Angle — Basic
7. Plane Angle — Variations
8. Fix
9. Address
10. Hinge Actions
11. Pressure Point Combinations
12. Pivot
13. Shoulder Turn
14. Hip Turn
15. Hip Action
16. Knee Action
17. Foot Action
18. Left Wrist Action
19. Lag Loading
20. Trigger Types
21. Power Package Assembly Point
22. Power Package Loading Action
23. Power Package Delivery Path
24. Power Package Release

—1—
GRIPS—BASIC

Des.	Term	Description
A	Overlap	Lower right hand overlaps upper left hand
B	Baseball	Any non-overlapping grip
C	Reverse Overlap	Upper left hand overlaps lower right hand
D	Interlock	Adjacent fingers of each hand interlocked
E	Cross Hand	All above grips with hand positions reversed

SUMMARY OF CHAPTER 10

—2—
GRIPS—TYPES

Des.	Term	Left Wrist Position	Right Wrist Position	Pressure Point Position
A	Weak Single Action	Vertical	Vertical	Top
B	Strong Single Action	Vertical	Vertical	Aft
C	Weak Double Action	Vertical	Rolled	Top
D	Strong Double Action	Turned	Vertical	Aft
E	Weak Underhand	Vertical	Turned	Under
F	Strong Underhand	Turned	Turned	Under
G	Triple or Quadruple	Variable	Variable	Variable

—3—
STROKES—BASIC

Des.	Term	Description	Combinations
A	Punch	Right Arm Punch	All except B&C
B	Pitch	Right Arm Slap	All except A&C
C	Push	Right Arm Push	All except A&B
D	Pull	Right Arm Passive	All except F
E	Putt	Absolutely No Body motion	All
F	Peck	No Arm Swing	All except D
G	Pick	Both Elbows Bent at Impact	All except H
H	Paw	Both Arms Straight at Impact	All except G
J	Pause	Zero Follow-Through	All
K	Bat	Right Elbow Hinge	A/B/E

SUMMARY OF CHAPTER 10

—4—
STROKES—TYPES AND VARIATIONS
(Accumulator Combinations)

A. Single Barrel
    1. 1st   Accumulator Only   (Right Elbow)
    2. 2nd   Accumulator Only   (Left Wrist)
    3. 3rd   Accumulator Only   (Left Hand)
    4. 4th   Accumulator Only   (Left Arm)

B. Double Barrel
    1. 1st & 2nd   Accumulators
    2. 1st & 3rd   Accumulators
    3. 1st & 4th   Accumulators
    4. 2nd & 3rd   Accumulators
    5. 2nd & 4th   Accumulators
    6. 3rd & 4th   Accumulators

C. Triple Barrel
    1. 1st, 2nd & 3rd   Accumulators
    2. 1st, 2nd & 4th   Accumulators
    3. 1st, 3rd & 4th   Accumulators
    4. 2nd, 3rd & 4th   Accumulators

D. Four Barrel
    1. 1st, 2nd, 3rd & 4th   Accumulators

—5—
PLANE LINE

Des.	Plane	Stance	Line of Flight	Pivot
A	Square	Square	On Plane Line	Full/Zero
B	Square	Open	On Plane Line	Delayed/Zero
C	Square	Closed	On Plane Line	Short/Zero
D	Open	Open	Pushed	Full/Zero
E	Closed	Closed	Pulled	Full/Zero

SUMMARY OF CHAPTER 10

—6—
BASIC PLANE ANGLES

Des.	Term	Club Shaft Angle
A	Elbow	Elbow
B	Turned Shoulder	Top Right Shoulder Location
C	Squared Shoulder	Squared Shoulder Location
D	Turning Shoulder	Squared Shoulder Location
E	Hands Only	Impact Hand Location

—7—
PLANE ANGLE VARIATIONS

Des.	Term	Starting Plane Angle	Plane Shift (Basic Planes) Up	Down
A	Zero	All	None	None
B	Single Shift	"A" (Elbow)	A-B	B
C	Double Shift	"A" (Elbow)	A-B	B-A
D	Triple Shift	"A" (Elbow)	A-B	D
E	Reverse Shift	"B" (Shoulder)	B/D	B/D-A
F	Loop	"A"/"B"	A/B	A/B-C
G	Reverse Loop	"C" (Squared Shoulder)	C	C-A/B
H	Twist	"D" (Turning Shoulder)	D	D-A

—8—
FIX

Des.	Term	Description
A	Standard	Full forward Press—left wrist F/L/V
B	Special	Entire body in an open stance—forward press with hands only
C	Half & Half	"Address" body position with left wrist F/L/V

SUMMARY OF CHAPTER 10

—9—
ADDRESS

Des.	Term	Description
A	Standard	Return from "fix" position to basic stance
B	Impact	Start backstroke from "fix" position
C	Half & Half	Return hands only (not body) from "fix" position
D	Special	From open stance "fix" (8-B above) return hands only

—10—
HINGE ACTIONS

Des.	Term	Description
A	Horizontal Only	Single Hinge—Closing Clubface—No lay-back
B	Vertical Only	Single Hinge—Clubface Lay-back—No closing
C	Angled	Single Hinge—simultaneous closing and lay-back
D	Dual Horizontal	Dual Hinges—Closing Clubface—No lay-back
E	Dual Vertical	Dual Hinges—Clubface lay-back—no closing

—11—
PRESSURE POINT COMBINATIONS

A Single Point Variations
  A-1 Pressure Point #1   A-3 Pressure Point #3
  A-2 Pressure Point #2   A-4 Pressure Point #4

B Two Point Combinations
  B-1 Pressure Points #1-#2   B-4 Pressure Points #2-#3
  B-2 Pressure Points #1-#3   B-5 Pressure Points #2-#4
  B-3 Pressure Points #1-#4   B-6 Pressure Points #3-#4

C Three Point Combinations
  C-1 Pressure Points #1-#2-#3   C-3 Pressure Points #1-#3-#4
  C-2 Pressure Points #1-#2-#4   C-4 Pressure Points #2-#3-#4

D Four Point Combinations
  D-1 Pressure Points #1-#2-#3-#4

SUMMARY OF CHAPTER 10

—12—
PIVOT

Des.	Term	Description
A	Standard	Move freely in both directions
B	Short	Damped follow-through turn
C	Delayed	Damped backstroke turn
D	Zero	Arm Swing (Pivot-zero or incidental)

—13—
SHOULDER TURN

Des.	Term	Description
A	Standard	Backstroke—flat/downstroke—on plane
B	Flat	Minimum rise (or dip) of right shoulder
C	Rotated	With reference to spine only
D	On Plane	Right shoulder follows line of plane angle
E	Zero	No shoulder turn

—14—
HIP TURN

Des.	Term	Up Turn	Up Shift	Down Turn	Down Shift
A	Standard	Free	Free	Free	Free
B	Slide	Zero	Free	Zero	Free
C	Shiftless	Free	Zero	Free	Zero
D	Reverse	Zero	Reverse	Zero	Zero
E	Zero	Zero	Zero	Zero	Zero

When using Turn Combinations, show Backstroke designations first.

—15—
HIP ACTION

Des.	Term	Description
A	Standard	Leads *and* powers shoulders up *and* down
B	Delayed	Lags shoulders up—powers shoulders down
C	Short	Leads and powers shoulders up—lags shoulders down
D	Zero	Leads but does not power shoulders up or down (no action)

SUMMARY OF CHAPTER 10

—16—
KNEE ACTION

Des.	Term	Top Left	Top Right	Finish Left	Finish Right	Plane of Hip Turn Top	Plane of Hip Turn Finish
A	Standard	Address	Straight	Straight	Address	Tilt	Tilt
B	Left Anchor	Address	Straight	Address	Address	Tilt	Flat
C	Right Anchor	Address	Address	Straight	Address	Flat	Tilt
D	Double Anchor	Address	Address	Address	Address	Flat	Flat
E	Zero	Address	Address	Address	Address	Flat	Flat

—17—
FOOT ACTION

Des.	Term	Top Left	Top Right	At Sit-Down Left	At Sit-Down Right	Finish Left	Finish Right
A	Standard	Roll and Lift	Flat	Flat	Flat	Flat and Lift	Roll
B	Flat	Roll and Flat	Flat	Flat	Flat	Flat and Flat	Roll
C	Flat Left	Roll and Flat	Flat	Flat	Flat	Flat and Lift	Roll
D	Flat Right	Roll and Lift	Flat	Flat	Flat	Flat and Flat	Roll
E	Zero	Flat	Flat	Flat	Flat	Flat	Flat

—18—
LEFT WRIST ACTION

Des.	Term	Back Stroke	Down Stroke
A	Standard	Turn and Cock	Roll and Uncock
B	Double	Turn and Double Cock	Roll and Uncock
C	Single	Cock without Turn	Uncock and No Roll
D	Half	Turn without Cock	Roll Only
E	Cut Shot	Turn and Cock	Uncock and No Roll
F	Special	Cock without Turn	Roll and Uncock
G	Zero	Selected Hinging	Selected Hinging

—19—
LAG LOADING

Des.	Term	Description
A	Drive Loading	Radial Acceleration only
B	Downstroke (or Float) Loading	Radial OR Longitudinal Acceleration
C	Drag Loading	Longitudinal Acceleration only

SUMMARY OF CHAPTER 10

—20—
TRIGGER TYPES

Des.	Trigger Description	Release Combinations	Types (11-24)
A	Hand Throw	B/C	A
B	Right Arm Throw	A/D	B/C
C	Shoulder Turn Throw	E	B/C
D	Delivery Path Throw	B	D/E
E	Wrist Throw	C	D/E/F

—21—
POWER PACKAGE ASSEMBLY POINT

Des.	Term	Description
A	Top	Hands shoulder high
B	Side	Hands below the right shoulder level
C	End	Hands at any point above right shoulder level
D	Downstroke Top	Hand at "Top" during "End" downstroke
E	Downstroke Side	Hands at "Side" during "Top" downstroke

—22—
POWER PACKAGE LOADING ACTION

Des.	Term	Description
A	Full Sweep	Gradual Loading from Address to Assembly Point
B	Random Sweep	Gradual Loading from any point between Full Sweep and Snap
C	Snap	Sharp Loading at Assembly Point

SUMMARY OF CHAPTER 10

—23—
POWER PACKAGE DELIVERY PATH

Des.	Term	Description
A	Straight Line	From "Top" position, drive Hands on "Straight Line" at the Aiming Point
B	Angled Line	Vertical Straight Line from "Top" Hand Position to "Elbow Plane" then angle off directly at the Aiming Point
C	Top Arc and Straight Line	From "End" Hand Position, bring Hands out to "Top" position, then straight toward the Aiming Point
D	Top Arc and Angled Line	From "End" position to "Top" position, then Vertical Line to "Elbow Plane" before angling off toward the Aiming Point
E	Circle	Swing Hands on a curve from "Top" or "End" position through impact

—24—
POWER PACKAGE RELEASE

Des.	Release Type	Release Point
A	Non-automatic	Full Sweep
B	Non-automatic	Random Sweep
C	Automatic	Random Sweep
D	Non-automatic	Snap
E	Automatic	Snap
F	Non-automatic/ Automatic	Flip

CHAPTER TWELVE

STROKE PATTERNS

12-0. A player's "Stroke Pattern" contains one Variation from each of the twenty-four Component categories in Chapter 10 and normally every one must be accounted for.

A Basic Stroke Pattern is a favorite, or Central, Pattern from which, normally, there would be deviation only in Zone #3 (Ball Control) with the possible exception of Stroke Type (Accumulator Combinations). Once a Basic Stroke Pattern is acquired, Variations may be added one at a time. If this process is pressed too rapidly the Basic Pattern can become shaky and produce a troublesome slump.

Stroke patterns 12-1 and 12-2 on the following pages are, as written, for Full Pivot Strokes. From those Patterns, Short Stroke and Putting Pattern should be drawn, so a player has only one Pattern to learn. That is, simply reduce or omit certain actions as needed, in the following order of preference—or in combinations—as gives gradual variation between maximum and minimum range:

1. Power Accumulators
2. Lag Pressure
3. Release Interval
4. Pivot
5. Arm Motion
6. Release Motions

Those steps must only shorten, not change 6-B-3-0. Keep *ALL* Full and Short Stroke alignments and paths identical. Chips and Putts are merely miniaturized — not altered. And each must have its own Total Motion (3-0). (Study 2-M-2 and 2-N.)

For those mincing their way into Golf, a Basic "Short Course" using Components 2, 3, 6, 10, 11, 18 and 19 from either 12-1 or 12-2, or the "Basic Motion Curriculum" in 12-5 — especially — 12-5-1 is recommended for a Starter Pattern. The rest of the Pattern can be added later — one Component at a time. Remember, continual improvement — not instant perfection — is the realistic program. A Stroke Pattern is a player's selected "MOTION." The Motion makes the Shots. As the Motion improves, shots improve — not vice versa.

STROKE PATTERNS

Non-beginners can do the same or merely spell out their present procedure on a copy of 12-4 and revise systematically (per 3-C or 3-D). Few of their Stroke Components will exactly fit any of the Catalog Variations but they can and should be adjusted to the nearest Catalog Variation most compatible with the rest of the proposed Basic Pattern. This Pattern need not be precise, but the Geometry (per Sketch 1-L), must be — which will incline the Pattern toward G.O.L.F. Those who know how precise it *can* be, know best how precise it *needs* to be.

In executing your Stroke Pattern, remember it is not Component location or position, but the alignments and relationships of their Motions and Actions that are central to this System and those who fail to squelch any compulsion to have it otherwise are, thereby, simply excluded because this System is based on Law and laws do not bend to fit intentions (9-0). You should not only be doing it "correctly" but also for the <u>right reasons</u> or its inconsistency will plague you endlessly. Garbage in—garbage out. Replace any inclination toward "Component Position and Location Feel" with "Component Alignment and Relationship Feel."

Finally, it is strongly recommended that, with or without an Authorized Instructor of The Golfing Machine, the first steps into this System be via the procedure set out in Chapter 12-5, regardless of your present level of play.

STROKE PATTERNS

12-1-0. DRIVE LOADING BASIC PATTERN (HITTING) This Pattern is based on Chapter 10-19-A in the Component Catalog and is most useful to the stronger players. Avoid "customizing" it with other Variations until it approaches the "expert" stage. Then follow 3-B.

No.	Component	Des.	Variations	Comments
1	Grip — Basic	A	Overlap	
2	Grip— Type	B	Strong Single	
3	Stro ke — Basic	A	Punch	
4	Stroke — Variation	C-1	Triple Barrel (1/2/3)	
5	Plane Line	A	Square-Square	
6	Plane Angle — Basic	B	Turned Shoulder	
7	Plane Angle — Variation	A	Zero	
8	Fix	A	Standard	
9	Address	A	Standard	
10	Hinge Action	C	Angled	
11	Pressure Point Combination	B-2	Double (1/3)	
12	Pivot	A	Standard	
13	Shoulder Turn	C	Rotated	
14	Hip Turn	B	Slide	
15	Hip Action	B	Delayed	
16	Knee Action	C	Right Anchor	
17	Foot Action	C	Flat Left	
18	Left Wrist Action	C-2	Single	
19	Lag Loading	A	Drive	
20	Trigger Type	B	Right Arm Throw	
21	Power Package Assembly Point	A	Top	
22	Power Package Loading Action	B	Random Sweep	
23	Power Package Delivery Path	A	Straight Line	
24	Power Package Release	B	Non-Auto Sweep	

STROKE PATTERNS

12-2-0 DRAG LOADING BASIC PATTERN (SWINGING) This Pattern is based on Chapter 10-19-C in the Component Catalog and is most useful to the more flexible players. Avoid "customizing" it with other Variations until it approaches the "expert" stage. Then follow 3-B.

No.	Component	Des.	Variations	Comments
1	Grip — Basic	A	Overlap	
2	Grip — Type	B	Strong Single	
3	Stroke — Basic	B	Pitch	
4	Stroke — Variation	C-4	Triple Barrel (2/3/4)	
5	Plane Line	A	Square-Square	
6	Plane Angle — Basic	B	Turned Shoulder	
7	Plane Angle — Variation	A	Zero	
8	Fix	A	Standard	
9	Address	A	Standard	
10	Hinge Action	D	Dual Horizontal	
11	Pressure Point Combination	C-4	Triple (2/3/4)	
12	Pivot	A	Standard	
13	Shoulder Turn	A	Standard	
14	Hip Turn	B	Slide	
15	Hip Action	B	Delayed	
16	Knee Action	C	Right Anchor	
17	Foot Action	C	Flat Left	
18	Left Wrist Action	A	Standard	
19	Lag Loading	C	Drag	
20	Trigger Type	E	Wrist Throw	
21	Power Package Assembly Point	C	End	
22	Power Package Loading Action	B	Random Sweep	
23	Power Package Delivery Path	C	Top Arc and Straight Line	
24	Power Package Release	E	Automatic Snap	

STROKE PATTERNS

12-3-0. MECHANICAL CHECKLIST FOR ALL STROKES This is a Section by Section (Chapter 8) checklist to improve the execution of the Stroke and reduce the Twelve Sections to a three station Total Motion (6-P-0). They are: A. The Address (8-3); B. The Top (8-6); C. The Finish (8-12). Be as prepared as possible before Start Up (3-F-5); as precise as possible through The Top (6-E); and, as smooth and complete as possible through Impact to the proper position at The Finish (2-N). (See 6-M-0.) To the degree that every step is improved, to that degree is the Total Motion improved. Note that no Zone #1 elements are listed — Educated Hands control The Pivot (9-1).

Specific Variations are not listed. Cross reference your Pattern and sequence the positions and actions of each listed item for each Section. Then Monitor them, per 5-0, toward mastery of the STAR SYSTEM TRIAD (Preface), per A, B and C above.

Section 1 — Preliminary Address
1. Stance — Balance
2. Ball Location

Section 2 — Impact Fix
3. Grip — Flying Wedges
4. Clubface Alignment
5. Approach Arc/Angle
6. Right Forearm Position
7. Clubshaft Alignments
8. Extensor Action

Section 3 — Adjusted Address
9. Practice Swing — Rhythm
10. Waggle — Alignments
11. Waggle — Pressure Points
12. Waggle — Hinge Action
13. Forward Press — Clear Right Hip

Section 4/5 — Backstroke
14. Extensor Action
15. Start Up — Line
16. Start Up — L/R Wrist Positions
17. Right Forearm Takeaway

Section 6 — The Top
18. Extensor Action — Waggle
19. Sweet Spot Loading — Lag
20. Delivery Line Prep
21. Delivery Line Uncocking Prep
22. DELIVERY LINE *ROLL* PREP
23. Right Forearm Position
24. Clear Right Hip

Section 7 — Start Down
25. Extensor Action — Rhythm
26. Aiming Point — Lag
27. Full Lever Assembly Prep
28. Left Wrist Position

Section 8—Downstroke
30. Aiming Point — Lag
31. Left Wrist Position
32. Delivery Line
33. Right Elbow Position
34. Rhythm

Section 9/10/11 — Impact
35. Right Elbow Position
36. Approach Arc/Angle — Lag
37. On Line Uncocking
38. On Line Release Swivel
39. ON LINE HINGE ACTION
40. Extensor Action

Section 12 — Finish
41. Finish Swivel
42. Left Wrist Alignment
43. Hand Location
44. Clubshaft Position
45. Balance — Body Position

STROKE PATTERNS

12-4. STROKE PATTERN FORM—FOR STUDENTS USE

No.	Component	Des.	Variations	Comments
1	Grip—Basic	...	....	
2	Grip—Type	...	....	
3	Stroke—Basic	...	....	
4	Stroke—Variation	...	....	
5	Plane Line	...	....	
6	Plane Angle—Basic	...	....	
7	Plane Angle—Variation	...	....	
8	Fix	...	....	
9	Address	...	....	
10	Hinge Action	...	....	
11	Pressure Point Combination	...	....	
12	Pivot	...	....	
13	Shoulder Turn	...	....	
14	Hip Turn	...	....	
15	Hip Action	...	....	
16	Knee Action	...	....	
17	Foot Action	...	....	
18	Wrist Action	...	....	
19	Lag Loading	...	....	
20	Trigger Type	...	....	
21	Power Package Assembly Point	...	....	
22	Power Package Loading Action	...	....	
23	Power Package Delivery Path	...	....	
24	Power Package Release	...	....	

STROKE PATTERNS

BASIC MOTION CURRICULUM
Non-Technical—Simplified

12-5-0. BASIC REQUIREMENTS Use a slow, smooth motion up-and-back, down-and-out and up-and-in the same distance in both directions and as continuously as possible. Your "Basic Motion" is a selected motion carefully maintaining the same characteristics of Angle, Pace, Rhythm and Posture to serve as your "Constant" on which Stroke Components can be hung without altering those characteristics for any unintentional cause (3-F-5-1).

1. Make no adjustment during the Stroke, for — or because of — Impact. *NEVER EVER.* That is "Hacking at the Ball" and produces only "Hackers"

2. Attach the items listed in the Three Stages, in sequence, without unnecessarily interrupting the Motion. Carefully develop the Address Routine (3-F-5)

3. Execute the items, single or in short series, first without a Ball and then with a Ball. Comply with 3-B, 5-0 and 12-3 — including the Triad

4. Observe the special instructions at the head of each Stage list

5. Where applicable, interpret the items per the basic Stroke Pattern, that is, Hitting or Swinging. Either 12-1 *OR* 12-2 — not both at the same time

6. The Strong Single Action Grip (10-2-B) is mandatory throughout

7. A lesson begins where the last one left off

8. Asterisks in list indicate items for an abbreviated version

9. The curriculum can stand alone for many students but may also serve as the curriculum for a Basic Certificate course. But most importantly, MUST be used in conjunction with all other G.O.L.F. curriculums

10. The information contained in the items in the two associated columns in Stage One, Two or Three may be presented "when and as" the instructor feels it to be the most effective

STROKE PATTERNS

STAGE ONE—SHORT IRON

12-5.1. BASIC MOTION About two feet in both directions. Zero out the Pivot, Shoulder Turn and Accumulator #3. This Stage concerns mainly the Basic Body <u>Positions</u> and the Basic Power Package Component <u>Alignments</u> and Arm Motion Power Accumulators.

NO.	COMPONENT	SKETCH 1-L	REFERENCE NO.
* 1.	Grip	1-L-3	10-2-B
2.	Stance Line	1-L-19	10-5-A
* 3.	Plane Line	1-L-16/18/19	10-5-A
4.	Foot Positions		10-17-B
* 5.	Foot Loading		7-17
* 6.	Knee Bend		10-16-C
* 7.	Waist Bend		9-1-1
* 8.	Stationary Head	1-L-1/2	3-F-7-C/D
* 9.	Left Arm Motion Accumulator #4	1-L-9	6-B-4
* 10.	Straight Left Arm	1-L-8	6-A-4
* 11.	Flat Left Wrist	1-L-8	4-D-1
* 12.	Right Elbow Bend Accumulator #1	1-L-7	6-B-1
13.	Right Forearm Position	1-L-10	7-3
* 14.	Pressure Point #2		6-C-1#2
* 15.	Pressure Point #3	1-L-7/12	6-C-1#3
* 16.	Right Forearm "Tracing"	1-L-10	5-O
17.	Right Forearm Fanning		10-3-A
* 18.	Extensor Action		6-B-1-D
* 19.	Pace		2-G
20.	Hand Motion — Hinging	1-L-4	4-D-0
* 21.	Rhythm		2-G
* 22.	"Closed Eyes" Hand Education		

Repeat Stage One with Putter and add Follow-through adjustment procedure, per 8-11.

* Items for an abbreviated version.

STROKE PATTERNS

STAGE TWO—SHORT IRON

12-5-2. ACQUIRED MOTION Motion not to exceed the level-to-the-ground position of Right Forearm; Zero to Minimal Pivot and add Accumulator #3 and any needed Shoulder Turn. This Stage introduces Body Motion and the Alignments and relations of the Hand Action Power Accumulators of the Power Package.

NO.	COMPONENT	SKETCH 1-L	REFERENCE NO.
* 1.	Weight Shift		10-14-A
2.	Flat Shoulder Turn		10-13-B
* 3.	Knee Action		10-16-C
* 4.	Foot Action		10-17-C
* 5.	Wristcock - #2 Accumulator		6-B-2
6.	Wrist Action		10-18-A/-C-2
* 7.	Wrist Roll - #3 Accumulator		6-B-3-0
8.	Clubface Manipulation		7-2
* 9.	On Plane Clubshaft	1-L-5	2-F
10.	Loading Action		7-19-1/-3
* 11.	Pressure Point #3		6-C-2
* 12.	Release		10-24-B
* 13.	Follow-through	1-L-13/-15	6-A-4
14.	Endless Belt Effect		2-K#6

STROKE PATTERNS

STAGE THREE—MIDDLE IRON

12-5-3. TOTAL MOTION This Stage should move slowly toward unrestricted motion but not to Full Power even with Long Irons and Woods. This stage is for the perfection of execution <u>prior</u> to Full Power.

NO.	COMPONENT	SKETCH 1-L	REFERENCE NO.
* 1.	Standard Pivot	1-L-2	9-1-1/-10/-12
* 2.	Finish		8-12
3.	Finish Swivel		4-D-0
4.	Delivery Path		10-23-A
* 5.	Delivery Line	1-L-6/-11	2-J-3
6.	Aiming Point		6-E-2
7.	Address Routine		3-F-5
8.	Adjusted TOP Position		8-6
9.	Trigger Delay		10-20-C
* 10.	Ball Location and Position		2-J-1/2-N
* 11.	Clubface Alignment	1-L-17	2-J-1
* 12.	Impact Fix		7-3
* 13.	Right Arm Takeaway		7-3
14.	Flying Wedges		6-B-3-0-1
15.	Centripetal Force		2-K#1, #2, #3
* 16.	Lag Loading		10-19-A/C
17.	Right Elbow Position		10-3-A

Repeat Stage Three using Long Irons and Woods.

CHAPTER THIRTEEN

NON-INTERCHANGEABLE COMPONENTS

13-0. Stroke Component Variations are not all 100% interchangeable with the rest of their category by their very definition. Some are interchangeable only in an awkward way — or within certain limits — or for certain special purposes.

Non-interchangeable Stroke Components must be eliminated. Incompatible components are faulty construction — mechanical improprieties, not legitimate variations.

For instance — Zero Hip Action is the Hip Action that is compatible with Zero Pivot. Again — Straight Line Power Package Delivery is not possible with the Shiftless Hip Turn. Again — Pull Stroke (Left Arm Swing) rules out the use of Radial Acceleration (10-19-A).

Personal preference should be considered, also. If Dual Hinge Action seems too complicated, use Angled Hinge Action and add the compensations which that requires — or put up with a Slice. This would label the Dual Hinge Action as incompatible with everything for that player.

CHAPTER FOURTEEN

THE COMPUTER

14-0. An invaluable ally is the Computer. This is a built-in analyzer that every one seems to have, though few are aware of it and even fewer use it and almost none of those use it consciously. It actually consists of two units: The Computer itself and the Incubator. In the latter, incomplete and underdeveloped concepts are stored AND PROCESSED — to a point where they can be at least partially programmed — missing elements are supplied through repeated review of the situation. It is a mysterious subconscious process that conscious thought only annoys. The egg always just lies there until the chick — not you — chips it open. So, never try to hurry the Incubator. When all is ready, the Computer will process it. Just remember to turn it over — in your mind — regularly.

It is a true computer. Information is fed into it which it will correlate and then adjust the mechanism to produce the intended result under the conditions at hand. Like any other computer — you'd better believe it. Or forget it. Don't try to second guess it; and don't change any condition without "reprogramming" the Computer. If you decide to Pitch instead of Chip, for instance, or change from a #3 iron to a #4 wood — reprogram the Computer.

"It" seems to work like this. The longer the experience of the player, the more information the Computer will have for comparisons as situations arise. "Post-mortems" of shots are good contributions to this library, too.

Then, when preparing for a shot, the programming is quite precise — in a loose sort of a way. That is — unless precision "surveying" in yards, mph, etc., is customary, there is no need to do so. Avoid programming negative orders. "It" will only "do." It just doesn't seem to have a "no-no" button.

The Computer's best use is, of course, for those less-than-full shot situations around the green. It is only necessary to scan the distance. Be sure there are no optical illusions involved — such as, elevated greens and hidden swales. That will take care of the distance if it is given full attention — a conscious effort to be fully "aware," even if only momentarily.

THE COMPUTER

The same procedure is followed in weighing every other factor — the wind, for instance; Its direction, force, steadiness — just a comparing sort of awareness. Omit no slightest factor: club number, uphill, downhill, heavy evening air, soggy grass, tilted green or fairway, new ball, how much hook or slice; just every little thing.

All this requires that the Computer control the entire mechanical operation. So, every Stroke Component must also be correctly programmed. If the Computer programming is neglected or erroneous — intentionally or unintentionally — it will make incorrect adjustments to mysteriously plague one's game. The longer an error continues, the stronger the Computer will push it.

It is much safer to isolate and program each element so the Computer can incorporate it correctly for each situation.

Computer Programmers must have, or develop, "visualization" to mentally SEE the causes and consequences of given action (1-L) and accurately translate those actions into a bodily equivalent (5-0). To teach (program), there must be accurate information available. But self-discipline is the catalyst for achievement. Set reachable goals and timetables and set to work.

Geometry and Physics must be clearly differentiated. "Alignments" (relationships) are Geometry. "Action" (energy) is Physics (Chapter 2). Together they constitute "Mechanics" — structurally "fixed" geometry and physics (1-L). "Feel" is the body's equivalent to structuring and its foundation is Educated Hands (5-0).

Geometry, being identical for every Pattern (1-L-20), is your Computer's basic program. All subsequent programming must agree with that basic. The Physics of Hitting or Swinging and their special Mechanics dictate the individual's basic TOTAL MOTION (12-1, 2 and 3). So the primary programming routine for your Computer must maintain the Feel of your basic procedure.

The second programming routine concerns the "positioning" of the Machine to the Ball (actually Ball location) to control direction under given conditions — wind, side hills, Hooks, Slices, etc.

The third routine is distance control data for Club selection — Lag Pressure, turf and wind conditions, etc.

THE COMPUTER

The fourth routine is the precise difference in "Feel" for selected Variations so they will not alter the basic geometry. That is — shift the Machine and adjust the Stroke alignments to the Target and establish the final pre-Stroke relationship of the Ball to the Target — both of which must be included and sustained from Adjusted Address to Follow-Through. That is being Target Conscious (3-B) without Downstroke Blackout of any portion of the whole. But don't forget — it's HANDS, HANDS, HANDS, that keep it all related and precise (5-0, 6-G).

The fifth routine is mental attitude — a button that wipes out of mind everything except the program — the non-emotional execution of a procedure. A complete and precise picture of what YOU will be doing — per 12-3. "Pressing the Button" is a complete shift from Ball Action to Hand Action. Don't move the Club until you are thoroughly conscious of yourself standing over the Ball with "All Systems Go." Shifting back from the "You Program" to the "Ball Program" during the Stroke is extremely hazardous for the learner. But finally may come the time when the intended Ball behavior could be all the conscious programming you'll need to do, and still produce the required Ball Behavior. So this is a point for relating the Alignments to the Target — Target Conscious execution of the selected procedure (3-F-5).

The completely scientific approach would require it to be recognized that the ball also is a computer. In four ten-thousandths of a second it can receive, analyze and respond to the impulses it is handed during Impact. Then obviously, Impact is the programming of the Ball-Computer. The false notion that impact is so fleeting that its programming is just unavoidably haphazard, encourages the wild flipping of Clubheads that passes for golf technique. So — as usual, a computer blindly complies with its programming and can be no more precise than its programming. In other words — "Precision in — Precision out."

Identically, "Garbage in—Garbage out." This book can only show you how good your game *can* be. How good it *has* to be is entirely up to you. And censure is unwarranted. However, penalties for non-compliance are built in and inescapable — impersonally revealing but comfortingly diagnostic. Remember — the time to hurry is between Shots.

CHAPTER FIFTEEN

GLOSSARY

15-0. Use this Glossary to understand that the mechanical application of a term is identical to its parallel golfing application and to see that there are no "Golf Laws" per se, but that both Golf and Mechanics operate under the same identical set of Principles and Laws. There is *ONLY* one set. Subject your every uncertainty to drawing its mechanical parallel — The Golfing Machine is a true machine and must be treated like one to act like one. The "Examples" selected are seldom total parallels but a parallel is there.

ACCELERATION *Example — toboggan ride.*
    Mechanical — A change in the product of Mass times Velocity.
    Golf — The Pressure Points increasing the Hand Speed or resisting Clubhead Deceleration.

ADDRESS ROUTINE *Example — starting a car.*
    Mechanical — Machine Set-Up. Adjusting and positioning a machine to take a selected series of actions for a desired end result or product.
    Golf — The *process* of establishing Component Alignments and Relationships as required for a selected Ball Response.

AIMING POINT *Example — bullseye.*
    Mechanical — A point at which Thrust is directed.
    Golf — A simulated or compensating change in Ball Location to offset Travel Time characteristics of different Clubshaft lengths.

ANGULAR FORCE *Example — wrecking ball.*
    Mechanical — The Kinetic Energy of Angular Momentum.
    Golf — The Kinetic Energy of the orbiting Clubhead.

ANGULAR MOTION *Example — merry-go-round.*
    Mechanical — An object rotating around an axis.
    Golf — The Clubhead RPM as differentiated from MPH.

ARC AND ANGLE OF APPROACH *Example — Suez Canal (go around or across).*
    Mechanical — The circumference of a circle passing through any two points — or the straight line chord drawn through the same two points as viewed vertically to a plane surface.
    Golf — The curved visual path of the orbiting Clubhead, visible on the ground, through Impact Point and Low Point — or the straight line drawn through the same two points.

ANGLE OF ATTACK *Example — lawn mower handle.*
    Mechanical — The relationship of the direction of thrust to an associated surface.
    Golf — The angle of the Inclined Plane as related to the playing surface.

GLOSSARY

ASSOCIATED PLANES *Example — floor and door.*
    Mechanical — The axis of a rotating motion must be mounted vertical to one of three possible planes — Horizontal, Perpendicular or Angled.
    Golf — The Flat Left Wrist must move vertical to one of three possible planes — Horizontal, Perpendicular, or Angled — and its motion takes the name of that Plane with which it is so associated.

AXE HANDLE/ROPE HANDLE *Example — power shovel vs. drag line.*
    Mechanical — Thrust against an Axe Handle can produce a centered motion. Against a Rope Handle it cannot.
    Golf — The continuous thrust against the Clubshaft moves the Clubhead radially. (The Axe Handle procedure.) The initial Thrust accelerating the Clubshaft longitudinally is the Rope Handle procedure.

AXIS TILT *Example — pouring tea.*
    Mechanical — To change direction, the helicopter Pilot alters the plane of the rotating blades by tilting their axis in the new direction.
    Golf — To change the plane of the Shoulder Turn without moving the Head, the golfer must tilt the Shoulder Axis by moving the Hips.

BACKSPIN *Example — a flying Frisbee.*
    Mechanical — A non-rolling rotation of a moving object.
    Golf — The non-rolling rotation of the Golf Ball produced by striking it below the horizontal centerline.

BALANCE *Example — a hula dancer.*
    Mechanical — State in which all opposing forces cancel each other out.
    Golf — Holding the center of gravity of the body inside The Stance without moving the Head.

BASIC MOTION *Example — driving tacks or spikes.*
    Mechanical — An effective, efficient repetitious motion always incorporating the same selected factors for the same purpose with the same results.
    Golf — An On Plane Lever Assembly Arc of equal length in both directions, incorporating Components always selected from the same list of options.

CENTRIPETAL FORCE *Example — whirling weight on a string.*
    Mechanical — The resistance of the Inertia in an orbiting object to change in direction.
    Golf — The effort of the Swinging Clubhead to pull the Primary Lever Assembly (Left Arm and Club) into a straight line.

CHECKREIN ACTION *Example — a leash.*
    Mechanical — A linear restraint limiting the possible distance between two moveable objects.
    Golf — Forcing the Right Elbow to bend by pulling in the Right Hand to an arms length from the Left Shoulder at all times.

GLOSSARY

CLUBHEAD LAG *Example — throwing rocks or feathers.*
  Mechanical — The stress occurring at the Point of Thrust by the resistance of Inertia to change.
  Golf — The information transmitted through the #3 Pressure Point by the resistance of the Clubhead to change.

CLUBHEAD THROWAWAY *Example — the sickle.*
  Mechanical — Allowing the Swingle of a Flail to pass its In-Line relationship to the Handle.
  Golf — Allowing the Clubhead to pass the Hands during Release, and set up a Centripetal Deceleration condition.

COEFFICIENT OF RESTITUTION *Example — splashing water.*
  Mechanical — The force of the return flow of a material after deformation.
  Golf — The speed with which the Ball will separate from the Clubface after Impact in relation to Clubhead Approach Speed.

CONCENTRATION *Example — the punch press.*
  Mechanical — The application of Force to a relatively small area.
  Golf — Keeping the attention focused alertly on alignments and relationships by monitoring the messages from the #3 Pressure Point.

ENDLESS BELT EFFECT *Example — moving targets at a shooting gallery.*
  Mechanical — The change between linear motion between pulleys to angular motion during the pulley encounter.
  Golf — The increase in clubhead speed of a Club as it moves from a Line Delivery Path into the Release Arc.

FLAT AND VERTICAL LEFT WRIST *Example — left hand karate chop.*
  Mechanical — The Paddlewheel blade relationships as vertical to its axis of rotation (crosswise) and vertical to its plane of rotation (lengthwise).
  Golf — Positioning the Left Wrist to be vertical to its Left Shoulder Axis and to its Associated Plane during Impact as though moving on Planes always at right angles to each other.

FLYING WEDGES *Example — multiple sails on sail boats.*
  Mechanical — Push-Pull rams on hydraulic excavators mounted 90 degrees to each other in position and hold the main beam.
  Golf — Maintaining the constant simultaneous In-Line relationship of the Clubshaft with the Left Arm and the Right Forearm positioned 90 degrees to each other along the Line of the Left Wristcock and the line of the Right Wrist Bend as though moving on planes always at right angles to each other.

GYROSCOPIC ACTION *Example — whirling weight on a string.*
  Mechanical — A spinning flywheel resists any effort to change its plane of rotation.
  Golf — A golf club swinging either On Plane or Off Plane, resists any attempt to change its Plane.

HINGE ACTION *Example — all types of swinging doors.*
  Mechanical — The blade of a hinge is always vertical to its Plane of Rotation.
  Golf — Holding the Flat Left Wrist vertical to one of the Three Basic Planes will impart that same *motion* to the Clubface.

GLOSSARY

HITTING AND SWINGING *Example — the catapult vs. the sling.*
    Mechanical — Continuous thrust producing steady acceleration of a hinged beam is a Hitting action. A rotating arm pulling steadily on a weighted line is a swinging action.
    Golf — Accelerating the Club radially with Right Arm Thrust is Hitting. Accelerating the Club longitudinally, with either Arm, is Swinging.

IMPACT *Example — bowling ball and "tenpins."*
    Mechanical — Objects meeting in collision.
    Golf — The meeting of Ball and Club.

IMPACT INTERVAL *Example — from billiards to bean bags.*
    Mechanical — The period during which colliding objects are in contact.
    Golf —The period between Impact and Separation of the Ball and Clubface.

IMPACT POINT *Example — darts on a dart board.*
    Mechanical — The *point* of first contact in a collision.
    Golf — The point on the Ball first contacted by the Clubface.

INCLINED PLANE *Example — a pitched roof.*
    Mechanical — A flat surface of any extent positioned somewhere between horizontal and vertical.
    Golf — The through-the-waist "Plane of Rotation" of the Clubshaft as established during Address Routine.

LAW *Example — burning fuel (piston engine vs. jet engine).*
    Mechanical — The Modus Operandi of a principle.
    Golf — The precision synchronization of interacting forces to control Ball behavior.

LEVER ASSEMBLIES *Example — nutcracker / vise grip pliers.*
    Mechanical — Any arrangement of two or more levers.
    Golf — An adjustable Radius for generating Kinetic Energy during the Downstroke.

LINE OF COMPRESSION *Example — bullet hole through a baseball.*
    Mechanical — The line through the center of that area from which material flows when displaced by a compressing force.
    Golf — The direction of the Impact Force, as related to the various centerlines, for determining Ball Behavior.

MOMENTUM TRANSFER *Example — the hammer thrower.*
    Mechanical — An appendage acquiring motion by reason of being attached to a large, central rotating body.
    Golf — The rotating Body (Pivot) accelerating and sustaining the Lever Assembly motion by the Throw-Out Action of Centripetal Force and reducing the effect of Conservation of Angular Momentum in proportion to the difference in Club and Body Mass.

PACE *Example — walking vs. running.*
    Mechanical — The miles per hour (MPH) of a moving body.
    Golf — The surface speed of the orbiting Clubhead as differentiated from Rhythm.

GLOSSARY

PIVOT *Example — revolving door.*
    Mechanical — That motion of a body moving around a center point.
    Golf — A multiple universal-joint assembly between the Stationary Head and the Stationary Feet. One of three sources of Rotation supplying the basic Hinge Motions.

PIVOT CENTER *Example — tetherball pole.*
    Mechanical — The point on which an assembly is suspended or erected to stabilize and limit that assembly's possible travel — the Hinge Pin.
    Golf — Some point on the body kept stationary throughout the Stroke, to stabilize the motion.

PLANE LINE *Example — eavetrough.*
    Mechanical — A line inscribed on a flat surface to be considered its Base Line and the line along which that Plane is to be rotated when changing its angle.
    Golf — A line inscribed on the surface of the Inclined Plane passing through the Ball location to serve as its Base Line and its center of rotation when changing its angle.

POTENTIAL AND KINETIC ENERGY *Example — the drop-hammer.*
    Mechanical — Potential Energy is the energy of position. Kinetic Energy is the Energy of motion.
    Golf — Loaded Accumulators are Potential Energy — the Orbiting Clubhead is Kinetic Energy.

POWER ACCUMULATION *Example — stretching a slingshot.*
    Mechanical — The process of assuming or acquiring a condition of Potential Energy.
    Golf — The process of Loading Power Accumulators during their Out-of-Line Configuration.

RESULTANT FORCE *Example — skipping rocks over water.*
    Mechanical — The single-direction Force equal to the multi-directional Forces being applied to an object but with less than the sum of the Forces.
    Golf — Regardless of the Vector Directions of unaligned Impact forces, the Ball moves in one direction with a Force less than the sum of the Forces.

RHYTHM *Example — crankshaft and connecting rods.*
    Mechanical — Holding all components of a rotating motion to the same RPM.
    Golf — Holding both Lever Assemblies to the same basic RPM throughout the Stroke while overtaking all other Components at a steady, even rate.

RIGHT FOREARM *Example — drawing a line between two points.*
    Mechanical — Any means by which a track can be provided to guide a moving object.
    Golf — The Right Forearm "Tracing" the Clubhead Delivery Line with the #3 Pressure Point.

STATIONARY HEAD *Example — a spinning skater.*
    Mechanical — Same as Pivot Center.
    Golf — Choosing the Head — rather then Between-the-Shoulders, as the Pivot Center.

GLOSSARY

STEERING *Example — guiding a rolling hoop along a curved path.*
    Mechanical — Forcing a Hinge Pin to give a straight line motion to its attachments.
    Golf — Holding the Clubhead Path and the Clubface, square with the Target during Release and/or Impact.

STROKE PATTERN *Example — a recipe.*
    Mechanical — Selection of possible materials or sequence for executing a procedure.
    Golf — The list of Stroke component Actions which can be properly executed in more than one way.

SWEET SPOT *Example — a plumb bob.*
    Mechanical — The longitudinal Center of Gravity of a length of material.
    Golf — That line on the Clubface through which a plumb-bob line would pass if both were suspended from the Grip area.

THREE BASIC PLANES *Example — floors, walls and pitched roofs.*
    Mechanical — Flat surfaces positioned horizontally, vertically or somewhere in between.
    Golf — The Three possible *Planes of Motion* which the Flat Left Wrist must simulate to give the Clubface a preselected *Motion* through Impact.

THROW-OUT ACTION *Example — leaning through a turn.*
    Mechanical — The action of Centripetal Force on a Rotating Body.
    Golf — The Law of the Flail producing or reducing Clubhead Power according to its In-Line relationship with the Left Arm.

WRISTCOCK *Example — fly casting fisherman.*
    Mechanical — The Flail producing Swingle velocity through a Hinge arrangement with the Handle.
    Golf — Shortening and lengthening the Primary Lever Assembly to reduce Clubhead Angular Inertia and to produce a rapid *rate* of increase of the Clubhead Surface Speed through Lever Assembly Extension.

CHAPTER SIXTEEN

INDEX

16-0. GENERAL This section is included to aid the cross-referencing of factors under consideration by locating the basic texts from which cross-referencing can proceed. If a subject does not appear under the expected title, try similar titles.

Subjects are located according to their chapter, sub-chapter, section and sub-section instead of by page number because this will most often cover and/or pinpoint the item better.

Subjects have identifying designations that have from one to five digits, using both numbers and letters. And these digits are always in alpha-numerical order—that is the numbers containing these digits follow each other according to normal numerical order of the numbers and according to normal alphabetical order of the letters.

All designations start with a number—the number of a chapter. The other designations may be either numbers or letters but not necessarily alternating. But any grouping will be consistent throughout any selected chapter.

Zeros ("0") appear only in the first or only appearance of a designation combination.

EXAMPLES

Subject	Reference Number	Interpretation
Power Package	6	All of Chapter 6
Power Accumulators	7-4	Sub-chapter "4" only (of Chapter 7)
Machine Concept	3-F-7	Section "7" only (of Sub-Chapter "F") which includes "3-7-0" to "3-F-E"
Extensor Action	6-B-1-D	Sub-section "D" only (of Section 1)

INDEX

Acceleration 1-D, 1-F, 2-C-0, 2-D, 2-E, 2-H, 2-K, 2-M-1, 2-M-2, 2-M-4, 2-P, 6-B-1-0, 6-B-1-D, 6-B-4, 6-C-0, 6-C-2-0, 6-C-2-A, 6-C-2-B, 6-C-2-D, 6-D-2, 6-F-1, 6-H-0-E #7, 6-H-0-F#7, 7-19, 8-7, 8-8, 8-9, 8-10, 10-1-B, 10-2-D, 10-19-A, 10-19-B, 10-19-C, 10-20-C, 10-23-C, 11-19-B, 11-19-C, 13-0, 15-0

Acceleration areas of: 8-7, 8-8, 8-9, 8-10

Accumulator Lag 6-C-0

Accumulators 3-F-5, 4-D-0, 6-0, 6-A-2, 6-A-3, 6-B-0, 6-B-4, 6-C-0, 6-C-2-A, 6-M-0, 6-M-1, 7-4, 7-11, 7-20, 7-22, 7-24, 10-14-A, 10-4-B, 10-14-C, 10-14-D, 10-11-0, 10-11-0-3, 10-24-A, 11-4-A,B,C,D; 12-0, 12-5-1, 12-5-2

Address 2-D-0, 2-D-1, 2-J-3, 3-B, 3-F-5, 6-B-2-0, 6-C-2-E,7-0, 7-2,7-6,7-8, 7-9, 7-10, 7-16, 7-17, 8-0, 8-1,, 3; 9-1, 9-2, 10-0, 10-6-C, 10-6-D-B, 10-8-0, 10-8-C, 10-9, 10-14-D, 10-16-D, 11-0 #9, 11-8-C, 11-9, 11-16, 11-22, 12-3-0, 12-5-0, 12-5-3, 14

Address Preliminary 8-0, 8-1, 9-1

Aiming Point 6-C-2-A, 6-E-2, 6-N-0, 6-R-0, 7-23, 10-3-B, 10-20-D, 10-23-A, 10-24-C, 10-24-E, 10-24-F, 11-23-B, 11-23-D, 12-3-0#26, Glossary

Alignments 1-C, 1-F, 1-L#20, 2-C-1, 2-E, 2-G, 2-J-1, 2-M-3, 3-C, 3-F-5, 3-F-7-E, 5-0, 6-D-0, 7-1, 7-5, 7-7, 7-8, 7-21, 9-1, 9-2, 10-2-0, 10-13-D, 10-19-B, 10-24-F, 12-0, 12-3-0, 12-5-2, 14

Angle of Approach 2-D-1, 2-H, 2-J-3, 2-N-0, 3-F-5, 3-F-7-E, 6-C-2-A, 6-E-2, 6-H-0-E#10, 7-2, 7-3, 7-12, 7-23, 8-4, 10-5-0, 10-24-0

Angle of Approach Procedure 2-H, 2-J-3

Angle of Attack 2-N-0, 6-B-2-0, 7-3, 10-6-A

Angular Force 2-L, Glossary

Application of Force 2-L

Approach Speed 2-E, 2-C-2-0

Approaching the Game 1-F

Arc of Approach 2-H, 2-J-3, 5-0, 6-H-0-F#10, 7-3, 7-15, 10-23-E

Arms 2-G, 2-K, 6-0, 6-A-2, 6-A-4, 6-B-0, 6-B-1-D, 6-B-2-0, 6-C-2-A, 6-H-0-C, 6-M-1, 7-10, 7-12, 7-13, 7-18, 8-11, 8-12, 9-0, 9-1, 9-2, 10-3-G, 10-3-H, 10-6-D-A, 10-23-E

Associated Plane 6-B-3-0, 6-H-0#8, 7-10

Attention Span 3-B

Axe Handle 2-K, 6-F-0, 10-3-K, 10-11-0, 10-19-A

Axis Tilt 2-N-0, 2-N-1, 7-13, 7-23, 10-13-C, 10-23-E

Balance (Essential) 1-L, 2-0, 2-C-0, 2-N-0, 2-N-1, 3-F-5, 3-F-7-D, 6-B-0, 6-C-2-D, 7-12, 9-0, 9-1. 12-3-0#1, 12-3-0#45

Ball Acceleration 8-10

Ball Control Foreword 2-B, 3-F-5, 6-B-1-D, 9-0#3, 9-3

Ball Location 2-C-3, 2-D-1#15, 2-G, 2-J-1, 2-J-3, 2-N-0, 3-F-6, 6-C-2-A, 6-E-2, 6-E-2#3, 7-2, 7-6, 7-10, 10-10-C, 10-24-F, 14

Ball Position 2-C-4-A, 2-J, 2-N, 6-B-3-0, 6-E-2, 7-3, 7-6, 7-7, 10-13-E

Basic Components 1-K, 7-0, 9-0, 9-1, 9-2, 9-3, 11-A

Basic Motion *Preface*, 3-0, 3-F-5, 3-F-7-B, 9-0, 12-0, 12-5, 12-5-1

Basic Planes 2-G, 7-2, 7-6, 7-10, 10-0, 10-2-0, 10-6-0, 10-6-D, 10-7-0, 10-10-B, 11-6

Basic Strokes *Preface* 6-B-4-C, 6-C-2-A, 7-0, 7-3, 7-4, 7-10, 9-2#3, 10-0, 10-2-0, 10-3-0, 10-3-K, 10-6-E, 10-9-D, 10-14-C, 11-A, 12-, 12-5-0#5

Basics 1-J, 1-K, 7-0

Bent Plane Line 2-D-1#6, 3-F-7-B

Body Control 9-0, 10-12-0, 11-A

Body Power 2-M -4, 6-B-4-0, 6-C-0

Brevity 1-H

Capitalization 1-H

Catalog XV, 1-K, 1-L, 10, 11

Centers 2-D-0, 2-H, 2-K, 6-M-1

Center of Gravity 2-F

Centrifugal Reaction 2-M-2, 2-N-1, 6-B-1-D, 6-B-3-0, 6-F-1, 7-2, 7-12, 10-18-B, 10-19-0,C, 10-24-F

Centripetal Force *Preface*, 2-E, 2-F, 2-K, 2-L, 2-M-2, 2-P, 6-B-2-0, 6-B-4-0. 6-C-0, 6-E-2, 6-F-0, 6-M-0, 7-1, 7-10, 10-2-G, 10-11-0, 10-18-B, 10-19-C, 12-5-3#13

Checkrein Action 2-M-3, 6-B-1-0, 6-B-4-0, 10-3-K

Circle 1-L#9, 2-D-0, 2-H, 2-J-2, 2-K, 2-N-0, 4-D-1, 6-E-2, 6-J-0, 7-23, 10-1-0, 10-14-A, 10-23-E. 11-23-E

Clear the Right Hip 2-H, 5-0, 7-13, 7-14

Closed Eye 3-B, 12-5-1#22

Club Control 9-0, 11-A

Clubface Alignment 1-L#4, 1-L#16, 2-G, 2-J-1, 3-F-7-A, 4-D-0, 6-R-0, 7-2, 7-8, 7-10. 7-19, 10-5-0, 10-18-B, 12-5-3#11

INDEX

Clubface Control 1-F, 2-G, 6-E-2, 6-F-1, 9-2
Clubhead Acceleration 2-M-2, 6-C-2-0, 8-9, 10-1-B
Clubhead Control 2-N-0, 3-F-7-B, 6-F-1, 9-2, 10-11-0
Clubhead Lag 2-0-B#2, 2-K, 2-N-1, 3-F-6, 4-0, 4-A-3, 5-0, 6-0, 6-B-0, 6-B-1-D, 6-C-0, 6-C-2-0, 6-C-2-A, 6-C-2-B, 6-C-2-C, 6-C-2-D, 6-C-2-E, 6-E-2, 6-F-0, 6-G-0, 7-11, 7-19, 7-22, 10-1-0, 10-2-0, 10-11-0, 10-19-0, 10-19-A
Clubhead Orbit 2-C-3, 2-J-2, 4-D-1, 7-13
Clubhead Path 2-C-1#2B, 2-J-2, 2-J-3, 3-F-5, 3-F-7-B, 3-F-7-E, 8-4
Clubhead Speed 1-L#12, 2-D-1#17, 2-E, 2-K, 2-M-2, 6-B-0, 6-C-2-B, 6-P-0, 7-23
Clubhead Throwaway 2-G, 2-K, 4-D-0, 4-D-1, 5-0, 6-B-1-D, 6-C-2-D, 6-D-0, 6-G-0, 7-19, 10-6-D, 10-19-A, 10-19-B. 10-19-C
Clubshaft Control 1-L, 10-6-0
Clubshaft Flex 6-C-2-A, 6-C-2-D
Clubshaft Plane 2-F
Coefficient of Restitution 2-E
Chronic Fades 7-10
Component Translation 3-0
Compression 2-0, 2-A, 2-B, 2-C-0, 2-C-1, 2-C-2, 2-C-3, 2-E, 2-H, 2-J-2, 3-F-7-B, 6-B-1-D, 6-B-3-0, 6-C-2-0, 6-F-1
Compression Leakage 2-B, 2-C-0, 2-E, 2-H, 6-B-1-D, 6-B-3-0
Compression Point 2-C-1, 2-H,
Computer 3-0, 3-B, 3-E, 3-F-7-A, 3-F-7-E, 5-0, 9-3, 14
Concentration 3-B, 6-M-0, 6-R-0,
Conservation of Angular Momentum 6-C-2-B, 6-E-2
Control 1-F, 1-H, 1-J, 1-L, 1-L#4, 1-L#16, 2-B, 2-D-0, 2-G, 2-H, 2-L, 2-M-3, 2-N-0, 3-F-5, 3-F-7-A, 3-F-7-B, 4-0, 5-0, 6-B-1-D, 6-B-2-A, 6-B-3-0, 6-C-0, 6-C-2-A, 6-E-1, 6-E-2, 6-F-1, 6-F-2, 6-G-0, 6-P-0, 6-R-0, 7-2, 7-3, 7-6, 7-7, 7-9, 7-10, 7-13, 7-14, 7-19, 7-21, 7-23, 9-0, 9-1, 9-2, 9-3, 10-1-C, 10-4-A, 10-4-D, 10-6, 10-10, 10-11-0, 10-12, 10-14-A, 10-14-C, 10-18, 10-21, 10-24-E, 10-24-F, 11-A, 12-0, 12-3-0, 14,
Cross Line 2-J-3, 4-D-0, 7-3, 7-23, 10-23-C
Cross Reference 2-R, 12-3-0,
Cut Shot 2-C-2, 2-C-2#2, 2-C-2#3, 2-C-3, 2-J-1, 2-J-3, 3-F-7-A, 10-2-D, 10-18-E, 11-18-E

Deceleration 1-F, 2-E, 2-K, 2-L, 2-M-1
Delivery 2-F, 4-D, 2-M-3, 6-E, 6-0, 6-B-2-A, 6-E-0, 6-E-1, 6-E-2, 6-J-0, 6-K-0, 6-L-0, 7-11, 7-20, 7-21, 7-23, 9-1, 10-13-D, 13-0
Delivery Lines 2-F, 2-H, 2-J-3, 2-N-0, 3-F-5, 3-F-6, 4-D-0, 5-0, 6-C-2-A, 6-E-2, 6-H-0-A, 7-3, 7-11, 7-12, 7-14, 7-23, 8-7, 8-8, 9-2, 10-11-0-3, 10-19-0, 10-20-D, 10-23-E, 12-3-0#20,21,22,32; 12-5-3#5
Delivery Paths 2-J-3, 2-K, 2-N-0, 5-0, 6-E-2, 6-J-0, 7-0#23, 7-11, 7-12, 7-23, 8-7, 9-3#23, 10-14-A, 10-19-C, 10-20-D, 10-20-E, 10-21-0, 10-23, 11-0#23, 11-20-D, 11-23, 12-5-3#4
Directional Factors 2-D-0, 2-D-1
Divots 2-D-0, 2-N-0, 3-F-7-B#3, 7-6
Down-and-Out 1-L#13,14, 2-J-2, 3-0, 3-F-7-B, 12-5-0
Down Plane 1-L#15, 3-F-7-E, 10-19-C,
Downstroke 1-F, 2-C-0, 2-F, 2-J-2, 2-M-3, 2-N-0, 4-0, 4-D-1, 6-B-1-D, 6-B-2-B, 6-B-4-0, 6-E-2, 6-N-0, 7-13, 7-17, 7-18, 7-23, 8-7, 8-8, 10-7-0, 10-7-B, 10-7-D, 10-7-E, 10-7-H, 10-13-D, 10-15-C, 10-18-0, 10-18-F, 10-19-0, 10-19-B, 10-21-AtoE, 11-13-B, 11-19-B, 11-20-D&E, 12-3-0-Section 8
Downstroke Blackout 3-F-5, 14
Downstroke Loading 9-2, 10-19-B
Downstroke Path 10-21-D&E, 10-23-AtoE
Downstroke Sequence 6-M-0, 6-M-1, 10-19-C
Downstroke Shoulder Lag 7-13
Downstroke Shoulder Turn 6-B-4-C, 7-14, 10-13-A, 10-13-B, 10-15-B
Downstroke Slide 7-16
Downstroke Thrust 6-C-0
Downstroke Turn 7-12, 10-13-C
Downstroke Waggle 7-20
Draws 7-10

Educated Hands 1-G, 3-B, 4-0, 6-E-1, 6-G-0, 6-H-0, 9-0, 10-2-0, 10-20-A, 12-3-0, 14
Elbow Position 2-N-0, 10-3-AtoC, 12-3-0#33&35, 12-5-3#17
Endless Belt Effect 2-K, 2-P, 7-18, 7-23, 12-5-2#14, Glossary
Execution 1-G, 1-K, 2-D-1, 2-N-0, 3-A, 3-B, 3-F-6, 3-F-7-E, 4-D-0, 6-B-1-D, 7-3, 8-0, 9-1, 9-2, 9-3, 10-1-B, 10-3-K, 10-19-0, 10-24-F, 12-3-0, 12-5-3, 14
Engineering 1-J, 2-L, 10-8,
Extensor Action 2-J-1, 2-M-3, 3-F-6, 6-B-1-0, 6-B-1-D, 6-C-0#2, 7-19, 10-9-C, 10-19-0, 12-3-0#8#14#18#25#40, 12-5-1#18

243

INDEX

Eyes 3-B, 3-F-7-E, 5-0, 12-5-1#22

Fades 7-10
Fanning 10-3-A, 12-5-1#17
Feel *Preface*, 1-J, 1-L, 2-E, 2-F, 2-G, 2-M-4, 2-N-0, 3-0, 3-B, 3-E, 3-F-4, 3-F-5, 5-0, 6-B-3-0, 6-D-0, 6-D-3, 6-E-2, 6-P-0, 7-8, 7-10, 7-14, 7-16, 7-19, 7-20, 7-21, 10-2-0, 10-2-C, 10-2-G, 10-6-D, 10-10-C, 10-11-0-3, 10-19-0, 10-24-F, 12-0, 12-5-0, 14
Finish 1-F, 2-G, 2-M-3, 2-N-0, 4-D-0, 6-M-0, 8-12, 9-3-12, 10-3-F#2, 10-7-D, 10-14-A#2, 10-14-B#2, 10-14-C#2, 10-14-D#2, 10-14-E#2, 1016-A, 10-16-A#2, 10-16-B#2, 10-16-C#2, 10-16-D#2, 10-16-E#2, 10-17-0-C, 10-17-A#3, 10-17-B#2, 10-17-C#2, 10-17-D#2, 10-17-E#2, 11-16, 11-17
Fix 2-D-0, 2-G, 2-J-1, 2-N-0, 3-F-5, 3-F-7-E, 4-D-1, 6-B-1-D, 6-B-2-0, 6-B-3-0, 6-E-2, 6-H-0#6, 6-K-0, 7-0#8, 7-2, 7-3, 7-6, 7-8, 7-9, 7-10, 7-11, 7-16, 7-19, 8-0, 8-2, 9-2#8, 9-3, 10-0, 10-2-0, 10-2-D, 10-3-K, 10-6-0, 10-8, 10-9-B, 10-9-D, 10-10-B, 10-14-D, 10-14-E, 10-18-C, 11-0#8, 11-9-AtoD, 12-3-0 section 2, 12-5-3#12, 14
Flail 2-K, 4-D-1, 7-19, 10-6-D, 10-19-0
Flat Left Wnst 2-0, 2-C-0, 2-G, 2-K, 2-P, 4-D-1, 6-B-1-D, 6-B-3-0-1, 6-E-2, 6-G-0, 7-2#3, 7-4, 7-10, 7-20, 9-2, 10-1-E, 10-10-A, 10-10-C, 10-19-0, 12-5-1#11
Flight Line 1-L#19, 3-F-7-A, 4-0, 6-E-2, 7-11
Flying Wedges 3-F-6, 6-B-3-0-1, 7-1, 7-20, 10-18-B, 12-3-0#3, 12-5-3#14,
Follow Through 1-L#15, 2-F, 2-J-3, 2-P, 6-A-1#3, 6-A-4, 6-B-1-0#3, 6-B-1-D, 6-B-4-0#2, 6-D-0, 6-M-0, 7-10, 7-20, 7-24, 8-11, 8-12, 9-3-11, 10-2-0, 10-3-J, 10-9-D, 10-10-D, 10-10-E, 10-12-B, 10-12-C, 10-13-C#3, 10-13-D#3, 10-13-E#2, 10-16-B, 10-16-C, 11-3-J, 11-12-B, 12-5-1, 14
Foot Action 1-J, 7-0#17, 7-17, 9-1#17, 10-0, 10-14-E, 10-16-E, 10-17, 11-0-A#17, 11-17, 12-1-0#17
Force 1-A, 1-D, 1-G, 1-J, 1-L, 1-L#10, 1-L#11, 2-0, 2-A, 2-B, 2-C-0, 2-C-1, 2-C-2, 2-C-3, 2-D-0, 2-E, 2-F, 2-K, 2-L, 2-M-1, 2-N-1, 2-P, 5-0, 6-A-2, 6-B-0, 6-B-1-0, 6-B-1-D, 6-B-2-0, 6-B-3-0, 6-B-4-0, 6-C-0, 6-C-1, 6-D-3, 6-F-0, 6-F-1, 6-M-1, 7-1, 7-2, 7-10, 7-12, 7-20, 7-21, 9-0, 9-2, 10-2-G, 10-4-B, 10-6-D, 10-11-0, 10-18-B, 10-19-0, 10-19-C, 10-24-F, 12-5-3#15, 14

Forward Press 3-F-5#3, 8-3, 10-2-0, 11-8, 12-3-0#13
Forward Lean 3-F-7-E
Fulcrum 2-N-1, 6-A-2, 6-A-3, 10-3-J
Full Extension 2-C-0, 2-D-0, 2-K, 2-P, 6-B-1-D, 6-B-2-0, 6-F-1, 7-18

G.O.L.F. 1-G, 2-0, 7-10, 12-0
Gear Train 6-C-0
Geometric Equivalent 2-J-3, 4-D-1
Geometry *Preface*, 1-A, 1-C, 1-G, 2-0, 2-H, 2-J-1, 2-K, 2-N-0, 2-N-1, 3-B, 3-F-6, 4-D-1, 5-0, 6-E-1, 10-13-E, 12-0, 14
Grips 6-C-2-E, 7-0#1, 7-1, 7-10, 9-2#1, 10-0, 10-1, 10-2, 11-0-#2, 11-1, 11-2
Gyroscopic 1-L, 2-N-1-C, 4-D-1

Hacker 2-F, 7-8, 12-5-0
Hand Acceleration 1-F, 8-8
Hand Action 3-F-5, 12-5-2, 14
Hand Controlled Pivot 5-0, 10-24-F
Hand Education 12-5-1#22
Hand Motion 4-D-0, 6-B-3-0, 6-G-0, 7-10, 7-18, 7-20, 10-2-C, 12-5-1#20
Hand Positions 4-D-0, 7-18, 10-1-E, 10-23-A, 10-23-B, 11-0-1, 11-23-B,C
Hand Speed 2-K, 6-B-1-A, 6-B-1-D, 6-B-2-A, 6-D-2, 6-E-2, 6-N-0, 7-23
Hands 1-G, 1-L, 2-C-3, 2-F, 2-G, 2-H, 2-J-1, 2-J-3, 2-M-3, 2-N-0, 2-P, 3-0, 3-B, 3-F-4, 3-F-5, 3-F-5-C, 3-F-6, 3-F-7-B, 4-0, 4-D-0, 4-D-1, 5-0, 6-0, 6-A-1, 6-A-3, 6-B-1-D, 6-B-3-0, 6-B-3-0-1, 6-C-2-B, 6-C-2-D, 6-D-0, 6-D-1, 6-E-1, 6-E-2, 6-G-0, 6-H-0, 6-N-0, 6-P-0, 6-R-0, 7-1, 7-8, 7-9, 7-10, 7-12, 7-13, 7-18, 7-19, 7-20, 7-23, 8-6, 9-0, 9-1, 9-3, 10-1-B, 10-2-0, 10-3-B, 10-3-C, 10-3-J, 10-6-B, 10-6-D, 10-6-E, 10-8-0, 10-9-0, 10-11-0, 10-18-A, 10-19-C, 10-20-A, 10-21-0, 10-23-0, 10-24-D, 10-24-F, 11-8-B, 11-9-C, 11-21-AtoE, 11-23-AtoE, 12-3-0, 14
Hinge / Hinge Acton l-L, 1-L#4, 2-B, 2-C-0, 2-C-1, 2-C-2, 2-C-3, 2-D-0, 2-G, 2-H, 2-K, 2-N-0, 2-N-1, 2-P, 3-F-7-E, 4-C-1, 6-B-3-0, 6-E-2, 7-0#10, 7-10, 7-12, 7-18, 9-0, 9-2#10, 10-0, 10-3-H, 10-6-C, 10-10, 10-18-A, 10-19, 10-24-F, 11-0#10, 11-3-K, 11-10, 12-3-0#12, 12-3-0#39, 13-0
Hip Action 7-10#15, 7-14, 7-15, 9-1#15, 10-0, 10-14-0, 10-15-0, 10-19-C, 11-0#15, 11-15, 13
Hip Slant 10-16-A
Hip Turn 2-N-0, 7-0#14, 7-12, 7-14, 7-16, 9-1#14, 10-0, 10-3-A, 10-13-C, 10-14, 10-15-B, 10-15-D, 10-16-E, 10-17-E, 11-0#14, 11-14, 11-16

INDEX

Hitters and Swingers 2K, 6-D-0, 6-R-0, 7-1
Hitting 1-G, 2-G, 2-J-2, 2-K, 2-M-3, 2-N-1, 3-B, 3-F-6, 3-F-7-B, 4-D-0, 6-B-3-0-1, 6-E-2, 6-F-0, 6-H-0, 6-R-0, 7-3, 7-19, 7-23, 10-3-C, 10-10-C, 10-11-0, 10-11-0-1, 10-11-0-3, 10-11-0-4, 10-19, 10-20-0, 10-20-D, 10-24-0, 12-5-0#5, 14
Hook Face 2-D-0, 2-G

Identity 1-A, 1-H
Impact 1-L#12, 2-A, 2-B, 2-C-0, 2-C-1, 2-C-2, 2-C-3, 2-D-0, 2-D-1#8#9#10, 2-E, 2-F, 2-G, 2-H, 2-J-1, 2-J-2, 2-J-3, 2-K, 2-L, 2-M-1, 2-M-3, 2-M-4, 2-N-0, 2-P, 3-B, 3-F-5, 3-F-7-A, 3-F-7-B, 3-F-7-E, 4-C-3, 4-D-0, 4-D-1, 5-0, 6-0, 6-B-0, 6-B-1-A, 6-B-1-D, 6-B-3-0, 6-B-4-0, 6-C-0, 6-C-2-C, 6-C-2-D, 6-C-2-E, 6-D-3, 6-E-1, 6-E-2, 6-F-0, 6-F-1, 6-M-0, 6-M-1, 6-N-0, 7-2, 7-3, 7-7, 7-8, 7-9, 7-10, 7-11, 7-12, 7-13, 7-16, 7-17, 7-18, 7-19, 7-20, 7-21, 7-22, 7-24, 8-0, 8-2, 8-7, 8-9, 8-10, 8-11, 9-2, 9-3, 10-1-B, 10-2-0, 10-3-A, 10-3-C, 10-3-J, 10-6-A, 10-6-D, 10-8, 10-9, 10-10-D, 10-10-E, 10-13-D, 10-14-D, 10-16-B, 10-16-C, 10-18-0, 10-18-E, 10-19-A, 10-20-A, 10-20-B, 10-23-0, 10-24-A, 10-24-D, 10-24-E, 10-24-F, 11-3-G, 11-3-H, 11-6-E, 11-9-B, 11-23-E, 12-3-0 section2, 12-3-0 section 9/10/11, 12-5-0#1, 12-5-3#12
Impact Alignments 2-E, 2-G, 2-H, 2-J-1, 7-8
Impact Fix 2-J-1, 2-N-0, 4-D-1, 6-B-1-D, 6-B-3-0, 6-E-2, 7-2, 7-3, 7-10, 7-16, 7-19, 8-0#2, 8-2, 9-3, 10-2-0, 10-2-D, 10-8-0, 10-9-B, 10-14-D, 12-3-0 section 2, 12-5-3#12
Impact Plane Line 2-N-0
Imperatives 2-0-B, 2-K, 2-N-0, 9-2
Inclined Plane 1-L-A, 2-C-0, 2-F, 2-J-2, 2-N-0, 4-D-0, 7-5, 7-7, 7-10, 7-13, 7-23, 10-6-0, 10-6-D, 10-10-C, 10-10-D, 10-10-E, 10-13-0
Inertia 2-C-0, 2-C-1, 2-K, 2-M-4, 6-B-0, 6-C-0, 7-19, 7-22, 10-19-A, 10-19-C
In-Line Condition 6-B-0, 6-B-2-0, 6-B-4-0, 6-C-0#4, 6-E-2, 10-19-0
Inside-Out 2-J-2, 2-J-3, 3-F-5, 3-F-7-A
Inside Out Cut Shot 3-F-7-A
Instruction 1-B, 1-E, 1-J, 3-A
Interchangeability 1-H, 10-11-0-5
Introduction to Mechanics 2-0
Introduction to the Game 1-0

Kinetic Energy 2-M-1, 6-C-2-B, 7-11

Knee Action 7-0#16, 7-16, 7-17, 9-1#16, 10-0, 10-16, 11-0-A#16, 11-16, 12-5-2#3
Knee Bend 7-2#4, 7-16, 10-16-A

Lag 2-0, 2-F, 2-G, 2-K, 2-M-1, 2-M-2, 2-N-0, 2-N-1, 3-F-6, 3-F-7-B, 4-0, 4-A-3, 5-0, 6-0, 6-B-0, 6-B-1-D, 6-B-3-0, 6-B-4-C, 6-C-0, 6-C-2-0, 6-C-2-A, 6-C-2-B, 6-C-2-D, 6-C-2-E, 6-E-2, 6-F-0, 6-G-0, 6-H-0-E#6, 6-H-0-F#6, 6-M-1, 7-0, 7-2#3, 7-9, 7-11, 7-13, 7-19, 7-20. 7-22, 8-6, 9-0, 9-2, 10-0, 10-1-0, 10-2-0, 10-9-A, 10-9-B, 10-9-C, 10-9-D, 10-11-0, 10-11-0-2, 10-11-0-3, 10-19-0-A,C; 10-24-E, 11-0#19, 11-15-B, 11-19, 12-0#2, 12-5-3#16, 14
Lag Loading 2-G, 6-B-3-0, 6-C-2-E, 7-0#19, 7-9, 7-19, 9-2#19, 10-0#19, 10-9-A,B,C,D; 10-11-0-3, 10-19-0, 11-0#19, 11-19, 12-5-3#16
Lag Pressure 2-F, 2-K, 2-M-2#1, 3-F-7-B, 6-B-1-D#4, 6-C-2-A, 6-C-2-C, 6-E-2, 6-F-0, 7-11, 7-19, 7-20, 9-2, 10-1-0, 10-19-0, 12-0#2, 14
Lag Pressure Point 2-0-B#2, 2-F, 2-K, 2-M-2, 2-N-0, 4-0, 5-0, 6-C-0#3, 6-C-2-A, 6-H-0-E#6, 6-H-0-F#6, 7-2#2, 7-11, 7-19, 8-6, 10-19-0, 10-24-E
Law *Preface,* 1-0, 1-A, 1-G, 2-0, 2-C-0, 2-D-0, 2-E, 2-K, 2-L, 3-B, 4-D-1, 6-A-1, 6-C-2-B, 6-E-2, 6-F-2, 7-19, 9-0, 10-19-0, 12-0, 15-0
Law of the Triangle 6-A-1
Left Arm Stroke 1-F
Left Shoulder 1-F, 1-L, 2-C-3, 2-H, 2-J-1, 2-N-0, 6-A-2, 6-B-4-0, 6-N-0, 7-8, 7-10, 7-13
Left Wrist Bend 4-D-1, 10-2-D
Lever Assemblies 2-K, 2-L, 2-M-3, 2-N-1, 6-A-2, 6-A-3, 6-B-0, 6-B-1-0, 6-B-4-0, 6-C-0#1, 6-C-1, 6-D-2, 6-N-0, 7-10, 7-20, 10-11-0, 10-20-B, 10-22-C
Lever Assembly Extension 2-P, 7-18, 7-20
Lever Forms 2-L
Line – Refers to the straight away direction of aim 7-2
Line of Compression 2-0, 2-A, 2-C-, 2-E, 3-F-7-B, 6-C-2-0
Line-of-Sight-to-the-Ball 6-B-1-C, 6-M-1
Linear Force 1-J, 2-C-0, 2-C-1, 2-C-2, 2-C-3, 2-C-4-A, 2-K
Loading 2-H, 2-M-1, 3-F-5, 6-0, 6-B-1-D, 6-B-4-C, 6-C-0, 6-C-2-E, 6-D-0, 6-E-0, 6-E-2, 7-0#22, 7-3, 7-9, 7-11, 7-17, 7-19, 7-20, 7-22, 7-24, 9-2, 10-1-B, 10-6-D, 10-11-0-3, 10-11-0-5, 10-18-0, 10-20-C,

INDEX

10-22-0, 11-0#22, 11-22, 12-3-0#19, 12-5-1#5, 12-5-2#10
Lob Shot 2-C-3, 2-D-1#10, 2-J-2
Low Point 1-L#13#15, 2-C-1, 2-C-2, 2-C-3, 2-D-0, 2-H, 2-J-2, 2-J-3, 2-N-0, 2-P, 6-B-3-0, 6-C-2-A, 6-E-2, 7-7, 7-10, 7-23, 10-18-B
Low Point Plane Line 2-J-3, 2-N-0

Machine Concept 1-L, 16-0
Magic of the Right Forearm 7-3
Mass 1-L#11, 2-C-0#2, 2-K, 2-M-1, 2-M-2, 3-F-7-B, 6-C-0#2, 6-C-2-B
Master Accumulator 6-B-4-0
Maximum Trigger Delay 6-B-1-C, 6-B-2-A, 6-B-2-C, 6-B-3-C, 6-B-4-C, 6-R-0, 7-20
Means 1-G, 2-D-0, 6-E-1, 9-0
Mechanical Advantage 1-H
Mechanics 1-F, 1-G, 1-J, 2-0, 2-R, 3-0, 3-B, 3-E, 3-F-3, 10-2-0, 14
Miles per Hour (MPH) 2-E, 2-K, 2-P, 7-18, 14-0
Momentum 2-A, 2-E, 2-J-3, 2-K, 2-M-1, 2-M-4, 2-P, 6-C-2-B, 6-E-2, 6-F-1, 7-12, 10-19-0, 10-19-C
Momentum Transfer 2-M-3, 10-24-F
Monitor 1-F, 2-N-0, 3-F-5, 5-0, 6-L-0, 7-20, 9-1, 9-2, 9-3, 10-19-0, 10-19-C, 12-3-0
Motion 1-A, 1-G, 1-K, 1-L#11#21, 2-0, 2-C-0, 2-C-3, 2-D-0, 2-F, 2-G, 2-H, 2-J-1, 2-J-2, 2-J-3-A, 2-K, 2-L, 2-M-3, 2-N-0, 2-N-1-C, 2-P, 2-R, 3-0, 3-B, 3-C, 3-E, 3-F-5, 3-F-6, 3-F-7-B, 4-0, 4-A, 4-B-0, 4-C-0, 4-D-0, 4-D-1, 6-B-1-0, 6-B-2-0, 6-B-3-0, 6-B-3-0-1, 6-B-4-0, 6-E-1, 6-E-2, 6-G-0, 6-K-0, 6-L-0, 6-M-0, 6-N-0, 6-P-0, 6-R-0, 7-3, 7-9, 7-10, 7-12, 7-13, 7-14, 7-15, 7-16, 7-18, 7-19#1#2, 7-20, 7-22, 7-23, 8-0, 8-4, 8-6, 8-7, 9-0, 9-1, 9-2, 9-3, 10-2-0#3, 10-2-C, 10-2-D, 10-2-E, 10-2-G, 10-3-0, 10-6-D-A, 10-7-D, 10-7-F, 10-7-G, 10-10-0-A,C; 10-11-0-5, 10-12-0, 10-13-0, 10-13-B, 10-14-0, 10-14-B, 10-14-D, 10-15-D, 10-16-C, 10-16-D, 10-19-0-A,B,C; 10-20-C, 10-24-0,D,E; 11-3-E, 12-0#5,#6; 12-3-0, 12-5-0, 12-5-1, 12-5-2, 12-5-3, 14
Muscle 2-K, 2-M-3, 2-M-4, 6-B-1-0, 6-B-1-D, 6-B-2-0, 10-19-0
Mutually Exclusive 10-19-0

Newton's Laws 2-C-0, 2-D-0
Non-interchangeable 13-0
Non-Pivot Stroke 3-F-5, 6-L-0, 7-23

On Line 2-J-1, 2-J-2, 2-J-3, 3-F-7-B, 7-23, 10-3-C, 12-3-0#37,#38,#39
On Line / Cross Line 4-D-0
On Plane 1-C, 1-L#11, 2-D-0, 2-F, 2-G, 2-H, 2-K, 2-M-4, 2-N-1-C, 3-F-5, 3-F-7-E, 5-0, 6-B-3-0, 6-B-4-A, 7-2#2, 7-3, 7-7, 7-9, 7-11, 7-20, 10-2-0, 10-2-B, 10-2-E, 10-2-F, 10-2-G, 10-3-G, 10-3-K, 10-6-A, 10-6-D, 10-6-E, 10-7-F, 10-13-0-A,B,C,D; 10-14-C, 10-14-D, 10-18-C, 10-21-0, 10-24-F, 11-5-A,B,C; 11-13-D
Orbiting Clubhead 2-D-0, 6-C-2-A
Out-of-Line 2-G, 6-B-0, 6-B-3-0
Outside-In 2-J-2, 2-J-3, 7-13
Over-Acceleration 6-C-2-D, 6-D-2, 10-19-A
Over Roll 2-G, 6-F-1
Overtaking 2-M-3, 2-P, 6-B-3-0, 6-B-3-A, 6-F-0, 6-M-1, 6-N-0, 7-20

Pace 2-G, 6-P-0, 12-5-0, 12-5-1#19
Paddlewheel 7-19
Paddlewheel Action 6-B-1-0, 7-18, 10-19-0
Paddlewheel Motion 7-20
Pass-the-Ball 6-B-1-C
Physics See Power, *Thrust,* Force – 2-0, 2-E, 2-G, 2-K, 3-B, 4-D-1, 5-0, 6-E-1, 7-18, 7-19, 14
Pictures 2-R, 2-S
Piston 1-L, 7-19
Pivot 1-L, 1-L#2, 2-D-1#2#4, 2-G, 2-H, 2-J-1, 2-P, 3-F-5, 3-F-7-D, 5-0, 6-B-4-0, 6-C-2-A, 7-0#12, 7-12, 7-13, 7-14, 7-15, 7-16, 9-0, 9-1, 9-2, 9-3, 10-0#12, 10-6-D, 10-7-F, 10-12-0 A,B,C,D; 10-14-A, 10-17-E, 10-18-C#1,#2; 10-20-C, 10-24-F, 11-0#12. 11-5-A,B,C,D,E; 11-12A-D, 12-3-0, 12-5-2, 12-5-3#1, 13-0
Pivot Controlled Hands 7-23, 10-24-F
Pivot Delay 6-B-4-C
Pivot Lag 6-B-0, 6-C-0
Pivot Power 6-B-4-0
Pivot Speed 2-M-4
Pivot Stroke 3-B, 6-K-0, 1, 6-K-0, 12-0
Pivot Train 6-B-0
Pivot Thrust 2-M-3, 2-M-4
Plane 1-C, 1-L#10,#11,#12,#16; 2-D-0, 2-G, 2-H, 2-K, 2-L, 2-M-4, 2-N-1, 3-F-5, 4-C-2, 4-D-0, 4-D-1, 5-0, 6-B-1-D, 6-B-3-0, 6-B-3-0-1, 6-B-4-A, 6-F-2, 6-G-0, 6-L-0, 7-2#2, 7-3, 7-7, 7-10, 7-11, 7-12, 7-13, 7-16, 7-20, 7-23, 10-2-0, 10-10-A,B,C,D,E; 10-14-C,D; 10-18-C#1,#2; 10-19-C, 10-20-E, 10-21-0, 10-23-A, 10-24-F, 11-13-D, 11-16, 11-23

246

INDEX

Plane Angle 2-C-0, 2-D-0, 2-D-1#14, 2-J-1, 2-N-0, 3-F-5-D, 6-C-2-A, 7-13, 10-13-A,B,C,D; 10-14-C, 10-23-B
Plane Angles-Basic 7-6, 3-F-7-E, 7-0#6, 7-2, 7-6, 9-3#6,#7; 10-0#6,#7; 10-6-0-A,B,C,D,E; 11-0#6,11-6
Plane Angle-Shift Hazard 10-6-B
Plane Angle-Variations 7-7, 10-7-A,B,C,D,E,F,G,H; 11-0#7, 11-7
Plane Inclined 1-L-A, 1-L#5, 2-C-0, 2-J-2, 2-K, 2-N-0, 4-D-0, 7-5, 7-7
Plane Line 1-L#6,#18; 2-C-2, 2-G, 2-J-2, 2-J-3, 2-L, 2-N-0, 3-F-5, 3-F-7-A, 3-F-7-E, 5-0, 6-B-3-0, 6-E-2#2, 6-G-0, 6-H-0-F#3, 6-R-0, 7-0#5, 7-2#4, 7-5, 7-9, 7-12, 7-16, 7-23, 7-23, 9-3#5, 10-0#5, 10-5-0-A,B,C,D,E; 10-12-A,B,C,D; 10-18-E, 11-0#5, 11-5, 12-5-1#3
Plane Line Bent 3-F-7-B#1
Plane Line-Confusion 3-F-7-E
Plane Line-Direction 2-D-0, 2-D-1#5
Plane of Motion 2-F, 10-10-0
Plane Line Straight 2-0-B#3, 7-7
Playing 3-B, 3-F-1, 3-F-6, 9-0, 9-1, 9-2, 9-3
Point of Separation 1-L#17, 2-J-1
Potential Energy 7-11
Power 1-H, 1-L, 2-K, 2-M-1, 2-M-4, 3-F-5, 3-F-7-A, 6-A-2, 6-B-0, 6-B-1-D, 6-F-2, 6-M-1, 7-8, 7-11, 7-24, 9-0#2, 9-2, 9-3, 10-3-C, 10-3-D, 10-3-K, 10-10-B, 10-15-B, 10-19-C, 11-15, 12-5-3
Power Accumulators 6-0, 6-B-0, 6-B-1,2,3,4; 6-M-0, 7-4, 7-11, 7-20, 7-22, 10-4-0,A,B,C,D; 12-0#1
Power Golf 9-2, 1-L, 9-2
Power Package 2-D-1#1,#3, 2-H, 2-P, 3-F-6, 6-0, 6-C-0, 6-C-2-A, 6-R-0, 7-22, 9-2, 10-3-H, 10-11-0-1, 10-13-C,D, 10-20-0, 12-5-1, 12-5-2
Power Package Assembly 7-0#21, 7-12, 7-20, 7-21, 9-2#21, 10-0#21, 10-21, 11-0#21, 11-21
Power Package Delivery 6-E-0, 6-J-0, 7-0#23, 7-23, 9-3#23, 10-0#23, 10-23-0, 11-0#23, 11-23, 13-0
Power Package Loading 6-C-0, 7-0#22, 7-22, 9-2#22, 10-0#22, 10-22-0, 11-0#22, 11-22
Power Package Release 6-M-0, 6-M-1, 7-0#24,7-24, 9-3#24, 10-0#24, 10-24-0, 11-0#24, 11-24
Power Transfer 7-12
Power Package Transport 7-12
Power Package Thrust 2-M-3, 6-C-1, 6-C-2-B, 6-E-0
Power Regulation 2-M-2
Power Storage 6-D-0

Practice Procedures 3, 5-0
Practice Ranges 1-J, 3-F-4
Practice Stroke 3-F-5
Preliminary Address 8-0, 8-1, 9-1
Pressure Points 1-L, 3-F-5, 6-0, 6-A-2, 6-A-3, 6-B-0, 6-C-1, 6-C-2-0, 6-C-2-C, 7-11, 10-2-0, 10-11-0, 10-11-0-5, 11-11-A,B,C,D; 12-3-0#11
Pulled Shots 3-F-7-E, 6-B-3-0
Pulley 2-K, 6-E-2, 6-N-0, 7-18
Pulley Diameter 2-K
Pulley Sizes 6-E-2
Pushed Shots 7-2, 11-5-D
Putting 2-C-4, 2-G, 3-F-7-B, 6-B-3-0, 6-G-0, 9-0, 10-6-C, 10-20-A, 12-0

Quitting 2-D-1#23, 2-M-1, 3-F-5, 3-F-7-B, 6-B-3-0, 6-D-3, 6-F-2, 10-19-B, 10-24-F

Radial 6-B-3-0, 6-C-2-A, 6-H-0#7, 10-19-B, 11-19-A, 11-19-B, 13-0
Reference Numbers *Preface* 2-R, 3-F-2, 16-0
Release 1-F, 2-K, 2-M-1, 2-P, 3-F-5, 3-F-6, 3-F-7-B, 3-F-7-E, 4-C-3, 4-D-1, 6-0, 6-B-0, 6-B-1-0, 6-B-1-C, 6-B-1-D, 6-B-2-0, 6-B-2-C, 6-B-3-0, 6-B-3-A,C; 6-B-4-C, 6-C-2-A, 6-D-2, 6-E-0, 6-E-1, 6-E-2, 6-F-0, 6-H-0-B, 6-H-0-F#2, 6-L-0, 6-M-0, 6-M-1, 6-P-0, 6-R-0, 7-0#24, 7-7, 7-18, 7-20, 7-23, 7-24, 8-0, 8-8, 8-9, 9-2, 9-3#24, 10-0#24, 10-3-B, 10-3-K, 10-6-A, 10-11-0-3, 10-14-A, 10-14-C, 10-18-A,B, E; 10-19-0, 10-19-B,C; 10-20-0-B,D,E; 10-21-E, 10-24-0,A,B,D,E,F; 11-0#24, 11-20-AtoE; 11-24-AtoF; 12-0#3,#6; 12-3-0#38, 12-5-2#12
Release Interval 2-G, 2-M-2, 6-F-0
Release Motions 3-B, 4-D-0, 6-P-0, 9-2, 10-24-0, 12-0#6
Release Roll 2-G
Release Sequence 6-M-1
Release Types 6-N-0, 7-24, 10-24-0
Resilience 2-A
Resultant Force 2-C-1, 2-D-0, 2-E, 2-N-1-C, 7-5
Revolutions per Minute (RPM) 2-G, 2-K, 2-P, 6-P-0, 7-18
Rhythm 2-0#3, 2-D-1#26, 2-G, 2-P, 3-0, 3-F-5, 3-F-6, 3-F-7-B, 6-B-3-B, 6-D-0, 6-F-1, 6-F-2, 7-10, 7-14, 7-20, 10-19-C, 10-24-F, 12-3-0#9,#25,#34; 12-5-1#21
Rhythm Control 6-B-3-0
Rhythm-Loss of 3-F-6, 3-F-7-B
Right Am-Active 6-B-1-0, 6-H-0-E#5, 7-1, 7-20

247

INDEX

Right Arm-Fanning 10-3-A, 12-5-1#17
Right Arm-Running out of 6-L-0
Right Arm or Left 1-F
Right Arm Participation 1-F, 7-3, 10-24-F
Right Arm Swing 7-19, 10-11-0-3
Right Arm Thrust 2-K, 2-M-3, 2-N-1, 2-P, 10-11-0, 10-19-A
Right Elbow 1-F, 2-F, 2-H, 2-N-0, 2-N-1, 2-M-3, 6-B-1-0, 6-B-1-C, 6-B-3-0, 6-B-3-A, 6-B-4-0, 6-C-2-A, 6-H-0-E#5, 6-M-1, 6-N-0, 7-1, 7-3, 7-10, 7-14, 7-18, 7-19, 7-20, 10-3-A, 10-3-B, 10-3-K, 10-4-A, 10-6-A, 10-14-A, 10-14-C, 10-19-A, 10-19-B, 11-3-K, 11-4-A#1, 12-3-0#33,#35, 12-5-1#12, 12-5-3#17
Right Forearm 1-F, 2-F, 2-G, 2-J-3, 3-F-5-F, 3-F-6, 4-D-1, 5-0, 6-B-3-0, 6-B-3-0-1, 6-C-2-A, 7-2#2,#3, 7-3, 7-7, 7-9, 7-11, 7-16, 7-20, 7-23, 10-3-B, 10-3-K, 10-6-A, 10-24-F, 12-3-0#17, 12-5-1#13, 12-5-1#16,#17, 12-5-2
Right Forearm Takeaway 2-F, 3-F-6, 5-0, 7-3, 10-24-F, 12-3-0#17
Right Hip 2-H, 3-F-5, 5-0, 7-13, 7-14, 10-14-A, 10-15-B, 12-3-0#13,#24
Right Hip Clearing 3-F-5, 10-14-A, 10-15-B
Right Shoulder 2-H, 2-M-3, 3-F-5, 6-A-1, 6-B-1-0, 6-C-2-A, 7-7, 7-12, 7-13, 7-15, 10-3-E, 10-6-B,C, 10-13, 0,D, 11-6-B, 11-13-B,D, 11-20-B,C
Right Shoulder Down and Back 7-13
Right-Wrist 3-F-6, 3-F-7-E, 4-D-1, 5-0, 6-B-3-0-1, 6-C-2-A, 7-1, 7-3, 7-9, 10-2-0,A,C,D,E, 10-3-K, 10-18-B, 10-19-0
Right Wrist Bend 4-D-1, 6-B-3-0-1, 6-C-2-A, 10-2-0,C, 10-2-D
Roll and Turn 4-0, 7-18, 7-10
Roll Power Control 6-B-3-0
Rope Handle 2-K, 6-F-0, 6-H-0#8, 7-19, 10-3-D, 10-11-0,2, 10-19-C
Rotating Pressure Point 10-H-0-F#6
Round Housing 2-N-0, 5-0, 7-14
Rubber-Properties of 2-A

Samenesses *Preface*, 1-J, 7-0
Scooping 6-F-2
Secret of Golf 2-0, 6-C-2-0
Separation Speed 2-E, 6-C-2-0
Set Up 2-J-1, 7-9, 7-18, 7-19, 7-19-B,C
Shanking 2-F, 2-H, 5-0, 3-F-7-E, 5-0
Short Course 2-0
Short Stroke Pattern 10-3-E, 10-14-D, 12-0
Shorten 2-J-1, 3-F-6, 3-F-7-B, 6-B-0, 10-19-A, 10-21-E, 12-0

Shoulder Acceleration 8-7
Shoulder Lag 7-13
Shoulder Motion 2-H, 2-N-1-C, 6-G-0, 7-13, 10-3-H, 10-13-0, *see backstroke*
Shoulder Turn 1-F, 2-H, 2-M-3, 2-N-0, 2-N-1-A, 5-0, 6-B-4-0.A,B,C, 6-C-0, 6-F-2, 7-0#13, 7-13, 7-14, 7-15, 9-1#13, 10-0#13, 10-6-B, 10-7-F,H, 10-19-C, 10-13-0,A,B,C,D,E, 10-14-C,D, 10-15-0,B,C, 10-20-C, 10-24-F, 11-0#13, 11-13-E, 11-20-C, 12-5-1, 12-5-2,#2
Simplification 2-P, 3 -F-3
Sit-Down-Position 7-16, 10-16-A,B,C, 10-17-0,A
Slicing 2-R, 2-D, 7-2, 1-F
Slide 3-F-7-E, 7-12, 7-16, 10-3-A, 10-14-B, 10-14-E, 11-0, 12-2-0
Soling the Club 2-J-1
Speed 1-D, 1-J, 2-D-1, 2-E, 2-H, 2-K, 2-M-1, 2-M-2, 2-M-3, 2-M-4, 2-P, 3-B, 3-F-6, 6-B-0, 6-B-1-A, 6-B-1-D, 6-B-2-A, 6-C-2-0, 6-C-2-A, 6-C-2-B, 6-C-2-D, 6-D-2, 6-E-2, 6-F-0, 6-F-1, 6-N-0, 6-P-0, 7-18, 7-22, 7-23, 9-2, 10-1-B
Spoke 7-23
Stance 2-N-0, 3-F-7-E, 6-E-2, 7-2, 7-5, 7-9, 10-5-0, 10-5-A, 10-5-B, 10-5-C, 10-5-D, 10-5-E, 10-9-D, 10-12-0, 10-12-A, 10-12-B, 10-12-C, 10-19-A, 10-24-F, 11-0, 12-3-0, 12-5-1
Start Down 2-F, 2-N-0, 3-B, 3-F-5, 5-0, 6-H-0, 7-14, 8-6, 8-7, 8-8, 10-15-B, 10-19-A, 10-19-B, 10-19-C, 10-24-A, 12-3-0
Start Up 1-F, 2-F, 3-F-5, 7-9, 8-4, 12-3-0
Starting-to Hit 6-G-0, 6-N-0
Stationary Head 2-H
Statement of Principle 2-0, 2-H
Steering 2-C-3, 2-D-1, 2-N-0, 3-F-7-A, 3-F-7-B, 4-D-0, 4-D-1, 6-F-2, 7-10, 9-3
Straight Left Arm 6-A-1, 6-B-1-0, 6-C-1, 12-5-1
Strokes-Basic 7-0, 10-0, 11-0
Stroke Patterns 1-0, 1-E, 7-0, 11-0, 12-0
Strokes – Types & Variations 7-0, 7-4, 11-0, 10-0
Structure 1-A, 1-D, 1-G, 3-F-6, 6-A-1, 6-B-3-0-1, 6-E-0, 6-E-2, 6-R-0, 7-16, 7-22, 10-19-B
Swaying 2-D-1, 3-F-7-D, 7-14
Sweet Spot 2-D-0, 2-F, 2-N-0, 6-E-2, 7-11, 12-3-0
Sweet Spot-Clubshaft 2-F
Sweet Spot-Plane 2-N-0, 7-11
Swing Radius 2-C-0, 2-H, 2-M-2, 2-P, 3-F-7-B, 6-B-0, 6-B-4-0, 6-B-4-A, 6-C-0, 6-C-2-B, 6-M-1, 7-17, 7-19

INDEX

Swingers and Hitters 6-F-0
Swinging 1-F, 2-G, 2-H, 2-K, 2-M-4, 2-N-1, 3-F-6, 3-F-7-B, 4-C-1, 4-D-0, 4-D-1, 6-B-3-0-1, 6-E-2, 6-H-0 (F), 7-3, 7-9, 7-10, 7-13, 7-17, 7-19, 7-23, 9-2, 10-11-0-3, 10-11-0-4, 10-19-0, 10-19-C, 10-20-D, 10-20-E, 10-24, 12-2-0, 12-5-0, 14-0
Swivel 2-G, 2-N-0, 4-0, 4-D-0, 7-10, 7-20, 10-2-0, 10-11-0-3, 10-18-A, 12-3-0, 12-5-3

Target-Line 2-D-0, 2-J-3, 3-F-5, 3-F-7-A, 3-F-7-E, 7-2, 7-5, 7-10, 8-2, 10-5-0, 10-5-A, 10-5-B, 10-5-C, 10-5-D, 10-5-E, 10-6-D (B)
Terminology 1-H, 2-0
Three Dimensional Impact 2-B, 2-F, 6-E-2, 7-10, 10-6-D
Three Essentials 2-0
Three Functions *Preface* 1-L
Three Imperatives 2-0
Three Zones 8-0, 9-0, 11-A
Throwaway Prevention 10-19-B, 10-19-C
Throw-Out Action 2-K, 6-B-3-0, 10-6-D (B), 10-24-F
Thrust 1-D, 2-H, 2-K, 2-M-1, 2-M-3, 2-M-4, 2-N-1, 2-P, 6-B-1-0, 6-B-1-A, 6-B-4-0, 6-B-4-A, 6-C-0, 6-C-2-A, 6-C-2-B, 6-C-2-D, 6-E-2, 6-F-1, 6-M-1, 7-3, 7-11, 7-23, 7-24, 10-1-B, 10-2-0, 10-11-0, 10-19-A
Timing 2-D-1#19, 3-F-7-D, 2-E-2, 6-F-0, 6-F-1, 6-F-2, 10-24-F
Top 2-G, 2-K, 2-N-0, 3-F-5, 4-D-0, 4-D-1, 6-D-0, 6-D-1, 6-E-2, 6-M-0, 7-3, 7-7, 7-19, 7-21, 7-23, 7-24, 8-5, 8-6, 10-2-A, 10-6-B, 10-6-D, 10-7, 10-11-0-3, 10-16-A, 10-17-0, 10-18-C, 10-20-A, 10-21, 10-23-A, 10-23-B, 10-23-C, 10-23-D, 10-23-E, 11-6, 11-16, 11-17, 11-21, 11-23, 12-3, 12-5-3 #8
Total Motion 3-0, 3-B, 3-C, 3-E, 3-F-5, 6-M-0, 9-3, 12-0, 12-3-0, 12-5-3, 14-0
Tracing 2-J-3, 3-F-5, 3-F-6, 5-0, 6-E-2, 7-20, 7-23, 10-23-C, 12-5-1
Trajectory Control 2-B, 10-10-C
Triangle Assembly 6-A-1, 7-20
Trigger 2-P, 4-D-1, 6-B-0, 6-B-1-C, 6-B-2-A, 6-B-2-C, 6-B-3-C, 6-B-4-0, 6-B-4-C, 6-D-0, 6-E-2, 6-F-0, 6-K-0, 6-M-0, 6-M-1, 6-N-0, 6-P-0, 6-R-0, 7-0, 7-18, 7-20, 8-9, 9-2, 10-0, 10-3-A, 10-3-B, 10-3-C, 10-14-A, 10-14-C, 10-20-0, 10-20-D, 10-24-A, 10-24-B, 10-24-C, 10-24-D, 10-24-F, 11-0, 12-1-0, 12-2-0, 12-4, 12-5-3

Trigger Delay 2-P, 6-B-1-C, 6-B-2-A, 6-B-2-C, 6-B-3-C, 6-B-4-C, 6-E-2, 6-F-0, 6-P-0, 6-R-0, 7-18, 7-20, 10-3-A, 10-3-B, 10-14-A, 12-5-3
Turn and Roll 4-0, 7-18
Twelve Section 2-N-0, 8-0, 9-0, 11-A, 12-3-0
Twenty Four Basic Components 1-K, 7-0, 9-0, 11-A

Uncompensated Stroke 3-A, 10-0
Underhand Pitch 2-N-0, 10-3-B
Under Roll 2-G, 6-F-1
Upstroke 2-J-2

Vectors 2-B, 2-C-0, 2-D-0, 2-E, 2-N-1
Velocity 2-B, 2-G, 2-E, 2-K, 2-M-1, 2-N-1, 3-F-7-E, 6-B-2-0, 6-B-3-A, 6-C-2-A, 6-C-2-B, 6-C-2-C, 6-M-1, 7-24, 15-0
Venturi 2-B, 2-D-0, 2-E
Vertical to the Ground 6-E-2, 7-10, 10-6-D, 10-10-0 10-10-D

Waggle 2-F, 3-F-5, 7-20, 8-3, 8-6, 9-2, 10-2-0, 12-3-0
Weight Shift 3-F-7-D, 7-9, 7-12, 7-17, 10-14-0, 10-14-A, 10-14-B, 10-14-C, 10-14-E, 12-5-2
Wrist Action 1-H, 2-C-2, 2-G, 3-B, 4-0, 4-D-0, 6-B-3-A, 6-D-3, 6-H-0, 7-0, 7-7, 7-10, 7-18, 9-2, 10-0, 10-2-0, 10-3-F, 10-6-D, 10-10-C, 10-11-0-3, 10-18-0, 10-18-E, 10-18-F, 10-19-A, 10-19-B, 11-0, 12-1-0, 12-2-0, 12-4, 12-5-2
Wrist Motion 4-0, 4-D-0, 4-D-1, 10-2-C, 10-2-G
Wrist Positions 4-0, 4-A-0, 4-B-0, 4-C-0, 4-D-1, 5
Wristcock 1-L, 2-M-3, 2-P, 3-F-6, 4-D-1, 6-B-1-D, 6-B-3-0, 6-B-3-0-1, 6-B-3-B, 6-M-1, 7-7, 7-18, 10-2-A, 10-2-B, 10-2-C, 10-2-D, 10-2-E, 10-2-F, 10-2-G, 10-6-D, 10-6-D (B), 10-19-B, 12-5-2
Wrist Bend 3-F-7-B, 4-D-1, 6-B-3-0-1, 6-C-2-A, 10-2-0, 10-2-C, 10-2-D
Wobble 1-F, 1-L #3, 2-B
Wobbly 3-B, 3-F-6, 9-2

X Classification 1-K

Zones-Three 8-0, 9-0, 9-2, 11-A

NOTES

NOTES

NOTES

NOTES

NOTES